# The Wrong Car

## The death of Lillie Belle Allen

## William Keisling

YARDBIRD

ISBN 1-882611-16-0
FIRST EDITION, second printing

This book was printed on acid-free paper. Set in Garamond 10/13 with Emigre Journal, Impact and Rubber Stamp display faces.

Yardbird Books can be found in any good book store. We encourage our readers to order books directly from us. A single copy can be purchased from us for $15.00, postage included. Pennsylvania residents please add six percent sales tax. Three or more copies of this book can be purchased for $11.95 each, including shipping, by calling Yardbird Books at 1-800-622-6044. Or write us at:

Yardbird Books, P.O. Box 5333, Harrisburg, PA 17110.

Digital versions of our books are available. E-mail orders can also be sent to: info@yardbird.com. Visit our web page at yardbird.com. For document downloads, videos and other materials associated with this book, visit www.yardbird.com/thewrongcar.htm

Library of Congress Cataloging-in-Publication Data

Keisling, William.
    The wrong car : the death of Lillie Belle Allen:
        a police murder mystery / William Keisling.
        p. cm.
    ISBN 1-882611-16-0
    1. Murder--Pennsylvania--York--Case studies. 2. Murder
victims--Pennsylvania--York--Case studies. 3. Criminal
investigation--Pennsylvania--York--Case studies. I. Title.

HV6534.Y587 K457 2002
364.15'23'0974841--dc21                    2002033853

This book is dedicated
to the memory of Abraham Lincoln

## Acknowledgments

My brother Craig provided invaluable assistance in the preparation of this book. Rick Kearns, old friend and collaborator, offered his usual great insights. Lynn Hamrick helped with the graphics. Lisa Westmoreland was our intern.

For research on the second part of this book, I'm indebted to the reporters working in 1968 and 1969 for the York Gazette and Daily and, to a lesser extent, the York Dispatch. If you want to learn about the York riots, these papers, particularly the now-defunct Gazette and Daily, are indispensable sources of information. Court records, in this case, are all but useless. A vibrant and free press, I've come to see, is not only a gift for today, but for future generations.

Warm regards to the family of the late Fred Speaker. Fred was a family friend and my confirmation sponsor in church. He was Pennsylvania attorney general at the time of the York riots. Always there for his family and community, Fred Speaker is fondly remembered and sorely missed.

Lastly, I'd like to thank the readers of my books, whose support and patience made The Wrong Car possible.

bk

# Contents

# PART ONE:
## 'What have we gotten ourselves into?'

"The past is not dead. In fact, it's not even the past."
William Faulkner

# 1
## Waiting for the Spells brothers

The Spells brothers got out of their Cadillac. They climbed the steps to the Messersmiths' porch and knocked on the door. Bobby Messersmith came out with his shotgun. He took in the two black brothers. He didn't like blacks, much less on his father's front porch. And he certainly didn't like the Spells brothers.

He saw James and Sherman Spells were angry, but resolved. He saw they weren't much impressed by his shotgun. They certainly weren't impressed with Bobby. They looked at Bobby Messersmith like he was a coward, the kind of coward who hid behind a hood, or shot kids in the back, or molested little girls, or threw firebombs at defenseless old ladies under cover of night. Which was what brought them here, in broad daylight.

The Spells brothers told Bobby someone had been tossing Molotov cocktails onto the porch of their mother's house. They knew Bobby and his gang were behind the firebombings. They wanted to put a stop to it.

James Spells told Bobby to leave their mother alone. If anything happened to their mother, he told Bobby, they were going to come back and personally take care of his cowardly ass.

Was that simple enough for him to understand?

The Spells brothers turned and walked back to their car. The white Cadillac belonged to Sherman. A large number of boys were milling about the street, and one of them yelled for Sherman to open the Cadillac's trunk. James asked Sherman what that was about, and Sherman said he didn't know. James didn't know whether or not to believe his brother. With that they drove off.

Cocky niggers, Bobby thought. Somebody ought to teach them a lesson. He stood on his porch, clutching his shotgun, watching them pull away in their white Cadillac. He'd get around to teaching them that lesson, once more of his gang was with him.

It was about four-thirty in the afternoon, Monday, July 21, 1969.

As soon as the Spells brothers drove off, Bobby Messersmith began planning to firebomb their mother's house again that night. Down in Bobby's basement they busied themselves making more Molotov cocktails. Pouring gasoline into empty bottles, stuffing the bottles with rags. They laid the bottles out back on the fence. Should the Spells brothers attack them from behind, someone would fire a shot at the bottles and ignite them.

While these plans were laid, Bobby and his family put out an alert. They needed help on Newberry Street. The message went out all over town, across the county. The niggers were coming back that night in their Cadillac. Boys with their guns were needed on Newberry Street. This time they'd be ready for the Spells brothers.

Hearing the call for help, white boys began arriving with their guns. Bobby's father, John Messersmith, assigned the boys to battle stations.

Then they told the police about the impending ambush.

Soon it was almost 9pm. The Cadillac full of coloreds would be coming before long. All was ready. Now they had only to wait for Sherman Spells.

## 2

### "What have we gotten ourselves into?"

All eyes fix on the Cadillac as it glides down Philadelphia Street. Neighbors sitting on their porches and stoops along Philadelphia Street watch expectantly. They know what's about to happen. Everyone in the neighborhood knows. They've been talking about it for hours.

First the car must turn the corner on to Newberry Street. On Newberry Street, many more expectant eyes watch.

The city and state policemen standing at the corner of Philadelphia and Newberry streets watch the car approach too. The police stand at a barricade in front of the Otterbein United Methodist Church, a gothic, dark structure brooding over the corner.

The car stops at the light behind a few other cars, its turn signal blinking. The light changes.

The policemen let the car pass their barricade. The cops watch the car round the corner and head down Newberry Street, toward the waiting, armed mob.

The car drives past Wentz's TV shop, at the corner opposite the church, cattycorner from the YMCA.

The car moves past the neighbors' homes. Neighbors with names like Strine, Koch, Slick. It rolls past the Haverstocks' house, past the Rupperts' house. All along the block, neighbors sit on their porches this warm summer evening, watching the car come down Newberry Street. It eases past the used furniture store, where a man sits watching out front. Until it reaches the railroad tracks.

At the railroad tracks twenty or more gun-toting kids wait. They're mostly teenagers. They're waiting for the car. The kids have been waiting all evening. With each hour their numbers grow. Many have brought guns. Guns normally used by the country boys to go hunting for deer or groundhog. Tonight they full well expect to kill men. For hours they've been running around the street with guns, under the eyes of police. More kids are stationed on the roofs of houses, and in windows, and elsewhere, their rifles and shotguns ready. In expectation, they've been drinking and drugging all night. The gun-toting teenagers suddenly are alerted that the car is coming.

What happens next is murder. Vicious, premeditated murder, committed in plain sight of at least a hundred eyes, some say hundreds of eyes. A murder committed in cold blood, in the shadow of a church, before the watching eyes of police. Down the street from the Young Men's Christian Association and the neighborhood store where kids are sent to fetch milk and bread, a murder committed in plain sight of the watching, expectant eyes of small town America.

The policemen, like the neighbors, watch the car drive into the ambush. The cops duck behind their cruisers and watch the murder they know to expect. That all their senses tell them to expect. That they have been told to expect. Then they turn their backs and run, not helping the people in the ambushed car. They have been running ever since, to this day.

Later, to explain why the murderers were never brought to justice, the police will lie and say no one saw the murder.

The simple yet painful reality is that at least one hundred eyes will see the murder. These eyes all watch expectantly as the car rounds the corner and rides into ambush at the railroad tracks.

This is the story of some of those watching eyes, and what they saw.

It's a very long story about a very short, ten or fifteen second car ride.

It helps to view the ten or fifteen second car ride cinematically, like a piece of film, or video tape, which can be stopped, fast forwarded, or reversed. Before the car reaches the murderous ambush at the railroad tracks, let's hit rewind, and back it up. The car glides to a stop short of the gun-toting mob of teens at the railroad tracks, and smoothly reverses. Our film runs backward now, backward past neighbors on their porches, past the Rupperts' house, past the used furniture store where a man sits out front, past the Slicks' house, past the

TV shop, past the watching cops at the barricade, rounding the corner backwards, stopping at the light, turn signal blinking. Then heading off backwards into the summer evening down Philadelphia Street.

Now let's hit play again. The car resumes it forward cruise, toward the cops at the barricade.

Among the first eyes that see the car coming are those of Helen Diaczun. She's sitting on her front steps on 249 W. Philadelphia Street, half a block away from Newberry. When the car passes her porch she sees "several colored people" inside. She watches the car stop at the light. She watches it pass the police barricade. She watches it turn right up Newberry Street.

The car approaches the stoplight at the corner of Philadelphia and Newberry streets, watched by the police stationed at the barricade. The barricade is made of yellow sawhorses. One city policeman and four Pennsylvania state police troopers stand by the sawhorses. Police have been stationed at the barricade for the past several days. More police officers are in the immediate area, walking the neighborhood of Newberry Street in roving patrols. There's been trouble in the neighborhood. There have been riots in the city.

The previous summer, police learned they could successfully head-off violence by sealing troubled neighborhoods. Sounds obvious, doesn't it? The cops have become good at setting up and manning their barricades. That's why they've manned the barricade at Newberry and Philadelphia streets. The job of these officers is to stop cars from going down Newberry Street, where a large gang of troubled white teenagers for days has been fomenting a race riot.

In the last few days, this neighborhood of Newberry and Philadelphia streets has seen several shootings of blacks and repeated mob attacks. It is a white neighborhood, whose residents feel they are at war with the city's blacks. The police too are at war with the city's blacks.

The policemen themselves are being shot at, and they are being hit. Several nights before, their fellow officer, Henry Schaad, was shot while riding through a black neighborhood in a poorly armored car. Schaad was a young rookie. He's the twenty-two year old son of a

York city police detective. Shot through the lungs, young Schaad lies dying in the hospital, on a respirator. Already the police have received the names of five young black men who they suspect of shooting Officer Schaad. They call these blacks the "militants." Sherman Spells is suspected of being at the scene of Schaad's shooting. Now here was Sherman and his brother, maybe more of the militants, riding into a trap. To say that the cops are mad is an understatement. They are out for blood.

Tonight the cops standing at the barricade wear bulletproof vests and riot helmets. Since the mortal shooting of the rookie cop, they have even been instructed to carry high-powered rifles.

Later, the police officers stationed at the corner will say they had no idea they were supposed to stop traffic at the barricade. They'd have us believe that they were there perhaps to collect dry cleaning, or perhaps to file their nails. They'd say they can't remember any instructions from supervisors about what to do at the barricade.

They have certainly received instructions from the white gang.

Manning the police barricade this evening are Pennsylvania State Trooper Gerald Roberts, Trooper Steve Rendish, Trooper Bill Linker, and rookie Trooper Michael Marchowski. With them is York city policeman Ronald Zeager. Trooper Roberts remembers a few more city and state cops coming in and out of the intersection from time to time, on roving patrol.

Suppertime on Newberry Street bleeds into evening. The smells of summer suppers and burning charcoal run into the smell of expectant death.

The cops watch as trouble foments before their eyes. They watch the growing mob of white teenagers running in the street with guns. It's pandemonium down there, and they do nothing. They've even received a phone call from a concerned neighbor who complains about the young snipers waiting in ambush on the roofs. Still the police do nothing. A few of the neighbors can't understand why the police don't seem to care that someone is about to get killed.

Before supper, Annabel Mae Kline, living on adjacent North Street, witnessed the Spells brothers confront Bobby Messersmith.

"At about 4:30pm I went out to get the garbage can in the alley to the rear of my house," she remembers later. "I saw a white boy, a teenager, standing in the doorway at 229 N. Newberry St. He was talking to two young Negro men. The white boy had a rifle in his hand. They seemed to be arguing about something. I went back into the house."

The hours pass and her concern grows. Annabel Kline sees the police turn a blind eye to another night of rioting on her block.

"After supper, I went out to North and Newberry streets," Annabel Kline remembers. "The gang of kids were congregating. They usually got together every evening at this time. I went back to my yard and sat down. I saw three fellows with guns on the roof at 231 N. Newberry. One of them was hanging on the chimney. This was about 8 to 8:30pm. I went into the house and called the city police. I told them there were snipers on the roof." In a short while, sitting in her back yard, Kline will hear the shooting start.

About the same time, seventy-year-old plumber Bill Boyer stands in the doorway of his shop, watching the mounting trouble and confusion.

"There were about seventy-five kids over there on the corner, kids seventeen or eighteen years old, running around with guns in broad daylight," Boyer remembers. "I don't know why the police didn't chase them kids off the street."

While the kids down the street prepare to kill the Spells brothers in ambush, police horse around at the corner barricade.

The officers notice someone's left a package at the corner of Newberry and Philadelphia streets. A little too close for comfort. City policeman Zeager cautiously goes to the package, looking it over. State Trooper Bill Linker playfully slams the door to his cruiser. Zeager thought he jumped two feet in the air. It turns out not to be a bomb.

It's almost 9pm, and the mob and the confusion grow by the moment. State troopers Gerald Roberts and Steve Rendish stand together on the corner, ensconced in riot gear. One of the young men waiting in ambush walks up from the railroad tracks, approaching the two troopers. He's white, in his early twenties, Roberts recollects.

"Turn your backs and everything will be okay," the young man winks at the state troopers. Turn your backs, he reassures the police-men, and the boys won't shoot *you,* just the Spells brothers. The young man hurries back to the railroad tracks.

Troopers Roberts and Rendish turn to each other.

"What have we gotten ourselves into?" Roberts remembers them both saying at once.

The policemen on duty this night at the corner are slow to pick up several crucial facts. They are slow to pick up on the fact that they are policemen, and the fact that the public expects to be protected in their presence. They are slow to pick up on the fact that the boys run-ning around with guns in front of their faces mean to kill someone. They are slow to pick on the fact that when they are told about a planned shooting, they should do something to stop it. They are not so slow to pick up on something else. They will notice the color of the skin of the people in the approaching Cadillac.

Not long after the young man came up and told the officers to turn their backs, Trooper Roberts sees the light-colored Cadillac approaching the barricade at the intersection. A couple of other cars sit in front of it at the intersection, waiting for the light to change. City officer Ron Zeager notices the Cadillac too. Zeager looks at the driver. He thinks he sees that the driver is a black man. He also notices passengers in the car. Later, he would curiously say he only saw they were black from behind.

The police, like the neighbors, expectantly watch the Cadillac waiting at the light. The light changes to green. The cars in front of the Cadillac go straight. The Cadillac reaches the corner and begins to turn at the barricade. The police make no effort to stop the Cadillac. Some would later remember that the cops actually move the barricade and wave the car through. One thing is certain: the officers make no effort to warn the blacks in the car of the ambush awaiting them. The ambush the police know to expect.

Years later, an occupant in the car would remember that one of the cops was smiling as he waved the car through the barricade.

At that moment, another York city police officer, Patrolman Charles Robertson, is listening to his radio several blocks away at

Farquhar Park. Robertson recalls receiving a police radio transmission from an unknown officer at the corner, advising that the Cadillac has passed the barricade. One of the boys waiting in ambush would later say that Bobby Messersmith's father, directing the mob of boys from his house on Newberry Street, is also listening to police transmissions, over a police scanner. Not only are the police at the barricade aiding in the ambush, turning their backs to the expected murder, witnesses say they broadcast a heads-up to the waiting mob that the Spells brothers are on their way down the street in the Cadillac.

All is set. In less than ten seconds, the car is halfway down the block to the waiting mob. In less time than it takes you to read this paragraph, the car ride is over. At the railroad tracks, trying to avoid the gun-toting mob, the car makes a sudden left turn. The police, and the neighbors look on as the shooting starts. The police take cover behind their cruisers, waiting for the shooting to stop.

Gunsmoke still lingers in the air while they learn the Spells brothers aren't killed. The Spells brothers aren't even *in* that Cadillac. The damn cops let the wrong car through the barricade. The fucking morons at the tracks opened fire on a preacher's family, on their way to the store to buy groceries.

They have all participated in murder. They have shot to death a young mother of two. A preacher's daughter. Later still they will learn her name. It is a name none of them will ever forget.

# 3

# The people in the wrong car

Who are the people in the wrong car?

Reverse the car ride as if it's a movie, this time in fast reverse, yanking it from the tracks, speeding it up the street backwards past the barricade, round the corner. Let the story of the people in the car rewind hours backward, and we learn this:

The day before the ambush at the railroad tracks, the people in the car had started out on their summer vacation. They are out-of-towners, unaware that York is in the throes of a race riot.

The family seems oblivious to another important event. The same day they start out on their vacation, Neil Armstrong and Buzz Aldrin land and walk on the moon. The Mosleys are on the highway on a day when most Americans are glued to televisions.

On Sunday, July 20, 1969, Reverend Jim Mosley and his family set out on their vacation by car from their home in Aiken, South Carolina. Jim Mosley is minister of the Cedar Grove Missionary Baptist Church in Aiken. He's held the pulpit there since 1965.

Aiken is a small southern town of mostly unpaved streets and deep-set segregation. Mosley and his wife Beatrice live in a small white house on Horry Street, where they raised their eight children and two grandchildren. On Horry Street blacks live on one side of the street, whites on the other. Children are forbidden to cross over to play on the other side of the street. The schools are segregated too, of course.

Rev. Mosley and his family planned a road trip. They'd drive to Brooklyn, New York, to see their son Benjamin. They'd stop in York, Pennsylvania, to visit their daughter Hattie and her family.

They bring with them two of their daughters, Lillie Belle, 27, and Gladys, age thirteen. Lillie Belle brought along her own two children,

Michael, nine, and Debra, eleven. Lillie Belle and her kids look forward to staying in Brooklyn, where they once had lived when her children were younger. She wants to get her kids out of South Carolina.

After attending church, the five drove out of Aiken, heading north for York. The family arrived at Hattie's by Sunday evening, and straightaway made plans to fish the next day. Lillie Belle likes to fish. Hattie's husband, Murray "Bubba" Dickson, had a favorite fishing hole a short way outside town at the York reservoir.

Bubba, himself from Bamberg, South Carolina, had several years earlier traveled north and found a labor union job in York. He sent for his family in 1966. They rented a small house on Pershing Avenue, near Penn Park. Enough money was coming in that Murray bought a light gray 1961 Fleetwood Cadillac.

The next morning, Monday, July 21, they packed fishing rods, some gear, and a picnic lunch into the trunk of that nice gray Cadillac. Thirteen-year-old Gladys was left in charge of her younger nieces and nephews. By 11am the Mosleys, Lillie Belle, Hattie and Bubba get into Bubba's Cadillac. They drive into the Pennsylvania countryside to fish. It was a pleasant, hot summer day.

Lillie Belle Allen is remembered as a quiet, good mother. She made her own clothes, and was a good cook. She wanted more for her kids than life in the South could provide. At times she's a little dreamy.

That afternoon, when Lillie Belle wasn't fishing, she dreamily walked among the rounded stones at the York reservoir.

She took to holding them up into the midday sun, rolling them over, watching the water curl around their smooth edges. Sun and earth and water. A warm summer breeze. On this pretty day on earth it crosses Lillie's mind to collect stones.

I can't help thinking Lillie was picking up the stones only a few hours after Neil Armstrong, on the moon, lifted his last lunar rock, and examined it with equal wonderment. She must have turned the rounded stones in her hands, her fingers dripping water.

The stones of each day are for the young to collect. I'd find that out, writing this book. The old no longer have an interest, and they'll tell you.

Lillie particularly fancied several larger stones. She brought them over to her mother, dreamily saying they looked pretty. Lillie wanted to take them home, and make bookends out of them. Beatrice had to laugh. Just what Lillie needs. More knickknacks to clutter things up. Rocks yet. Still Lillie Belle fancied them. She put the rocks into the trunk of Murray's Cadillac.

They prattled the pleasant day away like this, casting into the water, talking, looking around, eating. One of them would by and by feel a sharp tug on the rod, and they'd reel in a sunny. It was so pleasant, everyone being together, they began to talk about maybe coming back tomorrow.

The day slipped away so fast they hardly knew where it went. The fishing was good. At last the sun was going down and the moon was rising. Somebody must've said they better be getting back to the kids. Somebody must've said Gladys and Debra probably were doing fine with the kids.

At last Reverend Mosley sung out it was twenty-five minutes of nine, and they best be going. Driving home, they saw a little fruit stand off the side of the road. They stopped and bought some treats for the kids. Milk, ice cream, cookies.

Rev. Mosley had his eye on the prices at the fruit stand. He always had his eye on the prices. Had to.

"Is food high here?" he asked his daughter about York.

"Yes," Hattie told him. "But we shop at the J. M. Fields store." It was a big shiny new store on Route 30. The store had just unveiled a new fountain. When they got back to town, Hattie thought it might be nice to take her folks to the store and show off the fountain. They talked of spending another day fishing. They could get some supplies at Fields.

When they got home Hattie took the things she'd bought into the house. Rev. Mosley went upstairs to the bathroom. When he came back out of the house with Hattie, the others were waiting to go to the store.

There was a small problem. Hattie couldn't get Bubba's light grey Cadillac to start. She ground the engine but it wouldn't start.

Reverend Mosley suggested they take his car. Suddenly the Cadillac started, and Hattie bid them all to get in.

# 4

## What awaited the people in the wrong car?

They made these plans happily oblivious to the world spinning around them. They were oblivious to the televised spectacle of the first moon landing, oblivious to the sudden war raging around them in York, Pennsylvania.

In Europe, the joke goes, you never knew when to expect the Spanish Inquisition. In York, in the late 1960s, you never knew when to expect a race riot. And over the third weekend of July 1969, a bad one flared.

It wasn't just York seeing these troubles, though York's troubles certainly had been brewing. Race riots spread like wildfire across the country. Watts had already burned, and that very weekend Detroit and other, smaller towns were burning. At Easter time, in a strange premonition of things to come, the son of the 1930s actor Stepin Fetchit drove down the Pennsylvania Turnpike shooting at cars. Nobody was taking it anymore, not even Stepin Fetchit's kid.

For decades the white town fathers of York prided themselves in keeping blacks down. That's saying it charitably. The York city police force provided the primary muscle used to humiliate and subjugate blacks, though the police were by no means the only tool in the shed.

The rioting had started the Thursday before the Mosleys had rolled into town. An all-out race riot now was raging.

The city that night burned in all quarters, lit up by countless arsons and firebombings. Police cruisers and armored cars were shot. Black snipers aimed from windows all over town. They stuck potatoes on the ends of their gun barrels to hide the flash. The York police force — staffed by under a hundred men — quickly found itself out-gunned and overwhelmed. Thirty-five state police troopers already had been called in. Before the end of the night, another thirty-two state troopers would be added to bolster the glaringly poor local force.

On the previous Friday night, July 18, 1969 a young city cop had been shot and mortally wounded. While on patrol in a black neighborhood, twenty-two-year-old rookie Henry Schaad was hit by a high-powered sniper bullet. The armor-piercing round ripped through the armored car in which Schaad was riding. His father, city police detective Sgt. Russell Schaad, knew the identity of his son's shooters the next morning. For some reason, he never pressed for any arrests. Like many in the York police force, young Henry had followed his father into police work. Now young Henry lay dying in a hospital bed, hooked to a respirator, slowly dying from a bullet fired through both lungs. To the police, blacks were the enemy.

As young Patrolman Schaad lay dying, the largely incompetent and under-trained York police force stepped up to what can only be called a war footing in their rioting town.

The police began to ally themselves with young white street gangs, encouraging the youths to defend their homes from what they saw as black insurgency in their neighborhoods. With the blessing of police, several gangs of armed, white teenagers converged on N. Newberry Street, home turf of a gang calling itself the Newberry Street Boys.

Newberry Street in York for years enjoyed the reputation as the town's red light district. It's a working class, seedy area of town. Men came from all over to pick up working girls.

Open prostitution in this working class town went on for years. It's still going on, I'd learn. How is this possible? The girls worked under the noses of the police force, prosecutor's office and county court system. For years, policemen themselves received sexual favors above a bicycle shop on nearby South Duke Street. At the courthouse, a running story involved a pimp making regular visits to the county DA's office, where protection money was paid to the prosecutor. The judges in York County demand their share. Policemen as late as the 1980s warned each other to stay away from the parking garage at a downtown hotel. Informants told police they regularly stuffed money and narcotics into the trunk of a judge's car, parked in the garage.

York is a small industrial town, very set in class. You are what your daddy was, and you keep in place. There's also lots of old money hiding under the rocks in York County. The wealthy of York, like the robber barons of old, do little, and care less for their town. They languidly mate at places like the York Country Club. The York Country Club remains restricted to this day. No blacks or Jews allowed. It's one of the places the civic leaders, lawyers, and judges hang out. Oh, blacks are allowed in to cook, or to wash dishes. They, and Jews, are always useful as the subject of jokes.

Reverend Mosley could not have known what he and his family were riding into on their summer vacation. Did they imagine the American dream? They got the American nightmare.

In the 1960s, *South* Newberry Street was predominantly a black part of town. Philadelphia Street divided black from white. North Newberry Street, just across Philadelphia Street from the Y, remained a white enclave. Residents saw themselves as making a last stand against a rising black tide.

In July 1969, activity on Newberry Street buzzed around the home of John Messersmith, his wife and sons, Robert, Arthur, Michael and James. The Messersmiths rented a small row house at 229 N. Newberry, a few doors past the tracks of the Western Maryland Railroad. The Messersmith brothers formed a club of like-minded delinquents known as the Newberry Street Boys.

By all accounts father John Messersmith was a consummate York county urban cracker. Picture someone who sees himself as a beleaguered, racist Davy Crockett at the Alamo. Picture John Messersmith as a hairy, backwoods, foul-talking Fagin or Artful Dodger, barking orders to a brigade of stupid white street thugs. Toss in a fair dollop of your garden variety white-trash bigot, add a smidgeon of the wildness of the eye of Charles Manson, and the dull-witted temper of Huck Finn's pappy, and you've got a fair idea about self-proclaimed neighborhood guardian John Messersmith.

He was a drunk. He was often abusive. Neighbors, on occasion, complained to police that John Messersmith took pot shots from his front porch at passing black motorists. If he had accomplished nothing else memorable in life, he instilled a seething anger and hatred in his sons, particularly in the oldest, Bobby. The two were bookends.

Bobby Messersmith was a true neighborhood menace. He's walked off the pages of A Clockwork Orange, without the inventive language. Several days before, on Thursday, July 17, Bobby Messersmith, in the company of his brother Artie, almost single-handedly touched off the riots of '69 by sniper-shooting two young black men, wounding one seriously. This wasn't Bobby's first brush with trouble. Police knew he was trouble. When he was fourteen, Bobby had done time for sexually assaulting a six-year-old girl. Some neighborhood hero. No capes, just hoods.

Throughout these balmy days of July the Messersmith boys and their gang shot and firebombed their way into the hearts and minds of their fellow citizens. They planned commando raids into black neighborhoods. They schemed to draw unsuspecting blacks down to the singularly featureless Codorus Creek, a polluted drainage ditch running through the center of town, where they would ambush and shoot their hapless victims.

John Messersmith made the basement of their home the command center. The basement of the Alamo. From the bowels of chez Messersmith they initiated the firebombing of many black targets, including the home the of the Spells brothers' mother.

Late in the afternoon of July 21, 1969, in their bunker command center, their dank basement, Bob and Artie Messersmith and their father John busied themselves drawing up another half-baked plan for firebombing the Spells' mother's house. They put word out across town, and beyond, to youth and police alike, that the Spells and their militant black friends were expected back at any time with guns, looking to terrorize the neighborhood.

For once in their lives, the Messersmiths had a role, a raison d'étre. A self-appointed mission in life.

They were the neighborhood protectors.

Around suppertime on July 21, under the approving eyes of police, white teenagers from across town and beyond began converging on Newberry Street with guns to help defend the neighborhood from the expected attack.

Some of the boys who heard the call for help had military training, like twenty-year-old airman Mark Barr, or army men Dick Wales and John Duke. John Messersmith saw boys with military training as particularly useful. When Mark Barr arrives late that afternoon with a .22 rifle, AWOL from the Air Force, he goes to the cellar of the Messersmith house.

"I seen Bob in the cellar and he said that the colored people were coming up Newberry Street and burn it out," Barr remembered a few weeks later. Burn it out. Light it up. Good words for a young man when he's clearing the breach of his rifle.

John Messersmith proceeded to craftily draw up what he considered a fool-proof plan to defend their castle. He allowed that there had previously been serious security flaws in fortress Newberry. In the early days of the riot, boys had been stationed at the corner of Newberry and Philadelphia to signal when blacks neared. Approaching blacks then would be stoned, or beaten.

The arrival of the cops at the barricade over the weekend was supposed to dampen this behavior, but in reality the cops had taken over the job of gatekeepers and signalmen. John Messersmith kept a police scanner and sat listening for alerts broadcast by friendly cops.

Trouble was, the blacks had proved to be smarter, more wily, and better fighters than the Messersmiths and the police. It made a white supremist like Messersmith look bad.

Just the evening before, on July 20, a carload of blacks had snuck into the neighborhood through one of several side alleyways. When the white gang members approached the car, its trunk swung open and out popped an angry black man with a gun, firing away. Many said it was Sherman Spells. This much is sure: a brief and wild gunfight ensued in the alleyway beside Newberry Street. The white gang members shot back. One boy shot wildly into the cigar store on the corner. A white boy was shot in the arm. The car sped away up Newberry Street, pursued by a police cruiser suddenly appearing from the corner. In a town where one still hears the phrase "nigger in the woodpile," meaning the worst sort of unexpected treachery, the shooter popping out of the car trunk provided pure hair-straightening fright. The Messersmith gang wouldn't forget that lesson anytime soon.

This time, John Messersmith vowed, they wouldn't outsmart

him.

As the boys arrived, old man Messersmith assigned ambush stations around the house and the neighborhood. On the roof. The windows, front and back. The back yard, the railroad tracks, a nearby bridge or two. Covering all the side alleyways. Even a railroad car down the tracks a piece. They were ready, and they fully expected someone to get killed.

They'd keep an ear to the police scanner for an alert that "a car" was rolling into their trap.

This time, he thought, no nigger was going to make monkeys out of the Messersmiths.

## "Wait for this Cadillac, cause it's on the way"

"I remember it was real crazy," one of the boys present that night, Rick Knouse, recalls. "I remember being in (John) Messersmith's house, you know, going down into the basement and him giving orders. Like, 'Youse take these weapons and go there and this group take these weapons and go over there. And you man the window and you take the backdoor and you go across the street and all kinds of, you know, go here, go there.' And you know out of his mouth was 'Kill as many niggers as you can.' And you know that would ring and ring in a person's head. And you know that's what would happen and people would scatter."

Rick Knouse continues, "It was like an order. 'You go here. You, you, and you go down here and look for, wait for this Cadillac, cause it's on the way. And I think that (had) something to do with the police scanner....'"

The police were active allies, Knouse says. The day before, on the street near the Messersmiths, Knouse says he encountered a group of supportive police. "I'm talking about fifty people around these cops and they were talking just a lot of shit you know like white power and keep it together and protect yourselves and we're with you and we're behind you." It was, he recalls, a "rally type thing."

And it wasn't just a single policeman.

"It was a crew of police down there," he says, "hollering what kind of gun do you got and this and that." One of the cops, he says, asked him what he was shooting. Knouse says another boys gave him a 30-06 rifle. "I didn't know much about it and I don't know who it was said he's got a 30-06 and he had shells for it. He threw a box of them down."

Another boy on Newberry Street that night, Roger Kinard,

agrees. Kinard remembered some thirty years later that the kids on the street had "the impression (the) police wanted (the white street gang) to back them up."

Rick Knouse remembers his arrival on Newberry Street that night. He and fellow members of his gang received a plea for help from members of the Newberry Street Boys. Knouse had known some of the Boys Newberry since childhood. Knouse was a member of another, rival white gang, from Girard Park, called the Girarders. Since the rioting began, the white gangs had banded together to fight the blacks.

"Some of these guys I grew up with in the Parkway projects, before there was Newberry Street or Girard. We had childhood ties. Sonny Lutenge, Messersmith, and I think Teddy Halleran and maybe Jeff Flinchbaugh came over to Girard Park and asked us to come over there because you know they needed help. There were all these rumors that blacks were gonna run down there and just like terrorize this whole neighborhood and they were in fear. Four or five or six of us decided to go over there armed, except for me and except for maybe one other guy. Our thought process on that was let's go over there and keep the blacks over there so they don't make it over here. If there's gonna be this war of people living and dying we don't want it in our neighborhood. Let it happen on Newberry Street, and we'll help you guys out. We were over there in the day time so that we would be there without having the risk of getting caught for being out after curfew."

The day before, Rick Knouse proved to be an unreliable shot. Knouse was present when they'd all been surprised by the jumping-brother-in-the-trunk routine. Knouse was so shocked he'd fired the 30-06 into the cigar store. He later heard the bullet passed through some comic books and cup cakes, into the house beside the store, where it lodged in a woman's couch. The neighbor had complained, and John Messersmith had taken the gun away, saying it was the "kind of gun that somebody should have who knew what they were doing." In its place, John Messersmith gave him a shotgun loaded with buckshot.

Now, while waiting to hear the tip-off on the police scanner, Knouse and the other boys waited. And waited. And waited.

Where was that Sherman Spells?

Knouse goes on to describe this period of waiting: "And he gave me a shotgun I didn't like everytime I leave the house have the shotgun you know (sic). There was a lot of idle time you know sitting on the porch, drinking, smoking cigarettes this and that I mean getting tired. There was drugs. There was speed, there was crank, there was acid. I mean everybody wasn't like altogether upstairs mentally you know what I mean. There was a lot of getting high and craziness. I mean when I know myself I was under the influence."

# "It was insane"

At the barricade, meanwhile, a little after 9pm, Bubba Dickson's light gray Cadillac, on its way to the grocery store, had by this time stopped at the traffic light. Approaching the light and seeing the policemen, Hattie Dickson made it a point to flip on her turn signal. She kept coming toward the intersection.

Her mother was a backseat driver.

"Don't you see the red light?" Beatrice Mosley asked.

Hattie stopped the car. The policemen saw four or five blacks in the Cadillac, waiting at the light, behind a few other cars. The light changed.

The cops allowed the Cadillac to pass the barricade. Years later, Hattie would remember the cops talking and smiling as one waved her through.

By this time, amid all the mob confusion down the block at the railroad tracks and in the Messersmith home, witnesses report seeing several policemen mixed in with the kids running around with guns. Were these cops on roving patrol in the neighborhood, as mentioned by Trooper Roberts? Were they policemen responding to Annabel Kline's complaints of snipers on the roofs? One of the boys present that night, Stephen Noonan, remembers seeing a police car at the Messersmiths' about the time of the shooting. Noonan reports an officer told the boys to stay inside with their guns.

Newberry Street was also the family home of a policeman. York police officer Wayne Ruppert's mother, Miriam, lived at 121 N. Newberry, a stone's throw from the railroad tracks. Officer Ruppert and his brother lived at the family home off and on over the years, and often hung out there. Shortly after the shooting that night, Officer

Ruppert would be spotted on Newberry Street, talking to the murderers. Years later, Ruppert would become chief of police.

We have every reason to believe cops were all over the place on Newberry Street at the very instant the wrong car passed through the barricade and came down the block.

Several witnesses report the following: as the car rounded the corner at Philadelphia and Newberry streets, one of the cops stationed at the barricade opened the microphone of his two-way radio and broadcast an alert that the car was coming. He spoke through a police radio located either in his cruiser, or perhaps over a radio this officer was carrying. He broadcast an alert about the Cadillac. The identity of this officer is a mystery.

We know of this broadcast because, blocks away, in Farqurar Park, Patrolman Charlie Robertson says he heard the transmission.

Robertson remembers an officer at the barricade radioed an alert that a Cadillac had just run the barricade at a high rate of speed. "Oh shit a car got through," Robertson remembers hearing.

This is collaborated by Rick Knouse, who remembers John Messersmith listening to a police scanner for word of the arriving Cadillac.

Out on Newberry Street, a sudden relay of shouts alerted all that the awaited Cadillac full of blacks was coming, and everyone without guns get off the street. A hornet's nest of doped-up kids, most of them toting guns, with, witnesses say, cops standing among them, looked down the street and saw a light Cadillac emerging from the dusk, its headlights beaming.

It looked all the world like the Spells brothers' Cadillac. Some of the white boys began to run, taking off through the backyards and down the tracks to get away.

In the backseat the minister's wife, Beatrice, noticed a group of people sitting on a porch, then, by a railroad track a short distance ahead, she saw a state trooper with a gun. The trooper suddenly pointed his gun at the car. Murray Dickson, in the front seat, noticed another policeman pushing his motorcycle out of the way, off the street and onto the sidewalk.

A block from the barricade they had just passed, as the Cadillac approached a dip in the road where a railroad track crosses Newberry Street, Hattie finally noticed the large, menacing group of white men at the side of the road, pointing guns at their approaching Cadillac.

"Oh Lord, they're going to shoot!" Hattie yelled. Most of the young men with guns were off to the right, just on the other side of the tracks. One was a heavy-set looking cracker. They noticed an older man with a gun on the other side of the street. Other young men with guns hung out the second-floor window of the Messersmiths' row house, while still more clung to the roof and chimney above. All had guns pointing at the car rolling out of the dusk.

Hattie said she'd turn around and go back. Lillie Belle urged her to keep going and drive past the gunmen, but Hattie panicked and yelled she wasn't going that way and started to make a U-turn to the left on the railroad tracks. The big car made a wide turn, as the kids with the guns followed the car around. Now on the railroad tracks, Hattie encountered a cement barrier. Lillie yelled for her to be careful less she hit the pole. Hattie excitedly said she wouldn't hit the pole and put the car in reverse and started to back up.

Outside, in the street, the stoned and scared boys saw the trunk of the reversing Cadillac backing toward them. They fully expected Sherman Spells or one of his soul brothers to pop from the trunk and start shooting, as had happened yesterday. Looking down their guns at the trunk of the approaching Cadillac, the car suddenly stalled.

Inside the stalled car, Lillie Belle announced she'd drive. Lillie opened the left rear door, jumped from the car, and waved her arms, about to holler. She reached for the driver's door and began to pull it open.

What happened next would live forever in the memories of the many boys pointing guns at the car, at the many neighbors who looked on from their porches, and the many policemen who watched in plain sight from the barricade and the street beyond.

Lillie wore a blue and white-striped blouse. As she opened the driver's door, Bobby Messersmith bore down on her and pulled the trigger of his long-barreled shotgun. He had earlier loaded his shotgun with a huge slug. He had prepared the slug by carving a notch in its top, all the better, he explained, for it to blow apart on impact.

Messersmith's shotgun roared. Lillie Belle was thrown back and lifted by the blast, torn from her sneakers. She fell and leaned against the car, her face toward the front.

"Lillie Belle's been shot!" her mother cried. Hattie swung open the door and climbed out. She saw her sister on the ground, bleeding. In shock, Hattie started to run down the railroad tracks. Noticing she had left the headlights on, she went back to turn them off.

As she got back into the car someone yelled, "Get 'em, Neff!" at Girarder Greg Neff. All hell broke loose as at least twenty-five boys in the street, in the windows of the row house, and on the roof, opened fire on the car. It was by all accounts a furious and loud barrage. Muzzles flashed all along the street, from windows and roofs, and other places. Flashes lit the street, witnesses said. Each volley rocked the car.

Inside the car Murray Dickson pulled Hattie into the car and held her down in the seat. In the backseat Reverend Mosley also put his head down, but Mrs. Mosley went to the door to try to pull Lillie Belle to safety. She looked out and saw that Lillie Belle by this time had slumped under the car. The minister told his wife to take cover and lay down; only God could help their daughter now.

The boys kept firing. One boy blew out the back window, shattering the glass. They kept firing into the back and side of the car, into the trunk.

The minister and his family cried and prayed in the car. The Caddy's thick sheet metal (and everyone keeping their heads down) probably saved the lives of those inside.

Neighbors watched the ambush from porches and windows. Some ducked behind walls and cars and looked on. Other watched through their curtains. One bystander was peppered with shotgun pellets. The gunfire roared. The whole side of the block seemed to flash and roar with gunfire, and burn with smoke.

"I heard a lot of high power rifle and small .22 fire," one man, Harold Loss recalled. Loss sat on the porch of a second-hand store with its owner, John Nelson, just down the street, at 127 N. Newberry. During the shooting, Loss saw at least four policemen standing a short distance away, near the barricade on the corner of Philadelphia and Newberry Streets, by the church. The cops — state and local police — like the rest of the people up and down the block, looked on and watched the attack.

"It was insane," Rick Knouse later remembered.

Up at the corner barricade, state trooper Gerald Roberts remembers watching the Cadillac round the corner and head up Newberry Street. They watched as it made a sudden turn at the tracks and stop. Then all he heard was gunfire. He and his partner, Trooper Steve Rendish, took cover behind their cruiser while the shooting continued. They did nothing to help the family in the car.

York policeman Ron Zeager likewise remembers watching the car cruise down Newberry Street. When the shooting started, they "took cover behind their cruiser," he says. Zeager, like officers Roberts, Rendish, Linker and Marchowski, and whoever else may have been standing at the barricade, did nothing to come to the aid of the family that was being attacked in front of their eyes.

For some reason they would wait for another team of police, blocks away in Farquhar Park, to answer the call for help.

While the cops hid behind their cruisers, the fusillade finally stopped, but not before one last blast blew out a rear tire. Tire air hissed through the night, mixing with the soft sounds of whimpers and murmured prayers of Rev. Mosley's family hiding in the car. The stillness must've seemed uneasy. Gunsmoke wafted above the houses and hung over the block. The gunsmoke took on an eerie quality in the gathering moonlight. The shot-up car with the body lying in the road reminded the stoned boys of something out of the 1967 movie *Bonnie and Clyde.*

Lillie Belle Allen's mother remembered a policeman at this point coming up and looking into the car. "A police officer finally came up and wanted to know if anyone else was hurt and we said no, and he said to keep down," Beatrice Mosley would tell city police later that night at the hospital.

Who was this officer? He obviously was one the policemen who witnessed the mistaken ambush. Perhaps he was one of the cops

Beatrice spotted standing among the gang. Maybe he came down from the barricade. I asked retired Trooper Gerald Roberts why they had not helped the family in the car. "We did!" Roberts told me. "There's a lot that happened," Roberts went on. "You don't know. You weren't there."

In any event, this officer seen by Beatrice eyed the body of Lillie Belle lying in a pool of blood, and peered into the car. He was the first to understand the problem.

Sherman Spells wasn't in the car. James Spells wasn't in the car. These quivering people, their hair and faces sparkling with shattered glass, didn't seem to be armed. No one in this car had anything to do with the shooting of Officer Henry Schaad. There was only the most superficial, the most tenuous and unfair connection to the shooting of Henry Schaad. Blacks had shot Schaad, a white cop. Lillie Belle Allen, a black, had been shot by whites. From that moment a thought began to take root in the minds of York police. *They got one of us; we got one of them.* The score had been made even. Blood vengeance, blood justice.

The cops, as promised, would just have to back up the boys. The cops at the barricade and the cops in the street who participated in this and who witnessed this would need protection too.

Otherwise, they were all in deep shit.

It looked like hell. A real problem, particularly with race riot raging in the background.

After the policeman asked those inside if anybody else was hurt, and told them to keep down, he got the hell out of there, like the other cops who witnessed or participated in the ambush.

The kids who had done the shooting meanwhile moved around the car, their guns at the ready, taking in the shot-up Cadillac and the body in the street.

Rick Knouse, years later, remembers the aftermath. "I recalled myself walking down, not the whole way down, looking just you know like damn. You know seeing the car and it looked like Bonnie and Clyde. Like riddled, (a) bullet-riddled car and this person lying there and shit and then I hauled ass back up to the house."

Before long they heard the sounds of an approaching police

armored car. Somebody yelled that the armored car was coming and the kids scattered into the alleyways. Some ran back into the Messersmith house. One boy ran into the home next door to the Messersmiths' and chatted with the occupants. A man, two women, and several girls chatted as though nothing much of note had just happened.

The street was empty, save for the Cadillac and the bloody woman lying beside the car on the pavement.

# 7

# York police to the rescue

The armored car meanwhile rumbled up one of the side alleyways and stopped some distance from the Cadillac. One of the young patrolmen inside, Charlie Robertson, got out of the car and yelled for everyone not to shoot.

Robertson remembers it this way: he and three other officers had been several blocks away, northeast of Newberry Street, in nearby Farquhar Park. The police had an antenna in the park. Officers were stationed at the park to protect the antenna from rumored attack. Robertson and the others in the armored car were shooting the shit with the cops guarding the tower. They'd been chatting when, Robertson says, he heard the call over his police radio that a car had run the barricade at a high rate of speed.

Moments later, Robertson and the other cops heard a sudden barrage of gunfire. With that they started off toward Newberry Street. Robertson remembers driving the armored car down Jefferson Avenue with three other cops in the car. He turned south onto Pershing, turning onto College Hill heading west to Newberry. In route, they received a transmission from the dispatcher advising that shots were being fired on Newberry Street. They drove until they reached the area of the railroad tracks, parking some distance from the shot-up Cadillac.

Robertson remembers getting out of the armored car and yelling, "Don't shoot!"

"Who is it?" Robertson says a voice in the darkness called back.

"It's me, Charlie!"

"Come ahead!"

Neighbors looked on from their homes as Robertson and another patrolman, Dennis McMaster, approached the Cadillac with guns drawn. Neither of these two were the lone officer who had peered into the car and told the family to keep down.

Reverend Mosley would later tell the FBI, "When the shooting stopped for the last time I saw a red Army type truck drive up near our car. *Two* men in uniform approached our car. There was a third individual who remained in the truck." He hadn't noticed the fourth officer in the armored car.

They popped the bullet-riddled trunk and found not Sherman Spells, nor James Spells, not guns nor Blank Panther militants, but fishing rods and the stones Lillie Belle had fancied that afternoon at the reservoir while fishing. Now Lillie Belle lay in the street in a pool of blood.

For many years Lillie's murderers would circulate a false rumor that there had been a gun in the car. It's quite clear the police searched the car and found no guns.

"There were no guns in that car whatsoever," city public safety director Jacob Hose told the town paper, the Gazette and Daily, a few days later.

Lillie's mother told the paper there was nothing in the car but fishing rods, "and some stones which Lillie had picked while we were fishing. She thought they were an interesting shape and wanted to take them home to make bookends." Mrs. Mosley told the paper she intended to keep the stones, "because they are the last thing my daughter picked out and liked."

To the police Lillie appeared to be dead, though she wasn't. "From the waist up she was blown away," Robertson remembers. "There was nothing there."

They called for an ambulance. The preacher's family was in shock. The ambulance came and they loaded Lillie Belle inside. Her sneakers were left in the road. Afterward, kids would say Bobby Messersmith took the sneakers as a trophy. For years there would be stories circulating in the city that Messersmith asked his mother to keep the sneakers in a trunk with several Klu Klux Klan robes and the shotgun he'd used to commit the murder. Sometime in the year 2001 the police would get around to looking for the trunk, with no luck. Also in 2001, the state police would finally get around to searching for bullets on Newberry Street, more than three decades after the crime. They say they actually dug a bullet out of the cigar store directly in the line of fire where Lillie was shot, thirty-two years earlier. They wouldn't want people thinking they were letting the trail go cold.

Back on the night of the murder, in 1969, York Patrolman Dennis McMaster told Lillie's family to drive the shot-up car southward, the way they had come, toward the barrier where he knew police were stationed. It was then that he looked down the street and saw the barricade abandoned. No other officers in sight.

McMaster recalled, "I knew the Pennsylvania State Police had been stationed at a blockade one block away." Which was why, he'd testify in 2001, he'd told the family to drive south to get away. "I radioed to the state police up there," McMaster remembers, "but I didn't get a reply." Nothing but static. To this day there'd be a lot more static on that channel.

The cops at the barrier had vanished. The policeman who had been told to expect the ambush, who watched the attack on the wrong car, and had done nothing to help the family, now had run off. Somewhere in the city that night there must have been a very busy doughnut shop, filled with very nervous cops.

Looking down the street at the abandoned barricade, hearing only static on the radio, McMaster, Robertson, and the two other cops in the armored car saw they were alone. Indeed, they were more alone than they could imagine. The other cops had, in a word, fled, leaving them holding the bag. Three decades later, one of these officers would be charged with the murder.

Days would pass before anyone would bother to examine the crime scene, or take names of the many witnesses. (Decades would pass before they'd bother searching for physical evidence as trivial as bullets.) The Cadillac, permitted to leave the scene of the crime, wouldn't be examined for another three days. It would be destroyed. The bullets shot at Lillie Belle, recovered from her body and the Cadillac, would be lost.

But now, the night of the murder, the ambulance pulled away, heading for the hospital.

At that seemingly most lonesome of moments, the victims and the police in the armored car weren't really alone. Eyes were watching up and down the street. One neighbor would later say that as the police approached the shot-up Cadillac, Bobby Messersmith stood a short distance away, watching from his father's porch.

The cops instructed the family to follow the ambulance. The Cadillac drove away on the rim of the flattened tire. The armored car followed, but abandoned the family, responding, Robertson recalls, to an urgent call for help somewhere on Queen Street.

Normal police procedure at a shooting requires city detectives to arrive at the crime scene and relieve the responding officers. City detectives normally seal off the area and oversee the investigation, interviewing witnesses, collecting crime scene evidence, and so on. But this was not done in Lillie's case. This was far from a normal case. The city detectives, colleagues of detective Russell Schaad, were nowhere in sight.

Except maybe one.

Police officers themselves were running. They'd fallen down on the job. The depths to which they had fallen, I'd come to see, were bounded only by the dark depths of the human heart.

They had screwed up. Not, as they thought, by letting the wrong car through, but by forgetting their sworn oaths to protect and serve the public.

# 8

# Blood on the tracks

Rick Knouse remembers running from the tracks as he heard the police armored car approaching. "I was scared," he recalls. He walked back to the Messersmiths', went up to the second floor and watched from the window as the cops from the armored car, guns drawn, approached the Cadillac.

Once the Cadillac drove off, Knouse remembers, "everybody was pumped up, jumping up and down like you know, happy, like you know, they killed some people and shit like that."

Knouse adds, "You know it was real crazy." He says afterwards he heard some of the boys talking, saying things like, "'Bobby hit her so hard with pumpkin balls it knocked her out of her sneakers from here to here.'"

The boys had come out from hiding and were congregating in front of the Messersmiths' house. Bobby Messersmith seemed exultant. He told the others in the crowd, "Well, we got one." Then, after a piece, "I blew that nigger in half."

Gabriel Mark Barr recalled lingering on the roof for five minutes or so after the Cadillac drove away. Several other boys had been stationed with Barr on the roof: Donnie Altland, Dick Wales, and two others he knew only as Fireman Jim and Dave. The view down to the street was partially obscured, but Altland had managed to get off a shot at the car. "I heard this shot and I turned around and I see Donnie Altland holding a rifle in the direction of the car," Barr recalled. "I think it was a .30-30. By that time they stopped shooting and we both came down off the high part of the roof. I asked Donnie did he shoot and he said, 'Yes, once.' Then he told me he couldn't see very good but he thought he hit the back of the car."

A few minutes passed before Barr climbed off the roof to the balcony. From the balcony he went through a window into the second floor of the Messersmith house. In the front bedroom on the second floor boys with guns gazed out the windows. Other boys sat or lie on the beds. Rifles and shotguns were propped against the walls by the front windows.

Barr went down stairs and looked into the kitchen. Bobby Messersmith and his father sat at the kitchen table, casually eating, like nothing much had just happened. Guns were propped against the walls around them. In the living room Barr encountered Rick Knouse, Greg Neff and some other boys. Guns were propped all around.

Barr went outside into the hot night. The moon was rising. There was a fire on the moon. He walked down to the tracks to where the car had been to see if there was any blood. A dark pool of blood shimmered on the tracks in the moonlight. Barr returned to the Messersmiths' house. He went back up to the roof. Donnie Altland and Fireman Jim were still up there. Barr waited on the roof until he heard Jim Messersmith come into the house from work. Jim Messersmith had a job at Allis-Chalmers and had missed the ambush. He seemed surprised and put out by all the activity in his house, all the boys running in and out. Not upset about the innocent woman having just been killed, but by all the commotion in his house after a long day's work.

A policeman with a two-way radio stood in front of the house, mingling with the boys, watching them leave the scene of the murder. Barr walked across the street with Jim Messersmith to ask the cop if he knew what had happened to the woman who had been shot. The cop at first didn't say anything but as the boys were walking away they heard him say the woman died.

Make no mistake, they had intended to kill someone, but they didn't know what that meant. The reality sunk in. The horror of the blood on the tracks filled most of the boys with despair. After all, they were just teenagers, playing soldiers, led by a psychopath. When they saw the blood they realized it had gone too far. They had killed someone. It was no longer a game. It had been taken farther than most had intended. Bobby was different. "Well, we got one," he'd tried to reassure them.

Some of the boys began to leave Newberry Street, hurrying away with their guns, some of the rifles broken down into pieces as they ran back to their cars.

Barr never identified the policeman with a two-way radio who hung around the murder scene, watching the boys leave the Messersmiths' with their guns. We can be sure he was a policeman, since only a policeman would have a "two-way radio" capable of transmitting on the police band. Perhaps this was the policeman who had broadcast the alert that the Cadillac had passed the barricade.

Gabriel Barr and Jim Messersmith went back up to the roof to talk. Jim Messersmith spoke angrily about all the people going in and out of his house. After about an hour they came back inside. Barr lay down on the sofa in the living room and fell asleep.

It began to sink in that they had accidentally shot to death a young mother. The mood of the boys began to change. Soon there was a "change of emotions," Rick Knouse remembers. The exuberance bled away. "The mood kind of changed from that to getting really drunk," Knouse recalls. Knouse doesn't remember much after he started to drink. "I just started pounding a lot of drinks and shit like that." Pounding drink after drink as the night swung above Newberry Street, Rick Knouse has no idea when he finally left the Messersmiths'. Maybe it was that night, maybe it was the day after, maybe it was the day after that. "And I don't believe we went back."

So much for the neighborhood saviors. Soon they would be laughingstocks of the entire town.

Later that night, at the barricade, the police at some point finally decided to act like police again. They were working again behind a barricade, stopping cars. Trooper Steve Rendish stopped a man who was leaving Newberry Street with a shotgun in his car. After brief questioning, the man with a gun coming out of the area of the shooting was allowed to drive on.

That night state police superiors interviewed Rendish about the incident. Rendish died in 1993, of a heart attack. Rendish's partner,

Gerald Roberts, remembers stopping the man with the gun. The man with the shotgun in his car, Roberts remembers, was allowed to proceed past the barricade because he was the "brother of a York City Police officer."

As far as we know, only one cop had a brother on Newberry Street. The Polk City Directory records that Lt. Wayne Ruppert's brother lived on and off over the years with their mother at 121 N. Newberry Street.

Years later, the boy known as Fireman Jim, whose real name was James Frey, would recall that Officer Rupprt was standing at the murder scene shortly after the shooting, trying to reassure the boys. Frey had come down from the roof, and heard Officer Ruppert telling boys they had done the right thing. Years later Ruppert become chief of the York city police department.

# PART TWO:
## Mayor John Snyder's 'misbehaving darkie' problem

# 1
## Shooting at kids in the park

The out-of-towners in the wrong car did not know they were riding into trouble. They did not know trouble had been brewing
between police and blacks in York, Pennsylvania, for months, even
years before July 1969. For more than a year, police had been shooting and brutalizing defenseless blacks. More important to our story,
the York police department had adopted a strategy of turning a blind
eye and allowing white vigilantes to do the shooting for them.

A year before Lillie Belle Allen was shot, in July *1968*, there was
the telling incident in which police shot at kids who were running
from the playground in Penn Park.

Thursday, July 11, 1968 had been a hot day in the city,
approaching ninety degrees. Throughout the week it had been growing progressively hotter. Immediately surrounding the park many of
the houses were well kept, with porches and screen doors and windows propped with whirling fans. But the neighborhood beyond was
in decline. Many of the houses where the kids lived were owned by
slumlords. The houses were broken down, the streets were confining,
and no one had air conditioning. That night, like the other nights, the
kids had nowhere to go but the park to escape the heat.

The park at least was green and comparatively cool. It was a
shady green island surrounded by the hot city. The park boasted several rolling acres of grass. Paved walkways led to a large monument pro-
claiming gratitude to the men of the city of York who had given their
lives to the "War of the Rebellion, 1860 to 1865." As night fell, the
kids gathered.

As happened every other hot night that week, a police cruiser
pulled into the park and two officers got out. They told the kids to

leave. There was a 10pm curfew, they said. It was only 9:15.

That night the kids could see, as usual, hatred in the eyes of the policemen. They treated the kids with disdain. You could smell it. The police were bigots. They seethed with hatred. They hated everything about the kids. They ridiculed the way the kids looked, talked, walked and lived. Like many York countians, they called the kids "niggers," or, if they wanted to show sophistication, "coloreds." The mayor of York, John Snyder, had his own preference. In public Mayor Snyder would refer to blacks as "darkies."

In their hearts, the police wanted the kids not only to leave Penn Park, but also to leave the city, leave the country, the continent.

This was York County, sitting on the Mason-Dixon line in southern Pennsylvania. In the days leading up to the battle of Gettysburg, a scant thirty miles down the road, the mayor of York and its leading fathers once famously rode out to offer Robert E. Lee monetary gratitudes and keys to the city. It's said by some that they did this under duress, but they rode some distance in search of Lee. Already the blacks had come north, escaping slavery, and had set up shantytowns in York city, in the shadow of the halls where America's first congress had met. Other well-respected and even prosperous blacks had begun to call York home. The town fathers' fervent hope was that Lee would provide the necessary means for an ethnic cleansing. These hopes however soon were dashed as these town fathers found themselves altogether on the wrong side not only of decency, but history. Frederick Douglass, when speaking in Pennsylvania after the war, described York as a well-known problem.

By the 1960 census, the ghetto, or the tenement (as the section was called in the restricted country clubs up-county) had grown to house 4,747 blacks, in an industrial, gritty city of 54,504. That's about 8.8 percent of the population. By the late-1960s, the black population in the city had risen to ten percent. The two sides, living in segregation, nervously eyed each other.

What you had in York County was a little bit of Dixie just north of the Mason-Dixon line. That's how a good slice of the white folks hereabouts liked it and wanted it, then and now. Many had come north from Maryland and points south. They could not expunge from their hearts the social order dehumanizing blacks. In the city of York, in violation of law, restaurants and businesses refused to serve or wait on blacks until 1963, when Mayor John Snyder begrudgingly issued a proclamation ordering city businesses to obey state law. Some will tell you that blacks to this day feel uncomfortable in the outer-lying reaches of southern York County, in places like Red Lion and Dallastown.

Several chapters of the Klan operated in broad daylight around the county. One of the invisible empire's chapters was established in a country club a dozen miles outside town, in Red Lion. They burned their crosses on the lawn where today you tee off, a farmer tells me. Confederate flags flew all over the white countryside. Still do. Out in the sticks, York County was populated with backward, proudly uneducated bigots. Something about the rolling desolate acres of moonlit rural York County brought out the worst in the varmint-hunting good-old-boys. Not much else was handed down from parents and grandparents beyond a disdain for blacks. No cop or DA ever lost points up-county for chasing and maltreating blacks in town.

So on the night of July 11, 1968, the cops showed up at Penn Park to simply harass and push the kids around. The York police were unabashed bigots, and they were about to set a city on fire.

That night about fifty kids congregated in the park. The policemen ordered them to go. Having already endured several nights of this, the kids decided to resist. They refused. The two cops, angered at the defiance, began to push the kids toward the street.

A fourteen-year-old boy walking past one of the cops dared talk back. The cop took it as a wisecrack, and slapped the boy on the back of the neck. The young man could take no more. The heat, the harassment, the racist corrupt cops in the backward Johnny Reb county, the slum. He turned and struck the cop. A fuse lit. The two cops scuffled with the boy, and another fourteen year old joined in. The boys were subdued, arrested for disorderly conduct and thrown into the squad car.

Enraged kids began throwing rocks and bottles at the cruiser. The cops radioed for backup. Dodging rocks and bottles, cops began backing away from the enflamed kids. Two more cruisers arrived and drove into the park on the walkways, driving through the mob, breaking it up into smaller groups.

One of the kids lit a fire in a park trashcan. The Rescue Fire Company, located just east of the park, was summoned. Firemen quickly arrived. It was 9:43. The kids now had broken into two, smaller groups. Soon five police cars and twelve cops were in Penn Park. They kept trying to drive off the kids. The fire meanwhile was quickly extinguished, even as several of the kids began to stone the firemen. Walking back to his car, assistant fire chief Santo LaNasa found himself stoned, and had to duck for cover. The police again backed away. They got into their cruisers, and resumed driving through the crowd, hoping to disperse the angry kids.

Only now did the kids begin to leave, taking off into the streets and alleys surrounding the park, pursued by the police.

One group took off down College Avenue toward the center of town, the police driving behind. One of the kids threw a rock at a passing car, and the police got out of the car and began chasing the kids on foot. Soon it became apparent to the officers that they could not win a foot race. As the police approached a playground on College Avenue, two or three of them took out their revolvers and, ignoring public safety and the safety of the running children, began firing shots into the fleeing crowd of kids, demanding they stop. One of the bullets struck a doorstep. Passing bystanders were dumbstruck and dove for cover, yelling for the police to stop shooting.

With that the kids disappeared into the hot night.

Following the stoning in the park, fire officials retaliated against the blacks by closing The Rescue Fire House until eight the next morning. The station's lone overnight fireman was ordered off duty, and the fire truck was moved several blocks away, to the Laurel Fire Company. Should there be a fire overnight in the neighborhood of Penn Park, help would be slow to come, if help would come at all.

This was nothing new. In the poor neighborhoods of York, emergency services in the best of times were a joke. Often you would call the police for help and no one would come. You'd keep calling and no police would come. Now the fire department made itself unavailable.

Hearing their children had been shot at, enraged parents called the York Gazette and Daily, one of the town's two daily newspapers. A reporter telephoned Police Chief Leonard Landis at home. The chief told the reporter, "I don't want to talk to you tonight," and hung up.

2

## Talking in the park about maybe doing something

The next day, July 12, 1968, was another hot day. Word passed that concerned parents and other adults were holding an emergency meeting in Penn Park. A minister would be there. Parents began gathering in the park beneath the statue dedicated to the Civil War dead, beneath tableaus of Union and Confederate battle scenes. Some of the kids draped themselves over the statues of the solders, listening to the grownups talk while their chins rested on the bronze soldiers.

Earlier in the day, several blacks, including Rev. Irwin Kittrell, had tried to talk to Mayor John Snyder at city hall. The mayor wasn't in, they were told. Now Rev. Kittrell tried to facilitate the meeting in the park.

The growing assembly of worried parents had had about enough, they told the minister. They had endured years of indifferent or outright racist treatment by York authorities, and now the cops were shooting at their children. How would the authorities react if police shot at kids in the parks in their suburban neighborhoods? they asked.

The Gazette and Daily reports some of what they said: "I don't think we can just sit by and let police pull guns and start shooting at kids," it reports someone saying.

York authorities seemed unwilling or unable to provide for basic public safety. They seemed to *endanger* public safety. The problem ran deeper. The police and their higher-ups seemed incapable of doing the right thing. Qualities of basic decency and empathy seemed to be lacking in many York County whites. The authorities seemed incapable of applying the Golden Rule to the poor of the city. They seemed to be acting with no sympathy, no humanity. How would they like it if they were treated this way?

The group angrily swapped stories of other outrageous acts of the city police. Something had to be done, but what? One thing was certain, they agreed, if racist police kept harassing the kids, the parents would side with the children.

They looked around suspiciously and saw that two whites were present — a newspaper reporter, and a passerby. It wasn't a good idea to speak of plans in front of whites, someone said. Others shook their heads in agreement.

The passerby was friendly, someone said, and the newspaper had done a good job writing about last night's shooting. The paper had reported that seventeen witnesses had seen "more than one" policemen fire "more than one" bullets at the kids. The newspaper cast doubts on Chief Landis's version of events. Earlier in the day Landis had met with reporters and had defended his officers' actions, saying only a single policeman, whom he identified as Patrolman Wayne Toomey, had fired a "warning shot" into the air above the kids. The newspaper published a photograph of a bullet hole in the doorstep across the street from the playground on College Avenue. The bullet was lodged no more than three feet from the ground. If that was Landis's idea of firing "above the heads" of children, then those heads most have been pretty close to the ground.

The newspaper notwithstanding, some argued, no white could be trusted. Not even the five or six black policemen in the ninety-nine-man city police force. They were Toms, who did the bidding of the whites, and who worked for the white man's corrupt courts.

The meeting ground on. More talk, more anger, no solutions. At last a hush fell over the group. A whisper passed. Look who's coming—. Chief of Police Leonard Landis pulled up in a car and walked across the grass. Chief Landis, a tall man with thinning hair, walked up in a rumpled suit and tie.

Chief Landis had been on the job a little more than a month. He did not seem to understand the situation or the remedy, though he clearly was worried the anger and the volatility could worsen. He was there apparently to say he needed help from the community.

Earlier in the day, at his press conference downtown, Chief Landis had defended his department's handling of the fracas in the park. His officers had done "a good job," he told reporters. The chief went on, "Sure we make mistakes. And when I find out about them, I go about correcting them. I wouldn't take a chance of ruining a city like this. I don't want to see it burned down." He had noted that disciplinary action against Officer Toomey might be a possibility. First some citizen must swear out a formal complaint, he said. And no one had filed a complaint. Chief Landis said the violence at Penn Park had been organized by a militant group of blacks. The chief produced a mimeographed leaflet, which warned residents that police were beating and shooting "black children." It advertised the meeting at Penn Park that night, and was signed, "The Black Citizens Committee."

Now, in the park, Chief Landis shared his opinion with parents that militants had organized the violence there the night before.

Several disagreed. What happened was spontaneous, they said. The kids deeply resented being pushed out of the park by police before the 10pm curfew. For about a week before the shooting incident, they said, youths had been passively resisting the police. Emotions had boiled over Thursday night, when they'd actively defied the vacating orders.

Landis said it wasn't only a matter of the curfew. The night before, he said, five residents had reported acts of malicious mischief in the park. These five complaints had come in within three minutes of each other, and two patrolmen had been dispatched at 9:15pm.

It wasn't so, parents said. There had been no misconduct before police arrived. They admitted there had been trouble on two previous nights, due to the kids' anger at being prematurely thrown from the park. Even so, Officer Toomey had no justification for firing his gun at fleeing kids.

It probably had been a mistake that Officer Toomey had fired his gun, Landis allowed.

The parents had trouble holding back their anger. Mistake! Toomey was a dangerous cop who should be suspended from the force, someone countered.

"What you don't seem to understand," another told the chief, "is that you have racists in your outfit. Definite racists. Bigots."

It was no secret. It wasn't only Patrolman Wayne Toomey. In a force of almost one hundred cops, fifteen to twenty were known to be maddog racist. Take, for instance, Sgt. Nevin "Jigs" Barley, who made no secret of his hatred of blacks, and his readiness to inflict pain and worse. Mayor Snyder's point of view was that a cop like Barley earned his pay, as nothing, except maybe the dogs, could scatter a group of blacks like seeing Jigs Barley coming. Over the years Barley would be described as a "big-mouth bigot" by the county sheriff. A plaintiff in a 1969 civil rights suit described Barley as a man who treated blacks like "they were dirt." The federal judge presiding at the civil rights trial would refer to Barley as a "strong-willed individual with anti-Negro feelings."

Now, this night in 1968, Chief Landis would hear none of it. "I cannot control the minds of ninety-nine men," Chief Landis responded. "If I could, I'd be home mowing the grass."

We're a harassed minority, one man said. We need a coordinated strategy for dealing with unjust police violence against blacks.

Another turned and told him to shut up. It wouldn't do to discuss strategy with any white present. "It doesn't matter who he is."

The chief, the park passerby, and newspaper reporter felt the color of their skin.

Well, we aren't going to retaliate against racist police indiscriminately, another said. "We don't want to hurt anybody who's innocent."

Suggestions began to fly. What was needed was a black adult patrol of Penn Park to observe the police and to prevent a recurrence of police indiscretions.

"In other words, you don't want policemen in the park?" Chief Landis asked.

"No, this is no concentration camp," the chief was told.

Rev. Kittrell suggested that Landis's presence was an indication that the chief was trying to find solutions. Kittrell said that Chief Landis "would like to see something done, but apparently he can't control some of his men because of their prejudices."

"Does a cop have the authority to become a public executioner?" one man asked. He went on to say he understood departmental policy was that no York policemen could pull his gun or discharge it unless he had some reason to believe a felony had been committed. Chief Landis nodded that was so.

Well, how did that policy jibe with chasing fourteen-year-olds through a playground with guns drawn? the parents wanted to know.

Chief Landis countered that the shots merely had been "warning shots" aimed in the air.

Frustration began to build. If that was so, the chief was asked, how did a "warning shot fired in the air" produce a bullet that lodged in a brick wall near the College Avenue playground?

Another man added that he had found a piece of lead that he had seen fired from a police revolver. He said he'd witnessed the shooting incident. The policeman's revolver was not aimed in the air, but at the kids, he said.

"Why do they always have to disperse a group of blacks?" another asked. "What's wrong with congregating in a park?"

Rev. Kittrell felt the group splintering, losing focus. He worried aloud not only about the police, but of random acts of violence by a small, "militant" group of blacks that would further worsen an already dangerous situation.

The minister reminded everyone that the black community would have to act as single body to prevent provocations on all sides. Otherwise, Rev. Kittrell warned, "What's going to happen is we're going to have a bloodbath in our streets and it's gong to be ten black kids lying in the streets for every cop."

That's right, some agreed. "It's going to take a real commitment of black people and it's up to us," another said.

Some suggested using the courts, or appealing to the political establishment, but this only brought derision from others.

Trying to use "the system" to get justice won't work, because it hasn't ever worked in York, several people said. One added, "All the courts are white men's courts." No one had to be reminded that last night's incident in the park was just the latest in a long list of outrageous incidents perpetrated by the police against the black community in York County. If you were black you couldn't even get the police to answer an emergency call for help. Using the courts and "the system" had never produced any change in York County. It's been tried time and again. As for police transgressions, all that happens, at best, is that a policeman is suspended.

"And why get them suspended?" another man asked, "They're only going to make them detectives."

Still, some thought they at least had to try to use the system.

Perhaps the group should seek a meeting with York Mayor Snyder, some suggested. That brought laughter. Hadn't Rev. Kittrell and some others tried to talk with the mayor earlier in the day, only to be told the mayor wasn't in?

"Mayor Snyder has a bad habit of doing that," someone said. "He's never in when someone wants to talk with him. If you talk with the police chief you'll get the same old runaround."

Mayor Snyder was not only "never in." Often he was openly belligerent to the black community. He cared little and did nothing about community development to eradicate the worsening slums of York, or to help the sinking city schools. He'd even recently refused to channel community development funds to the Crispus Attucks association's effort to rebuild the blighted community center. The Crispus Attucks center was the town's black community organization named, ironically, for a black who was killed in the Boston Massacre, which the British characterized as a riot.

Frustration and anger rose. York officials and judges had a great talent for sidestep and hot air. But now things were getting out of hand. They were talking about issues of public safety, the safety of children. Sidesteps and hot air are sometimes harder to fight than bullets, and can be endlessly more frustrating.

Some were disgusted with the indecision and inaction of the others. We have to fight back, someone muttered. "The youngsters more or less fight back and this is what the cops don't like." And the kids might be right. "If they're right, they're going to stand up for their rights, and we have to back them up."

The police were out of control. "They ran through a black neighborhood, shooting with no discretion. This is serious," someone said.

How would residents in suburbia react if police came into their neighborhoods, firing guns at fourteen-year-old children for breaking streetlights? another asked.

Another pointed out that the York police had time and again proved themselves to be untrustworthy liars. They'd even lied yesterday when they first said they didn't know anything about the police shooting at the kids. Now they say one officer fired his gun.

Chief Landis repeated that was correct, that Officer Toomey had

apparently fired his gun, but that Toomey's reaction was not warrant-
ed. The chief said he would like witnesses to the incident to come
down to the police station to file formal, signed complaints.

A teenager stood nearby. Chief Landis asked the teen to tell him
what kind of mistreatment black youth were subjected to by police.
The youth shied away. Well, Chief Landis said, he'd like the boy to
come down to the police station to talk to him in private. That drew
outright laughter. Some said anyone who spoke with the police would
be subject to recriminations.

Chief Landis said he guaranteed that if the boy, or any others,
spoke with him alone, he'd keep their statement confidential.

"I'm running a confidential investigation," Landis promised. He
said he didn't always tell the rest of the force what he was doing.

You better do something about Officer Toomey, the chief was
told. "This is a dangerous man. He shouldn't be on the force."

"We don't want to see our kids shot down in the streets," another
said.

A half dozen teenagers stood off to the side, conferring between
themselves while the adults spoke. They were downcast, impatient by
the indecision. One boy at last addressed the meeting, "If the
grownups don't do something, we will."

Chief Landis seemed at a loss. He described the 10pm curfew at
Penn Park as an "outdated ordinance." Other parts of the city have a
*midnight* curfew, he said. The chief told the group, "Go down and see
your city council and tell them you want the curfew changed."

What time had his officers arrived at the park last night to
enforce the 10pm curfew? the chief was asked.

Police started clearing out the park at 9:30pm, to enforce the
10pm curfew, Chief Landis said.

It turned out Chief Landis didn't know what he was talking
about. Over the weekend the city solicitor, John Heller III, would
announce that the 10pm curfew the police had been enforcing didn't
even exist in city ordinance. The only 10pm curfew on the books
involving city parks had been repealed thirteen years earlier, in 1955.
Police had been enforcing the non-existent ordinance out of habit, the
solicitor said. It clearly had been a bad habit.

# 3

## Generational divide widens

Those who walked home through the heat after the meeting that Friday night had a building sense of dread, building with the stifling heat wave. Something bad hung in the air.

Roving bands of kids began menacing the city, taxing the police's ability to handle the crisis. Police were put on overtime, but it wasn't enough. That Friday night police received three reports of cars being stoned in the city. One man's car was hit with a bottle. The man stopped and was threatened by a group of kids. Also that night, two city homes had their windows broken by rock-throwing groups of kids.

Saturday night was even worse. As darkness fell, wildness gripped the city. At 9:30pm, the police received an anonymous call complaining of youths breaking windows in a workshed at Penn Park. When police arrived they found the door and floor of the shed ablaze. Kids had broken in and torched the shed with gasoline they'd found inside. The Rescue Fire Company was summoned to put out the fire, and three public works employees were called to temporarily repair the shed.

A few minutes later, at 9:50pm, several blocks away on South George Street, kids threw a sewer grate through three display windows at a downtown jewelry store. A few blocks away, on Duke Street, a white boy was assaulted and robbed of sixty-five cents by five black boys.

At 11:35pm, at George and South streets, a forty-five year-old man was beaten and robbed by a gang of kids. Patrolman Charles Marrow witnessed the assault, and chased the kids, who ran off with the man's wallet.

Mrs. Nancy Heaps, an out-of-towner from Maryland, drove

through town that night with her twelve-year-old son. At Duke and Maple streets at 11:40pm a broken bottle was thrown into their car, cutting their arms. They required treatment in the hospital.

Duke and Maple streets that night erupted into a hail of rocks and bottles. One black officer who was called in, Elmer "Chip" Woodyard, age twenty-seven, recalled his amazement and anger at what he saw. Woodyard was one of only six blacks on the force. He was on patrol on the west end of town when the officer in charge sent a cruiser to pick him up and take him to Duke and Maple.

The neighborhood was in an uproar. Residents were excited, shouting, some throwing rocks. Cops on the scene indiscriminately swung their sticks and menaced anyone in their path, adult or youth, with snarling dogs.

There seemed to be a dozen to fifteen officers on the force who simply hated blacks, Woodyard later would remember. They considered any youth with long hair or an Afro a "militant," and their hatred seemed to override their judgment and professionalism. The racists cops, "seemed to let emotions override understanding in making arrests, while racism dehumanized their treatment of prisoners following arrests," Woodyard would remember.

Patrolman Woodyard watched as the police were pelted with rocks and stones, even as they swung clubs and threatened neighbors with dogs. Woodyard witnessed several officers simply go inside a home and pull out two teenagers. At last an order came over the radio to clear the area where the police had been stoned. Arrest or clear the area, the radio ordered, but the police had already been clearing.

While Woodyard looked on, two white officers without warning grabbed a neighborhood black barber who'd been sitting in front of his shop in a lounge chair, watching the turmoil. The barber had simply been "sitting on a lounge chair at his place of business," and suddenly two policemen were grabbing him and placing him under arrest.

There was a struggle, and a gun suddenly appeared in the hands of the barber. The barber had a permit, but the two white officers took the gun from him. The barber kept fighting. Woodyard stepped in and escorted the man to a cruiser, and told him to please stop fighting.

Woodyard asked the barber to get into the squad car. The barber complied, but not before a white policeman came up from behind Woodyard and slammed the door on the barber's foot. All the while rocks and stones were raining down.

Returning to headquarters in the cruiser, Woodyard vowed he would make no more arrests of blacks in this disturbance. At the height of the full-scale riots the next year, Woodyard would resign the force citing institutionalized "racism and bigotry" in the York police department, and a double standard of justice for whites and blacks. The Gazette and Daily would run a detailed front-page story. The other paper, the Dispatch, would run a short wire service report filed from Harrisburg.

The heat wave built. Late Sunday night, going into early Monday morning, some fifty kids broke windows near Queen and Duke streets, and hurled bottles and rocks at police and firemen. A newspaper reporter encountered a black youth who bragged of hitting a cop with a bottle. Why are young blacks throwing rocks and bottles at policemen? the kid was asked. Why do the police hit people on the head with their clubs? the youth responded.

Afterward, two white men came to the mostly black area and fired guns at the kids running in the street. Police never bothered to officially identify or apprehend the gunmen.

Dreading violence, and certainly mindful of retaliatory attacks from an angered white community, older blacks and community workers began to hold meetings with the young people. Why were they doing this, the elders asked the young. Didn't they realize where this could lead?

The events unfolding in York would later be remembered as a conflict between black and white. But it was just as much a divide between young and old. The turmoil between the generations, to understand each other, was just as pitched, though not nearly as celebrated.

On Tuesday, July 16, 1968, a black recreation leader in his twenties held a neighborhood meeting with a dozen or so kids. The older man tried to speak of the importance of non-violent civil disobedience, but the kids scoffed. They said they'd tried that, and it failed.

They had been beaten and chased by too many policemen in the past. Vitriol began to overflow.

The kids explained they had tried non-violent civil disobedience, and passive resistance, in Penn Park the week before, and it only led to the shooting incident. One young man explained, "I was sitting in the park the other night with my girlfriend. A police car pulled up. A bright light shone in my face. I said, 'Take that light off my face. We're minding our own business.' A cop gets out of the car, comes over with a billyclub and says, 'Get moving.' We get up and I start walking like this—." He demonstrates a slow walk. "He put the end of the club in the middle of my back and shoves. He says, 'I said get moving.' What am I supposed to do, run? So I say, 'Let's go,' and we walk away. Like nothing happened. Am I supposed to take that forever? What would you do? Last night I threw a bottle at a cop."

Had they attempted to create better relations with the police? the young were asked.

"What can you do?" another replied. "The cops are out shooting at people or busting heads, and you go down to city hall and they say they didn't do it and that's all there is to it. You can't buck city hall. We've been going to city hall for years. Somebody's going to have to get hurt, and that's all there is to it."

The next night, the Gazette and Daily would report that, on Tuesday evening, July 16, a man identified as Robert Simpson hosted a meeting of about thirty-five young and older blacks at his home at 114 S. Newberry Street. The purpose of the meeting, Simpson explained, was to get the kids to see the consequences of violence.

"Suppose some white man decided to shoot your sister or brother or mother and father just for being black, stemming from the disturbances here lately?" the paper reported one adult asked.

"That's just a chance we have to take," a youth responded.

"Why wait until it comes to that?" Simpson asked. "Let's stop now before someone gets hurt."

"We are going to try to stop these militant guys who seem to be bent on destruction," another adult told the kids, "and find another way to iron out our differences with the white man."

While some continued lobbying city hall, others had already

taken off in directions that in those days were called "militant." Various groups had sprung up. In 1967, for example, several dozen young York blacks formed a loose association, which they called The Black Unity Movement, or The B.U.M, modeled after the Black Panthers. They were avowed anti-white, and their influence would grow in the coming months. Young York blacks were tired of waiting. They were ready to fight. One flyer distributed by The B.U.M., titled, "Things for Brothers and Sisters to Remember," counseled blacks not to talk to the police, and to defend themselves "by any means necessary."

After nearly a decade of knocking their heads against Mayor Snyder's city hall, and being kicked around by his police, the time for talk seemed to have run out. Still, at the meetings like the one at Robert Simpson's, alarmed adults tried to keep the young people talking to officials.

"Why? We already went to city hall and talked to the chief of police and he told us there was nothing we could do, it had to go to city council," one youth responded.

Why deface your own property and parks? an adult wanted to know. Didn't the kids know that they couldn't burn down buildings near homes and molest people and expect sympathy for their cause from blacks or whites.

A young black answered, "The black man is not part of the white civic structure in York at all. There are no black men on city council, no black doctors, lawyers or civic leaders in high offices. So what can we destroy that is really ours?"

The kids pointed out that the housing was owned by white slumlords who never fixed the properties, and that they wouldn't sell to blacks. The streets were in disrepair, the schools were falling down, and a black man could only get a laborer's job.

"Right now as young teenagers you think as you do," the paper reported Simpson told the kids, "but when you get older and begin to look for a job and raise a family, you will find doors closed to you for hot-headed acts you do now." The kids didn't want to think of the future. There didn't seem to be a future worth thinking about.

So there it was on the table, the standoff between the young and the old. Older blacks were growing scared.

Those old enough to have lived through Jim Crow America knew the risk of cataclysm had always been there, the fear of the final American blow-up, the long-suppressed urge to violence now enticing the kids.

The older among them knew it wasn't just about deplorable living conditions, jobs and schools. It was about attitudes, often handed down from parent to child. It was easier to level mountains with dynamite than it was to change attitudes. God knows in many of their minds there'd always played the dark itch to pick up a rock or bottle and hurl it. The older among them, those who had grown up with lynchings in the South, knew with dread that an angered white majority could always muster more violence. They had grown up at a time when even northern heads turned from everyday atrocities. The New York Times through much of the twentieth century perpetuated a policy of covering lynchings in a "balanced" way. In a famous 1894 editorial explaining its stand, the Times decried whites taking the law into their own hands, saying such behavior was savage, but, it editorialized, on the other hand, "the crime for which negroes have frequently been lynched (rape), and occasionally been put to death with frightful tortures, is a crime to which negroes are particularly prone."

So they had gone through their lives, worked their jobs, raised their families as best they could, enduring. They went on with their lives, hoping the explosion wouldn't come. A tree lives in the same place all its life, never moving. Funny thing, so can some men and women. And now, before their eyes, the explosion seemed to be coming, heralded on the lips of their children.

They had seen some change come, slow as it was. Martin Luther King had demonstrated they could win using Gandhian non-violence, acting as one people, always seeking the moral high ground. True change can only come to the world in the hearts of your adversaries, Gandhi taught. Violence could only lead to more violence. To bring love into the world, you must love your adversary. You must be the change you want to see in the world. Yet to many of the kids, these seemed to be no more than fruitless slogans.

The barriers against change were formidable. Martin King had wondered aloud why it was a nation could send a man to the moon, but black and white children couldn't join hands as brothers and sisters. Attitudes about the color of skin were buried deeper in the hearts of some than the moon was high.

Only a few months before the shooting in York's Penn Park, on a spring evening in Memphis, King told a crowd that he, like any man, wanted to live, to attain old age, to have a nice home, but he somehow knew those things were out of his reach. He wanted them to know that he had been to the mountain top, and he'd looked over to the other side, and he wanted them to know he'd seen that we as a people would get to the other side, even if he might not make it with us.

The next night Robert Kennedy, running for president, broke the news to a campaign crowd in Indianapolis: "I have bad news for you, for all of our fellow citizens, and people who love peace all over the world, and that is that Martin Luther King was shot and killed tonight," Kennedy announced. "Martin Luther King dedicated his life to love and to justice for his fellow human beings, and he died because of that effort. In this difficult day, in this difficult time for the United States, it is perhaps well to ask what kind of a nation we are and what direction we want to move in. For those of you who are black — considering the evidence there evidently is that there were white people who were responsible — you can be filled with bitterness, with hatred, and a desire for revenge. We can move in that direction as a country, in great polarization — black people amongst black, white people amongst white, filled with hatred toward one another. Or we can make an effort, as Martin Luther King did, to understand and to comprehend, and to replace that violence, that stain of bloodshed that has spread across our land, with an effort to understand with compassion and love."

In Penn Park, there had been a gathering to honor Martin King. The police chased them from the park because they didn't have a permit.

It's a wonder all American cities, not just York, didn't burn. After King's shooting there'd been trouble, sporadic though it was, in York and north, into inner city Harrisburg. Bottle throwing, street violence, gang thuggery. No great flare up. But an uneasy peace.

On June 6, 1968, Robert Kennedy was gunned down. The brightest lights seemed to be going out.

What could you say to these kids who were tired of waiting? Kids who had just seen Martin King shot off a motel balcony? A great minister, thinker and orator shot down like a dog. It was getting hard to preach non-violence to them. There were other, harsher and louder voices. Malcolm X, before his violent death, challenged young blacks: "We want freedom by any means necessary. We want justice by any means necessary. We want equality by any means necessary." Huey Newton and Bobby Seale hadn't just stood around a park talking about maybe going down to city hall. They'd founded the Panthers, whose militancy was feared by the white establishment. Just the year before, in 1967, Newton had been arrested for killing an Oakland police officer.

The Tet Offensive in January seemed to have spun the Vietnam War into some nightmarish twilight zone. The front page of the York newspapers, besides the local stories of rising tensions, carried the news: "1,370 Men Killed in War Last Week."

Campuses were reeling. Soviet tanks had already rolled that spring in Czechoslovakia. What next? The Democratic National Convention in August. The black power salute at the Mexico City Olympics in October. A man around the moon in December....

For now, in York, in the hot July of 1968, there were those, like Reverend Kittrell and Robert Simpson, who were trying to keep a lid on the coming explosion. Still trying to talk to the kids. Still trying to talk to the mayor. Trying to vent passions by working the system.

Mayor John Snyder seemed on the surface unruffled and oblivious to the coming explosion. His opinion of the problem of race relations remained unfazed, and his approach to dealing with the problem had been the same throughout his term of office, dating from the early 1960s. He knew what many York countians wanted. They had a predilection, in general, to keep things pretty much the same, and, in particular, not to better the condition of blacks. This after all was the formula that had helped Snyder win the mayor's office in 1961.

By occupation, Mayor John Snyder was an insurance agent. He knew what the customer wanted, and he knew the risks. He'd previously served as York mayor from 1944 to 1947, when the city had a weak-mayor form of government. Under the old charter, dating from 1913, city council and the mayor formed a commission, governing with dual-executive and legislative powers. Snyder served on city council for eight years, from the mid-1950s to 1961, when he again stood for mayor.

In 1959 city voters approved a strong-mayor city government, a reform which Republican councilman Snyder opposed. Upon his swearing in, Snyder ironically found himself York's first strong-mayor.

Snyder pretty much liked things the way they were in York. He wanted to keep things pretty much the same. This applied to the "Negroes."

Snyder's Democratic opponent in the 1961 mayoral race was attorney Henry B. Leader. Leader was the brother of Pennsylvania Governor George Leader, also of York. He'd served in his brother's 1950s administration as legislative secretary and advisor. Returning home from Harrisburg, Henry Leader became a force for reform in York. He headed the York Redevelopment Authority. During the campaign Leader drew fire for helping blacks with urban renewal projects. A group calling itself the York County Conservative Democratic Committee sprung up to help rally a protest vote against Democrats like Leader. It worked, and Leader lost the election, despite a significant Democratic registration edge. The York Gazette and Daily reported the election results as follows:

"Graphic evidence of the protest against the Leader-led urban renewal program was the almost two-to-one swamping he took in the third precinct of the Eighth ward where a Negro Elks lodge was built to replace the old Princess street quarters demolished under the Park Lane urban renewal project.

"The Democrats had little expectations of taking this district where anti-Negro sentiment was made known."

Another explanation for election results appeared in the city papers the day after Snyder's election. Black city residents complained to the district attorney that they had been offered two dollars apiece to vote Republican.

Mayor Snyder understood (and owed his office to) the black and white facts of York County. Most white voters did not want to help blacks. The niggers can go to hell, as my neighbor still says. In York County, it's always smart politics to be dumb. These boys here go to school dumb, and come out dumb. Snyder won by 9,197 votes to 8,335. At the time of his 1961 election, Snyder was sixty-seven years old.

Mayor Snyder believed he knew how to handle the "darkies," as he often called blacks in public. In private there were harsher words. Over the years he'd been an avid student of how the problem was handled down South by sheriffs in places like Alabama. The darkies, he knew, hated the dogs. You saw it for yourself in the evening television news. Nothing scares a darkie more, Snyder thought, than setting a big vicious dog on his ass.

In 1963 Mayor Snyder organized the city's first canine corps. The dogs would prove to be his most memorable reform. The dogs were purchased by like-minded downtown businessmen, many who reserved the right to refuse services to anyone with an unapproved skin tone. There quickly arose accusations that the dogs were used solely on blacks, and were part of a larger systematic plot to keep blacks down. To this day, York residents are still haunted by the attack dogs.

In one incident all the way back in 1963, police allowed a dog to attack a defenseless black man who couldn't get off the ground. This had been witnessed by school children. The police had been in process of forcibly arresting two men, on the grounds that they had obstructed a police officer from performing his job.

"I remember a police dog attacking a man," Wayne Wilson told a city newspaper in 1999. Wilson, who by 1999 had become the city's block watch coordinator, in 1963 lived in the Freys Avenue neighborhood and was attending elementary school. "The man was on the ground, defenseless, and the dog was chewing him up."

This 1963 incident rallied blacks. They formed a group, timidly called The Peaceful Committee for Immediate Action of York. To the Jim Crow-jaded ear of a York County cracker this committee might as well have been called the Kill The Whitey Association. In a July 1963, meeting with Mayor Snyder, the committee demanded an immediate disbanding of the canine corps, and a biracial police oversight committee. Mayor Snyder refused, all the while referring to the blacks as darkies. Three hundred blacks thereupon marched on the strangely gothic and dark York city hall, prompting a second meeting with Mayor Snyder. At this meeting a spokesman for the committee complained to the mayor that blacks were routinely treated as second-class citizens. Mayor Snyder responded to the comment in a July 22, 1963 letter addressed to the committee and the citizens of York. Snyder wrote, "It is unfortunate to have them called thusly because I know so many of the group who well rate first class citizenship. Regardless of race, all of us may choose for ourselves whether to be first class, second class, third or fourth, or whether to become the scum of the earth."

The police attack dogs wouldn't be needed in a well-behaved society, Snyder wrote the committee. A well-behaved community would be required before he'd disband the canine corp, he vowed. Besides, Snyder wrote, police dogs are "one of the greatest assets to the police department," and, "are also a support to a policeman when necessary to cope with a group."

While Mayor Snyder throughout the '60s saw himself as benevolently coping with a group of misbehaving darkies, the black community began to deepen and strengthen its organizational roots. They tried to drag the mayor kicking and screaming into civilized twentieth century society. The mayor tossed a bone. Following the second meeting with the committee in 1963, Mayor Snyder had announced henceforth all city businesses must comply with the state's anti-discrimination laws. There was a growing sense of two distinct communities. The divide and the mistreatment seemed to grow, as did the anger.

Two summers later, in July 1965, police arrested a woman named Mary Brown and two men on Freys Avenue. Police beat the woman's face with a club, and put the dogs on one of the men. This time area churches and the County Labor Council joined about one hundred blacks marching on city hall. Letters were written to the state attorney general, and the FBI promised a preliminary investigation. We're still waiting. Nothing seemed to happen, and no change seemed to come. Conditions seemed to worsen. Throughout '65, the mayor and the all-white city council continued to refuse to create a biracial police oversight board. There were no racial problems in York, Mayor Snyder insisted. Nor were there problems with his police force, he said. For that matter, there were no problems in the black community, as far as he could see.

But housing was falling apart. Whole areas of York were shamefully neglected by city hall. Most of these homes had been neglected and falling apart long before blacks moved in. In February 1965, blacks again rallied at city hall, this time to protest deplorable living conditions. The state Human Relations Commission would later report that even though the city received thirty complaints a month about substandard housing, only one arrest had ever been made, and only one landlord fined in the eleven years of city codes enforcement.

Some of the neighborhoods were shamefully squalid. Some houses had no running water, had collapsing walls, unsafe wiring, bad roofs and floors, and outdoor toilets. Fire hazards abounded. Streets were pocked with potholes, and were never properly mended. Basic public safety was ignored due to racism, indifference and corruption. Mayor Snyder all the while minimized and scoffed at the problems. The day finally came when Mayor Snyder grudgingly agreed to tour some of the blighted neighborhoods. On a tour of one occupied house, as the mayor trod the rotten floorboards, he was greeted with a sudden crack. The surprised mayor suddenly sunk. The bottom had finally dropped out.

Mayor John Snyder had fallen through the rotten floor.

By the summer of 1968, Mayor Snyder had refined his favorite approaches in dealing to what he characterized as his "misbehaving darkie" problem. On Monday, July 15, Mayor Snyder again downplayed the significance of the street fighting, and scoffed at the idea of declaring an emergency. Earlier that day police and firemen had been stoned and windows broken during the early-morning explosion on Queen Street. The same day, forty black community leaders met at the Crispus Attucks center to discuss the deteriorating conditions and to propose addressing grievances with the city and the police. Blacks wanted to talk, while the authorities kept pushing them away.

Mayor Snyder and his police force had their own time-tested ideas about how to handle city blacks. The next day, on Tuesday, July 16, police arrived at the home of a woman named Carmella Hudson.

Without a warrant, they entered her home and, under the guise of searching for weapons, unleashed their attack dogs in her house.

The same day, Mayor Snyder quipped that the black community didn't have as many problems as it thought it had.

The next day, Wednesday July 17, 1968, the city's public safety director, Jacob Hose, whose own son was on the police force, defended the police. Lacking directives from the mayor, Hose found himself in the position of being the man in charge. York police, Hose said, "have been blamed for a hell of a lot they've had nothing to do with. The police didn't create the ghetto, they don't own those properties." Still, Hose tied many problems to deplorable living conditions in York city. The city council the night before had passed legislation moving the responsibility for housing from the department of community affairs to Hose's public safety department.

Hose said he would not use the word "ghetto" to describe any section of York. Nevertheless, he said, some neighborhoods of the city shared similar problems with "some areas of New York which I've seen. I would say that some areas of Freys Avenue were as close to Harlem as you could get.

"Those tenement houses up there I wouldn't want to live in," Hose allowed. "I don't know the solution to it. I don't know where you're going to get the money to demolish those areas, or where you're going to put the people in the meantime. Those questions somebody better answer who's closer to the housing problem than I am." Hose spoke of Hope Avenue, whose residents were demanding a playground. "If they want a recreation area over there, they've certainly got to tear down the houses. But where do they put the people?"

Would Hose change code enforcement policies if he found himself in charge? he was asked. Hose pointed back to the mayor, saying his department might not have any support for changes. "I don't usually jump across the creek unless I know I have support," he said. To get along in York you had to go along, and Hose wondered aloud why everyone else didn't live by the same easy-going, good-old-boy philosophy. Was this then an impossible situation? the public safety director was asked.

"I have never seen any situation that was impossible to correct,"

Hose said. "The improbability might be there, but when you get to the point you think it's impossible to correct a problem, it's time to fold up your wings and leave for parts unknown."

# 4

# Chilling

That Wednesday, thereabouts, adult blacks began patrolling the streets, hoping to stop the fighting. The patrols, consisting of some eleven men and eighteen youths, seemed to work. The police opined that things were quieting down. No false fire alarms were reported. "Things have been quieter around here than they have been for over a week," a police spokesman reported.

A different spin was given the mood by young blacks. Rumors swirled that police had been given orders for a crackdown. Worse, the National Guard might be called in, and a curfew placed on blacks. Older blacks warned that the National Guard would shoot first and ask questions later. "Everyone felt that if guardsmen were called in, it would give them a reason to just shoot down black people for no reason at all," a young black man told a Gazette and Daily reporter. "The kids talked a lot about the rumor and decided to cool things down," one adult added. The general consensus was that any calm wouldn't last. "It's quiet for a while—. A while," one young man told the newspaper. Some youth began signing petitions to send to city council.

Others disputed any notions of quiet. Residents of East Maple and South Queen streets reported, "things were not that calm all night." One witness reported having seen a group of black youths sitting in the middle of the intersection of East Maple and South Duke, "forcing a police car to ride around them."

A teenage girl reported witnessing a resident hit with shotgun pellets on the corner of East Maple and Queen streets. The gunfire had come from an apartment building on the corner, she said, though no arrests were made.

All the while there was no escaping the heat. In the Susquehanna

Valley of central Pennsylvania there is a kind of muggy heat that can be oppressive beyond description. Under a hot sustained sun the normally lush countryside and wide shallow river evaporate into a humidor of torture. The sweat doesn't seem to want to leave your body. Everyone's hair curls. If it's a good year for black flies, which brood around the river and creeks, you'll have them buzzing your face and clinging to your skin. Conditions become unbearable one week at least every summer. In York, in 1968, this looked to be the week.

The city found itself in the grips of a ten-day, July heat wave. Mercury in thermometers hit a near-record ninety-three degrees F., at 4:15 in the afternoon that Wednesday, nearing the ninety-four degree F. July record. Brownouts and blackouts dimmed streetlights all over town, and knocked others out altogether. The local power utility, the Metropolitan Edison Company, blamed the power failures on an increase in use of air conditioners, presumably in suburban realms of the county.

Walter Creitz, a Met-Ed division supervisor, blamed the blowing of utility circuits breakers on the air conditioners. York had seen a ten percent increase in electrical usage over the same time the previous year, Creitz observed.

In July 1968, Walter Creitz felt pressure to keep the lights on, yet this would not be the greatest crisis of his career. Not even close. Eleven years later, in 1979, Walter Creitz had risen to the presidency of the Metropolitan Edison Company, when the utility's nuclear generating station at Three Mile Island suffered a massive coolant leak. Creitz would then become famous for, in true York-officialdom fashion, threatening public safety by issuing one bald-face lie after another about the status of Three Mile Island, to protect company profits. Just a little water spilled on the floor, was Creitz's famous lie to the public. It would of course turn out to be America's worst commercial nuclear disaster to date. Scientists estimated Three Mile Island Unit Two's meltdown had come close to a Chernobyl-type radiation-release disaster. Creitz would lose his job over Three Mile Island. Three Mile Island Unit One is still in operation. In central Pennsylvania, money traditionally comes before public safety.

# 5
## Police allow disgruntled white to shoot blacks

The heat wave hung on through July that year and rolled into August, bringing unrelenting ninety-degree-plus weather to the neighborhoods of the city. Saturday night, August 3, 1968, was more than just another hot evening in the neighborhood of South Penn Street. The area at the time was described charitably as a tenement. It was a predominately black, rundown neighborhood west of downtown. Junk cars and burned-out houses lined the street. The only playground consisted of a dirt lot with broken basketball hoops and horseshoe stakes shoved awkwardly into the dust.

At about 11:30pm, a 58-year-old white truck driver for the York division of Borg-Warner named Chester Roach came out from his second-story apartment, above the Hoffman Brothers Meat Market at 226 South Penn Street. Honest, his name was Roach. One imagines his apartment, like the other apartments on the street, ungodly hot and noisy. No air conditioning, only open, screen windows partially obscured by Venetian blinds. The neighborhood is out on the street. The only escape from the heat was the porches, the alleyways, the sidewalks. It's noisy and hot in Chester Roach's small apartment, which he shares with his wife.

There would be two distinct versions of what happened that night. York's two newspapers would tell the story in two very different ways. The Gazette and Daily has reporters on the street, and for the most part takes the side of the people, and the neighborhood blacks. The Dispatch, the Republican business paper, becomes a mouthpiece for the police, has no reporters on the street, and seems to have an open phone line to the chief of police. This would be the case for much of the disturbances to come.

From the Gazette and Daily we learn the following:

Chester Roach had been drinking beer. He seems to have snapped from the heat and the noise of laughter and conversation in the street below his apartment. An air rifle in hand, he comes down to the street and yells for the "niggers" with their "black asses" to clear out of "his" alley.

The kids in the street begin to taunt him and yell back, at which point Roach began firing the pellet gun at them.

Fifty-year-old Buck Jones about this time ran down to Sammy's Pizza at Princess and Penn Streets to call the police. He told the dispatcher trouble appeared to be brewing. He got back to the meat market only to find no police cars had arrived.

"It was terrible in those days," one elderly black man told me recently on south Penn Street. "You'd call the police and they wouldn't come."

Chester Roach, taunted by the kids, went back up to his apartment and leveled a 12-guage shotgun out his window to the street below. The kids at whom he aimed kept taunting him, not believing he'd fire. With a roar, Roach fired, injuring several youths.

By this time Buck Jones had run down to Sammy's Pizza to again telephone the police. Jones later would recount that he called police four times between 11:30pm and midnight, when Sammy's closed.

Another neighbor, James McNeil, an anti-poverty worker and former policeman, arrived at the meat market shortly after midnight and immediately telephoned the police. McNeil later would say that the police didn't seem to want to act on the complaint. The police "seemed to want trouble to start," McNeil said.

Upon hearing the gunfire, Dorothy Sweeney, of Princess Street, walked to corner of Penn and Princess streets, a half block away from the meat market. She witnessed two police cars finally arrive. Wearing riot helmets, the policemen escorted Roach's wife from the scene, and drove her to safety, *leaving Roach behind in his apartment,* firing the shotgun at the young blacks below.

The police having left a sniper in their neighborhood, the youths began throwing bricks through the windows of Roach's apartment and the meat market. Roach kept firing the shotgun. Several kids set fire to a shed behind the meat market, hoping to smoke out Roach.

Roach at last appeared on the street, with his shotgun and a .38 caliber revolver. He began firing both guns, hitting eighteen-year-old Earl Smith in the lower back with a slug from the revolver. Emergency vehicles were not dispatched, and a critically wounded Earl Smith had to be driven to the hospital in a taxi. He was admitted into the intensive care unit with a bullet lodged in his intestines.

A scuffle ensued between Roach and those on the street. Roach was disarmed, clubbed over the head with his shotgun, and shot with his own revolver. His injuries from the .38, miraculously, were only of the flesh-wound variety. All told, in addition to Roach, ten blacks would be hospitalized with gunshot wounds.

With the shooting of Chester Roach, police again arrived at the meat market. Roach was not charged with any crime, but was allowed to file a complaint against his "assailants," whom Roach said had provoked the fight by throwing bricks through his window. Roach, contrary to all witnesses of the event, claimed kids were breaking into the meat market and he had simply defended himself. Police would say that they had received a call, apparently from Roach, saying that the market was being vandalized and bricks were flying through windows, but this call apparently came after Roach had gone down to the street with firearms.

Roach nevertheless was given a ride to the hospital in an ambulance, while the meat market burned. The police arrived in force in one of the department's makeshift armored cars. They weren't true armored personnel cars, but delivery trucks on loan from a local bank. These trucks weren't even what you'd call properly armored. Quarter-inch steel plates had been fastened to their sides. They looked like overgrown milk delivery trucks. Their bullet-worthiness had never been tested.

In an uncharacteristic display of whimsy, the York police had nicknamed their three armored cars Bonnie, Clyde, and Big Al, the last presumably named after Al Capone. The twisted psychology of naming their equipment after three of America's most notorious killers is beyond the scope of this book.

The police parked an armored car in front of the burning market. They aimed the barrels of their guns from the slits in the armor plating, peering out as though on the moon.

Angered kids, meanwhile, turned over and burned the car of longtime resident Robert Goodling, who vowed to pack up and move. He'd been living in the neighborhood for fifteen years and now he'd had enough. Police at last barricaded the area, allowing only residents to enter.

The other newspaper, the Dispatch, relates these events much differently. It accepts Roach's story that he merely had been responding to a break-in at the meat market below. With no reporters on the scene, the Dispatch treats the police blotter as gospel.

It relates, "Police reports indicated that Roach noticed the burglary in progress at the meat market and was seen through his window by eight youths on the street. A brick hurled through the window knocked down a Venetian blind and struck Roach. This was followed by a shotgun blast from the street that also struck him."

The Dispatch casts Roach as responding as would any white, gun-loving York County truck driver whose life and limb was threatened by the dark swarm below. "Roach replied with a .12 gauge shotgun fire and then left the apartment to go to Sam's Cafe, 254 South Penn Street, to obtain help," the Dispatch reports.

"He was intercepted, police said, by the youths who 'jumped him' and took his .38 caliper revolver. Percy W. Smith, 65, of 300 South Penn Street, attempted to aid Roach and was also beaten. Smith was treated at the hospital for broken ribs."

This version of event of course is suspect. No one but Roach reported a break-in at the meat market below. It omits the police evacuating Mrs. Roach and leaving Chester behind to go on shooting. It doesn't mention that Roach obviously had been down on the street with weapons more than once, and so on.

Violence spread through the city with word that Roach had not been arrested. Saturday night into Sunday morning hundreds of young people lurked in the streets and alleyways, engaging police with guns and firebombs. This was the first mention I've found of guns wielded by a black mob.

The police brought out armored cars, Bonnie and Al. They used the armored cars to patrol streets and to block intersections, including

Newberry and Princess, Green and Princess, and College and Penn, "employing a tactic which proved helpful the previous night," the Dispatch observed. Detective Lt. Charles McCaffery directed the task force charged with sealing the troubled area.

Rock and bottle throwing again flared. The Dispatch makes mention of guns wielded by blacks, reporting, "Police said that cursing youth began to mill at various places and guns were seen. The largest crowd, about 150 persons, began threatening officers about 9 p.m. at Princess and Penn where one shot was fired by a member of the crowd, police said."

Blacks now had turned to guns. A milestone. Of course, Chester Roach had been firing at them, with what appeared to be police blessing. In such circumstances, hadn't blacks every right to defend themselves? What's also interesting here is the Dispatch's description of the police being "threatened" by a dark, ominous throng. A Southern white man's worst nightmare.

It's no surprise that what followed was a long weekend of trouble. Arsons, thrown objects, hospitalizations. All clearly caused by Chester Roach and the monumental bad judgment, if not outright complicity, of police.

On Monday, police announced they would arrest Chester Roach, after all. Roach was charged with aggravated assault with intent to kill, and aggravated assault and battery. He was arraigned and released on five thousand dollars bail.

Too little, too late. On Monday about noon, York police corporal Peter Chantiles arrived at the burned out meat market and found kids picking through the debris. Earlier, the owner of the market, Edward Hoffman, had been to his store with an insurance man. The kids and other witnesses, including a photographer for local NBC affiliate WGAL TV-8, said Hoffman told the kids they could take what they wanted. The WGAL photographer was at the scene asking locals to simulate riot conditions for his newscast, though he later promised nothing of the sort would be aired.

Upon his arrival, Cpl. Chantiles grabbed an eleven-year-old boy and kicked him in the back, forcibly knocking the boy through the door. Cpl. Chantiles then fired his gun at escaping children and adults, scattering them, injuring a nine-year-old girl in the ensuing panic. The girl was hospitalized for lacerations of the knee.

A neighborhood worker with the Community Progress Council, Vincent Williams, age twenty-five, grabbed Chantiles' arm to prevent another firing. Why had Chantiles discharged his weapon "with all these children around?" Williams asked. Whereupon Chantiles arrested Williams for "interfering with a policeman in riotous conditions."

A newspaper reporter, meanwhile, ventured upstairs to the gutted apartment Chester Roach until the evening before shared with his wife. He found the floor littered with shotgun shells and beer cans.

At about 3:15 in the afternoon, Cpl. Chantiles returned to the store with Patrolman Wayne Toomey and another officer. Chantiles soon fired one, and possibly two, canisters of tear gas at a group of kids standing on the corner.

A large, angry mob formed, at which point one of the armored cars was called. Sergeant Wayne Ruppert, the Newberry Street denizen, parked the armored car in front of the store, got out, and began speaking with a handful of kids.

Ruppert was "acting like a cop—talking to us and telling us how we can avoid situations like this," one of the youths later told the newspaper. Ruppert went back to his car. Witnesses said Ruppert was approached by Cpl. Toomey, who told Ruppert that if he was any kind of policeman he'd give Toomey the name of the kids with whom he'd just been speaking.

Events by now were so much out of hand that District Attorney John Rauhauser had come to the Penn Street area to talk with, and try to assuage, residents. He moved down the block talking to the crowd. Neighbors complained bitterly of Cpl. Chantiles firing his gun at children. They complained that no one paid attention to their complaints.

Cpl. Chantiles was a dangerous man who should be jailed or, at the very least, suspended, neighbors told DA Rauhauser. Rauhauser, a balding, mid-sized man in a light, well-tailored suit, considered the situation.

Leaving Penn Street, Rauhauser drove to the office of Mayor Snyder and asked that Chantiles be suspended. The mayor complied. DA Rauhauser returned to meat market at 4:30pm and told the crowd: "I just left the mayor's office and Chantiles has been officially suspended for ten days pending an investigation. I had demanded or very strongly suggested that he be suspended after receiving many complaints on his actions today."

Shortly after Rauhauser returned, a small fire broke out in the rear of the meat market. By now it was about 5pm. A police car arrived and two officers, including Sergeant Wayne Ruppert, stood guard for a few minutes at the front and back doors of the store. After about fifteen minutes, the guards took off, leaving Sgt. Ruppert talking with a group of fifteen or so youths at the front of the store. While the sergeant spoke with the kids, another group removed items through the store's back door. Getting wise, Ruppert drove his car around back. There he got a flat tire. While he changed the tire, looters carried goods out the front door. It was now about 6pm.

Throngs began to clear out the store. Children as young as eight years of age, and adults, carried whatever remained from the shelves. Some filled their arms with groceries and fresh meats and distributed the goods to the throng out front.

After a few minutes, some began throwing their booty at passing white motorists. Several cars were hit with bottles of prune juice and cleaning fluid. Several received cuts from flying glass. One motorist was accosted by a youth wielding a can of shaving cream, and was sprayed in the face.

Once Sgt. Ruppert had finished changing his tire, he drove around to the front of the store. He made several kids return goods they had stolen. Then he left.

A short while later another fire broke out in a garage fifty feet down Hope Alley, behind the meat market. Fireman arrived, guarded by fifteen policemen. It was about 6:50pm. Two policemen stood with dogs at Penn and Hope Alley. Others, toting rifles and tear gas, mingled with firefighters. The line of policemen ran from Hope Alley down Penn Street to Princess. When the fire was extinguished, the cops left.

Disturbances like this raged for several days, building to Monday evening. Someone set fire to the York Bedding factory on Queen Street. Again, police stood by with rifles as firemen from two companies fought the blaze.

Troubled areas around Penn and Princess streets were sealed off. Police used barricades to block traffic from entering or leaving. Shotgun toting policeman patrolled the areas in full riot gear, wearing plastic face shields. They brought out twelve dogs.

At midnight police reported hearing shots in the area. But a newspaper reporter witnessed "the arbitrary firing of weapons by police."

There was mayhem on the streets. Not only were the police doing nothing to stop the escalation, they unquestionably added to the mayhem. Some argued that the police, wanting to see black blood flow, intentionally whipped up the storm.

Shots were reported emanating from 202 South Penn Street. Witnesses said one policeman recklessly pointed his weapon into the window of the building and fired at point-blank range. Others said policeman chased children through an alleyway. At last, police fired tear gas into the building, which turned out to have been occupied by Cleo Holmes, his wife, and their 15-month-old baby. After several minutes, Mrs. Holmes came out into the alley screaming, clutching her baby. No sniper was found.

At 11:15 Monday night, more shots were fired at Green and Princess streets. Police used a spotlight to illuminate rooftops, and brought out both armored cars. At 11:30pm, someone smashed the rear window of a police cruiser.

City resident John Nolan reported that police entered his home without a warrant and unleashed three police dogs. A pregnant woman was in the house at the time, Nolan complained.

Not far away, about this time, two newspaper reporters witnessed police running amok at Penn and Princess streets. "Kill them! Shoot them!" the reporters heard the police yell.

"The police, both reporters said, seemed to have lost self-control," the York Gazette and Daily reported.

The police had lost control not only of the streets, but also of themselves. Nine people were arrested over the weekend of trouble. Among them, a newspaper reporter, charged with failing to follow a policeman's order.

Police began to take out their wrath on the local newspaper reporters. Patrolman Wayne Toomey, whose gun firing at Penn Park had started the trouble, attempted to block reporters from entering the police station. In Toomey's eyes, it must not have been a public building.

Sunday evening, Patrolman William Hose, the son of the public safety director, said to a local newspaper reporter at the police station, "You dirty son of a bitch. I hope you get in my way over there." Hose at the time was carrying a box of bullets and a high-powered rifle. Hose was never charged for these threats. He would later go on serve as York's chief of police. Today, Bill Hose is York County sheriff, overseeing a department known for corruption, false arrests and brutality.

This clearly was not a race riot. It was a police riot.

Newspaper reporters also began to face hostility from the public. The Gazette and Daily reported on Monday, August 5, 1968, "Earlier in the evening, while questioning witnesses on South Penn Street, a reporter was shoved by a group of youths and told that his life was in danger 'because you're white.'

"A reporter was later slapped several times in the face and hit in the stomach by youths. 'You aren't safe on the street, white man,' he was told. The reporter left the area.

"During the afternoon, a reporter had his notepad taken by a resident who remarked that the residents 'were tired of honkey reporters coming down here and writing lies about us.'

"Another reporter, confronted with a similar situation, escaped injury when a black adult intervened and defended the reporting accuracy of The Gazette and Daily."

Throughout this latest round of trouble, clearly caused if not instigated by police, Mayor John Snyder refused to declare an emergency. Nor would he ask for help from state police or the National Guard. His police had the situation well in hand, he'd drool. Most York cops worked twelve-hour shifts, and some seemed to relish the opportunity to shoot at blacks.

Other York residents weren't so sanguine. Fourteen members of the county's advisory council to the state Human Relations Commission put their names to a telegram asking Pennsylvania Governor Ray Shafer for "immediate action" in York.

The group wrote the governor about the incident involving Chester Roach. "On Saturday, August 3, 1968, ten black persons, pre-dominantly teenagers, were shot by one alleged white man in two reported separate shooting incidents by the same alleged white man," the telegram to the governor read. "Following the first incident in which several were wounded, the York City police reportedly arrived, they did not arrest nor disarm the white man but merely removed his wife for her own safety, thereupon the police left, and the alleged white shooter resumed shooting, wounding several more, one critical-ly.

"We demand to know why the York City police department did not apprehend nor arrest nor disarm the alleged white shooter when they had the full opportunity to do so and further why that man remains at large even now. York is in crisis. We request immediate action by you as you deem appropriate."

Governor Shafer, a quiet, retiring man from Meadville, didn't get the telegram that day, and provided no immediate protective action. An aide explained the governor was in Miami Beach, Florida, at the Republican National Convention.

Richard Nixon was about to receive the nomination for the presi-dency of the United States.

# 6
## "Get him Sarge, kill that black nigger!"

Summer headed into fall of 1968, and troubles didn't stop. The first weekend in September after Labor Day traditionally marks the start of the York Fair. It is one of the country's oldest and largest country fairs. The fair features old-fashioned carnival rides, grease-soaked country foods, and big-name entertainers. At the York Fair, to this day, you can feast on such down-home delicacies as hog mawl, funnel cakes and barbeque ribs. Enough fat-heavy food to clog your arteries and help you fine tune that belt-overhanging paunch that no York County squire seems without.

In recent years big-name entertainers have included such white country acts as Alabama, Billy Ray Cyrus with his mullet hairdo and his Achy Breaky Heart, and other down-home, cracker delights. There are chain saw competitions and swine races. Ferris wheels, carnie acts and barkers.

In 1968 the York Fair seems to have sought a wider appeal.

I called the fairgrounds to inquire about the entertainers in 1968. A gruff-sounding though patient man spoke with me. His voice was quintessential York. No hint of Madison Avenue polish. Gritty and earthy. He seemed to know what I was asking, and why.

He read the 1968 York Fair entertainment bill to me: The head-line entertainers that year included New Orleans horn player Al Hirt, the Lawrence Welk singers, Bobby Vinton, comedians Allen and Rossi, and The New Christy Minstrels. The star attraction of the 1968 York Fair was no less than the godfather of soul, James Brown. In his gruffness I detected an unspoken, "Why can't we all listen to James Brown without bashing in each other's heads?"

James Brown's presence at the York Fair no doubt brought out a large black audience to the Fair Grounds, just outside the confines of the city. This culture clashed with the often under-educated whites who frequented the fair.

Throughout the run of the York Fair that year, rumbles and fights broke out between rival white gangs, and between black and white. Knives and guns were flashed at the least provocation. Look at somebody the wrong way and a fight could break out.

Among the rowdy gangs police had to deal with at the 1968 York Fair was a group of whites calling themselves the Newberry Street Boys. Like many gangs in York, their home turf gave them their names. Gangs had names like Swampers, Girarders, Roosevelt Park Inc., and Yorklyn.

One former member of a gang explained to me that territory and home turf triggered a large part of the gang fighting. "Kids come over from another neighborhood, taunting you, and next thing you know you and your neighborhood friends are out on the street, defending your street."

But it wasn't only about territory. A good bit of York County gang activity was for entertainment, plain and simple. This wasn't just in the city, but also in the outer-lying countryside. A friend of mine grew up in Hellam, a small York County borough ten or fifteen miles outside York city. My friend remembers rumbles regularly taking place in Hellam in the 1960s, when he was growing up. "Word would go out there was going to be a rumble somewhere outside town that evening, and everybody would show up to fight or to watch. It was what we did for entertainment when I was a kid," he told me. "We'd show up and watch the older kids fight."

It wasn't only the guys engaged in fighting. An old-time York countian tells me girls traveled with each gang, "sort of their ladies' auxiliaries." Between bouts, the girls would fight.

These kids liked to fight and the York police seemed unable to control them, and unwilling to provide alternative recreation. They would give the kids what they wanted.

Mayor Snyder and his public safety director, Jacob Hose, spent no extra money on recreation for the kids, or community outreach. Instead, they relied on the old standby: more dogs. The first week of

September 1968, just in time for the York Fair, they announced the despised canine corps would be expanded to include eleven officers — increased by four men — and thirteen dogs. A reciprocal training agreement with surrounding townships and counties made forty-one dogs and their handlers available "in case of trouble."

The use of dogs was not only inhumane, and ill advised, they provided a false sense of security, a Maginot Line against the gathering explosion.

The same day the acquisition of more dogs was announced, residents learned that the dogs had mauled a twenty-three-year-old city man. Police waited more than two hours to take the man to York Hospital.

George Linrock Elliot, of the 200 block of Green Street, was bitten, police said, after he refused to produce identification. Police accused Elliot of refusing to get in the squad car after he was arrested. "At that point George Elliot pulled away from me and tried to strike me," said one of the canine officers, Patrolman Ronald Heist.

Heist's dog then attacked Elliot. This happened at 3:40pm. York Hospital records indicate Elliot was not admitted to the emergency room for treatment of a dog bite of the lower leg until 5:50pm. Elliot was allowed to suffer and bleed in the city jail for two hours. Magistrate George Chantiles, brother of the officer suspended in the meat market shooting incident, gave Elliot thirty days in prison.

Soon even the high school sporting events would turn into orgies of police brutality and gang rowdyism. On the evening of September 20, 1968, fights broke out following a football game between York's William Penn High School and Cedar Cliff High School at York's Small Athletic Field. Even before the game, York High's principal, Dr. O. Meredeth Parry, had heard rumors of expectant gang rumbles at the game.

The atmosphere felt charged with violence. Skirmishes broke out. Police confiscated a length of chain used as a blackjack in the grandstands. Cedar Cliff disputed a call, and resumed play under protest, a fact not announced for fear of worsening the violence. The game ended with a come-from-behind victory by York. Fights suddenly erupted between young blacks, broken up by older blacks. Chants of "fight! fight!" rumbled the stadium. As the crowd spilled out of the athletic field, more fights started.

All available police officers were called in, including the canine units. Police arrived in full riot regalia, bringing along an armored car and tear gas.

The rowdy crowd spilled onto George Street. Motorists were pulled from cars and beaten by youths, and windows were smashed. The police responded, by all accounts, with even more brutality. Neighbors sat watching on porches and front steps.

Before the night was over, ten people would be treated for dog bites, and fifteen arrested. One fifteen-year-old boy, Calvin Stokes of Jessup Place, later dictated a first-person account of his treatment by York police and their dogs. Stokes statement, which was published anonymously by the Gazette and Daily, reads:

"I was returning from the football game about 10:30 Friday night, walking on the east side of George Street where, at Maple, I started across George Street on my way to my home on Jessup Place. I was walking alone but there was a group of black kids behind me that turned east on Maple.

"I stepped into the street, when I saw a police cruiser car slowly following kids up George. As I stepped into the street the cruiser picked up speed and came at me as though it was trying to run me down. I stepped back on the curb, a cop jumped out and yelled at me cursing, and said, 'If you ever try a stunt like that again I'll run over you.'

"I don't know his name but he was alone, a short and stubby cop. I guess he meant stepping in the street, because I hadn't done anything else. He said, 'Where are you going?' and I said home, pointing in that direction. He said, 'No you're not,' and grabbed me around the neck and tried to hit me with a night stick.

"I grabbed for the stick to keep him from hitting me. Another cop came on the scene and grabbed me from the back, around my neck. The two cops tried to pull me toward the cruiser and I knew I could not struggle any more to protect myself so I just gave up.

"A third cop came on the scene with a dog while the other two were holding me. The cop yelled, 'Get out of the way — Sarge will get him.' The two cops holding me slammed me to the ground and jumped out of the way. I was on my back when the cop holding the dog on the leash moved closer, yelling, 'Get him Sarge, kill that black nigger!'

"The cop had the dog on the leash but gave the dog enough slack to leap on me. The dog went for my throat, and I covered my face and neck with my arms. He grabbed my right arm, bit fast, clinging to it with his teeth and shaking his head from side to side, tearing at my flesh.

"I broke free from the dog by grabbing the dog's neck in a head-lock with my other arm. I believe I cut off his wind as he appeared to get weak and let go my right arm. I thought I was okay now, and started to crawl away from the dog, but one cop pushed me right over again, while the cop who had released the dog while I was first struggling with him, kept commanding the dog to 'get that black boy, kill him.'

"The dog leaped on me again. My right arm was already badly chewed, so I raised my left arm again to protect my head and neck. He grabbed my left arm, in front of my throat and chewed it up.

"A Gazette and Daily newsman saw what was going on and started taking pictures of the dog chewing my arm. The cop then pulled the dog off. In the meantime about a dozen cops had gathered at the scene.

"Three other cops, not those first involved, grabbed me and pushed me to the cruiser, where one of them pushed my head face down on the rear floor of the cruiser.

"Another holding the door open kept saying, 'You're one of those smart niggers, tough guy.' Every time I lifted my face from the floor of the cruiser to get air, one of the cops would smash my face back against the floor.

"During this period, in the cruiser, one of the cops said, 'There's a reporter from the Gazette over there taking pictures of what's going on.' Another said okay and left the cruiser. Three cops took me to city hall in the cruiser. I was bleeding badly. They took my name at city hall and then the cops took me to York Hospital.

"I waited at least 45 minutes in a small room for treatment.

Finally a nurse came in and gave me a shot in the back and in the left arm. A doctor came in to sew up my arm and I asked him if he would give me a pain killer of some sort before sewing me as my arm hurt real bad.

"He said no because it will only take three stitches to close each hole. I don't know exactly how many stitches he put in but it must have been at least twelve.

"The nurse bandaged me up and I was put in a wheel chair and wheeled to the X-Ray room where I was X-rayed. I waited at the hospital for about fifteen more minutes until the cops took me back to city hall. I went to the juvenile office, and there I waited for my mom who had been told about what had happened by my cousin, who was on the opposite side of George Street when the cops attacked me.

"My mom, dad and uncle came to city hall and took me home. One of the cops involved had a badge 109 on."

It turned out that while a badly bitten Calvin Stokes was transported to city hall, the police turned their attention, and one of their dogs, on the Gazette and Daily reporter, Arthur Magida, then twenty-three years old.

Magida would later tell Magistrate George Chantiles that he had been documenting police misdeeds when Corporal Jack Blum took his camera away from him, and then Officer Nevin "Jigs" Barley ordered his dog to attack. Only after he'd been accosted by Blum and attacked by the dog, Magida testified, had he been told he was under arrest.

While "Jigs" Barley sicced his dog on Magida, Corporal Blum twice threw Magida's camera on the ground, jumped up and down on it, and tore out the film. Then they arrested the young reporter. Magida was treated at the hospital for both deep dog bites of the upper right arm and chest.

At a hearing before Magistrate Chantiles, Cpl. Blum would say there were about fifteen cops at the scene of Magida's attack. Police witnesses backing up Blum at the hearing included "Jigs" Barley, brothers William and Jacob Hose, Jr. (sons of the public safety director), and William Farrell III.

Magida and police would relate two completely different accounts of the event. The four police officers testified that Magida dropped the camera, and the reporter was arrested for "getting in the way."

Magida would testify that his camera was taken from him after he'd photographed the four officers "manhandling a black youth."

Each officer had no problem lying to back up Cpl. Blum's story. Each said that Magida had been some sort of threat to the four of them. Here we see within the York police force not only a conspiracy to commit unlawful brutality, but also a conspiracy to keep quiet and, if necessary, a willingness to lie about it.

Public defender Harold Fitzkee, Jr., defended reporter Magida. Fitzkee had spent a considerable amount of time at city hall the night of the football riot.

Cpl. Blum first testified that he had told Magida to "get out of the way." Under examination from Fitzkee, Blum testified that Magida had been arrested "when he started to move back away from us."

How had Magida "made things hard" for police? Fitzkee asked Cpl. Blum.

"Well, he was with us," Blum replied.

Fitzkee told Magistrate Chantiles that Magida had only been attacked because he was a newsman documenting events the police didn't want the public to see.

Magistrate Chantiles nevertheless sided with the police, finding Magida guilty, fining him fifty dollars or twenty days in county jail. Magida paid the fine. Magida was the fourth newsman in seven weeks to be arrested and convicted. Magida, now a writer living in Baltimore, declined to talk with me about the incident.

Years later, remembering that night, York County Sheriff Bill Hose would question the use of the dogs, but would add that it had been a comfort for the police to have them since, Hose said, people were acting like animals.

These were not law enforcement officers. These were thugs with guns, badges, and big mean dogs. They had no problem acting like this because they knew they had the backing of the mayor and the public safety director, the DA's office, and, as I increasingly came to see, the courts of York County.

The day after the unrest at the football game, a "visibly shaken" Rev. "Adam" Kittrell visited the offices of the Gazette and Daily to protest what he described as police abuse.

"The way things are going now," Kittrell told the newspaper staff, "we're really going to have full-scale trouble."

Police dishonesty, incompetence, mean-spiritedness and brutality following the football game set off another wave of unrest. The weekend brought seven more dog attacks, twelve assaults, and six reports of property damage.

The next Sunday morning, a drive-by gunman shot out the windows of police headquarters in city hall.

Later that Sunday night, police pulled a black man named Willie House from his car on south George Street and arrested him, supposedly for drunkenness, a charge which House and his friends denied. Thirty-five young blacks descended on city hall and milled about police headquarters. Police cruisers gathered outside, while the dogs were readied. Finally the angry youth left city hall, but not before cops and the kids exchanged threats of violence.

Mayor John Snyder and Public Safety Director Jacob Hose employed a strategy based on unlawful police conduct, stupidity, brutality, and court acquiescence. Their plan clearly was not working.

# 7

# State report: York police conspire to break laws and harm blacks

Following the incident at the Penn Street meat market, where police allowed Chester Roach to shoot blacks, York blacks petitioned the Pennsylvania Human Relations Commission to look into matters. All eight members of the commission voted to hold investigatory hearings in York, which were held in August and September 1968.

The findings of the commission were released in a hard-hitting, sixty-eight page report issued in December 1968. The report covered practically every abysmal aspect of what it described as an "apartheid" life suffered by blacks in York, not only at the hands of the police, but including substandard or non-existent schooling, housing, recreation and medical treatment.

For the purposes of our story, the most interesting and telling aspect of the report centers on the unlawful, racist activities of York police. The report suggests these unlawful police activities were made possible due to the complicity of the administration of Mayor Snyder, and a corrupt and detached York County court system.

"Repeated testimony by both black and white witnesses attested to racist attitudes and actions of a recognizable portion of the Police Department of York," the report states. The police were "operating with more concentration of effort to maintain the status quo than to maintain the peace, (and) has become the focal point for expressions of hostility toward insensitive authority.

"This police community relations situation has deteriorated to the point where a recognizable fraction of black youth of the community has totally 'seceded' from and is combatively alienated against the 'whitey' dominated community structure."

The report went on to relate the obvious, that the dogs were making a bad situation worse. The commission criticized a depraved "game" played by police, reminiscent of cock or dog fights, but involving black youth. "Testimony revealed instances of canine usage such as 'letting a black youth fight the dog,' that reflected extremely poor judgment and a callous racist attitude on the part of canine officers." The dogs "constitute an increasingly employable means of inflicting physical injury on black residents by racist police.... The black resident cannot understand why he, and his child, should be terrorized by dogs in the hands of white police."

The report goes on, "Police officers of the City of York have demonstrated extremely poor judgment in the use of firearms. The discharge of weapons by police in unwarranted instances has added to crowd hysteria and endangered the lives of residents in no way involved in the disturbance at hand."

Extremely poor judgment certainly. Yet behavior this bad and long-lived was not only a product of a "portion" of the police force. It could only be kept alive *systematically,* as a coordinated policy of the city administration, the DA's office, *and* county courts.

The state Human Relations Commission's report amply details unlawful activity and monumental "bad judgment" involving what it flatly calls "a recognizable portion of the Police Department of the City of York."

The reader is left to wonder, between the lines, whether this same "recognizable portion" of police are allowing white vigilantes and street gangs to threaten to harm or kill blacks, and to perpetually obscure the murderous truth. This cuts to the heart of our story.

All told, "The City of York has a high potentiality for racial tension and violence," the state commission warned in December 1968. The commission put the blame for a coming explosion squarely at the feet of Mayor John Snyder.

The Snyder administration implemented exactly none of the commission's twenty-five pages of recommendations. Mayor Snyder and his police force were playing with fire. Increasingly, it looked as if certain individuals wanted fire.

The match would literally be lit the following summer, on a night in July 1969.

# 8
## The fire last time

On the hot Thursday evening of July 17, 1969, two young black boys played a dangerous game with lighter fluid in Penn Park. They practiced sucking lighter fluid into their mouths and spitting it out across a match to make themselves human flamethrowers. One of the boys, twelve year-old Clifford Green, messed up as he blew the fluid across the match. His face caught fire, and police were summoned to take him to the hospital. It was about 7pm.

Green at first lied to police about the cause of his burns. He told the cops he had been doused with gasoline and set afire by members of the white Girarder gang. The boy soon recanted the story but not before the false rumor had spread across the black community. As evening gathered a large group of angry black youths set out for the white neighborhoods to find the Girarders to avenge the supposed attack.

The Girarders not found, the black youths by 11pm descended on North Newberry Street, where they encountered the Messersmiths and their white gang, the Newberry Street Boys. A rumble broke out in front of the corner cigar store. Rocks were thrown, and several store windows were smashed before the police arrived and the kids scattered. Bobby Messersmith meanwhile ran home for his shotgun, which he loaded with a rifled slug. He took off with one of his brothers through the backyards to the railroad tracks.

A block away, at the corner of Philadelphia and Pershing streets, plain clothes York police Detective George Smith stopped a group of black boys hurrying home from the rumble. Smith spoke to the boys about the curfew. Some distance away, Bobby Messersmith crouched near the tracks with his gun and fired a shot at the boys talking to Smith.

Bobby's slug grazed the arm of fourteen-year-old John Washington, then hit seventeen-year-old Taka Nii Sweeney in the back. Sweeney went down, bleeding badly.

Bobby tried to get off another shot but his shotgun jammed. He ran home through the darkness and hid his gun in his house.

Detective Smith told Sweeney to lie still, and summoned an ambulance. He could not see who had fired the shot.

Rumors began flying in the black community that Sweeney and Johnson had been shot by Detective Smith or another white cop. Black men hopped into cars with their guns. The town exploded in full-scale riot.

After years of provocation, blacks were going to shoot back. It seems obvious now that the cops and the white gangs had picked on the wrong men. In the history of the United States, some of the finest fighting units have been composed of blacks. From the buffalo soldiers out West, to the Battle of the Bulge, to Vietnam, blacks soldiers have proven themselves time and again. Now full-blown warfare erupted in the streets of York.

For the next week, snipers fired from buildings and alleyways at police and white passersby. Countless firebombs were thrown, and ambushes were sprung on firefighters and police responding to the blazes. Police brought out their armored cars. They renewed the strategy from the previous summer of erecting barricades to seal troubled neighborhoods. They quickly kenneled the police dogs. They knew the dogs would be shot. In the end the vicious dogs, so much a provocation, proved worthless.

For years the identity of the black fighters has by and large remained a mystery. Some have held that out-of-town black "militants" came into York and started the shooting. I don't think so. To this day, if you ask a black in York about the snipers and the street fighting you will invariably be greeted with silence. Similar troubles spread to Harrisburg, my hometown, in the following weeks. Blacks in Harrisburg aren't so secretive about the disturbances there, perhaps because no one was killed, perhaps because the scars don't run so deep. My black friends in Harrisburg tell stories of their fathers and uncles shooting from windows in the capitol city. I'm convinced it was the same story in York. If you were young and black you picked up a rifle and you fought. Enough was enough.

A strong case can be argued that the blacks, after years of abuse, provocation and injustice, simply were defending themselves. An equally strong case can also be made that the second amendment to our constitution, guaranteeing our right to bear arms, a right so near and dear to the hearts of the county's whites, was meant to protect the public from a government acting like the York County establishment.

By all accounts the blacks proceeded to outfight and outsmart the police and the white gangs.

At nightfall the following evening, Friday, July 18, 1969, York found itself lit up by uncountable arsons and sniper shootings. That night at about 10:15pm a police armored car passed the intersection of Penn and College streets, near a bridge passing over the Codorus Creek. A group of blacks came out from behind Sam's Cafe. They wanted to teach the cops a lesson. One crouched down with a high-powered Krag .30-40 military rifle, loaded with an armor-piercing round. The shooter took aim at the armored car and fired. The gun sounded like a cannon. The round hit the armored car nearly a block away, ripping through the jury-rigged steel plate.

Three York policemen were riding inside the armored car. The bullet passed through the steel plate and struck twenty-two year-old Officer Henry Schaad below the armpit, ripping through his lungs. Schaad had been on the force less than a year. Other shots bounced off the armored car. A motorcyclist riding near the armored car on the bridge also took a hit. The unharmed officers pulled the motorcyclist into the armored car and hurried off to York Hospital with the two wounded men.

Another motorist, Calvin Sims, driving over the College Avenue bridge, was hit by sniper fire. Attorney Richard Noll, driving across the bridge, saw Sims slumped over the wheel. Noll jumped from his car and stopped Sims' drifting car. He pulled Sims out, placed him in his car, and sped off to the hospital.

That night eight men, including Officer Schaad, would be treated for gunshot wounds.

Mayor Snyder saw the day of reckoning was at hand. All city

police officers were ordered into emergency duty. Officers were told to carry heavy weapons and wear full riot gear. Still it wasn't enough. The state police were called at 1:30am Saturday morning to reinforce the overwhelmed city force. Mayor Snyder on Saturday declared a state of emergency.

At the hospital Officer Schaad was placed on a respirator, where he would struggle for life for the next two weeks. Before he died Schaad would gasp to his family that he knew he wasn't going to make it. He'd leave behind a wife and a young daughter. His father was York City police detective Russell Schaad.

The day after young Henry Schaad fell mortally wounded, Saturday, July 19, 1969, detective Russell Schaad's boss, Detective Captain Charles McCaffery, wrote an internal police report in which Capt. McCaffery detailed events of the previous two nights.

"With Lt. Wasser," Capt. McCaffery writes, "(I) interviewed Rev. H.G. Knight... and also Rev. Adam Kittrell. Both men gave us the same information regarding information they had received concerning Negro youths having guns and the fact that they were going to use same. We were unable to obtain any names of the youths as the informants would not give the Reverends same."

Capt. McCaffery next mentions the obvious growing trouble on Newberry Street. McCaffery writes, "Spent considerable time on Newberry Street, between Gay and North talking with several Hundred youths with regard to their throwing rocks, bottles, etc. at passing vehicles and other disorderly acts they were doing. With Lt. Wasser we explained what could and would happen and we convinced the youths to get off the street – which they did." (Underlined emphasis by McCaffery.)

"The men of the Detective Bureau, in Units 21 and 22, toured the entire City, trying to find out who was doing the shooting, what type of guns were being used, and who had the guns. Also received information regarding a dark colored Mustang that was driving around the areas of the shooting at our armored trucks, patrol cars and other vehicles. Information received was that Vincent Williams and Robert 'Bobby' Simpson were responsible for this.

"Det. Sgt. Chatman received information as to the names of 5 youths who might be responsible for the shooting of Officer Henry Schaad (see confidential Directive typed on Mustang and information as to names of youths.) <u>This information is to be kept within the Police Department so as not to mess up our investigation.</u>" (Underlined emphasis by McCaffery.)

McCaffery continues, "Dets. Chatman & McIlvain with Cpl. Sherman Watner spent several hours at the York Hospital where 11 complaints were received of shooting incidents.

"Assisted Captain Koontz, Lt. Bortner and other officers at College and Grantley where considerable shooting was going on.

"Spent considerable time checking other areas regarding disorders and shootings.

"With regard to guns which were brought in by the Uniform Division, Det. Border dusted all guns for prints but were unable to come up with any prints."

Several retired York police officers have told me in 2002 that the "5 youths who might be responsible for the shooting of Officer Henry Schaad," were identified almost immediately, as indicated by McCaffery's report. Det. Russell Schaad knew who shot his boy the next day, one retired cop after another told me. These five suspects for some mysterious reason would not be arrested. Instead, police singled them and others out for blood retaliation.

Outspoken Bobby Simpson was long suspected by police of witnessing Schaad's shooting. Rather than arrest Simpson, police at the height of the riots tried to kill him, his wife and five-year-old son. Simpson and his wife had just gone to bed when they heard two police armored cars pull up outside the Simpsons' Green Street row house. The cops came in the armored Bonnie and Clyde. One armored car parked out front, the other to the side. Without warning they opened fire on Simpson's home. Simpson pulled his wife and child to the floor as bullets strafed through the windows, shattering glass, ripping through plaster.

Police soon were accused of this and countless other retaliatory strikes against blacks in response to Schaad's shooting. After the riots, a federal civil rights suit was brought against the city by a group of York blacks. Federal Judge William Nealon, sitting on the 1970 civil rights trial, recounts one incident occurring that Saturday night. The judge writes, "At approximately 12:30 A.M. an armored vehicle appeared at the intersection of West College Avenue and Green Street; someone in the vehicle shouted, 'Okay, you black bastards, if that's the way you want it, you're going to get it...' whereupon a continuous volley of shots rang out from the vehicle, spraying Green Street and sending those on (Bennie) Carter's porch scrambling for cover. Mr. (Clarence) Ausby was shot three times in his right thigh and lay help-less by his car, parked at the curb, and called out to Mr. Carter, 'Dodo, I am hit.' Mr. Carter crawled out and pulled Ausby toward his house when he also was shot in the back. Mr. Ausby was taken to the Carter kitchen and a call for help was made to City Hall. Subsequently, in response to the call, an armored vehicle pulled up in front of the house and while shouting racial epithets, someone in the truck stated, 'If you want him to go to the hospital, you put him in the truck because we are not coming out there with all you niggers there.' Neighbors then put Ausby into the truck, but the police would not allow anyone to accompany him to the hospital. While in the truck, Ausby testified that he was kicked and threatened and then transferred to an ambulance which transported him to the hospital, where he remained thirteen days." Carter and Ausby weren't even at the scene of the Schaad shooting.

Judge Nealon later would write in 1970 that allegations that York policemen "were emotionally upset over the Schaad shooting which motivated the purported wanton and reckless shooting on Green Street merits careful consideration." Reports like this fill page after page of the judge's findings of fact. For exmaple, the next day of the riots, Sunday, Judge Nealon reports, "Sgt. Nevin Barley remarked to fellow officers that he 'had two shotgun shells for Lionel Bailey.'" Like Carter and Ausby, Bailey wasn't even at the scene of Schaad's shoot-ing.

The judge noted, "It became obvious during the course of testi-mony that Lionel Bailey is viewed in a different manner by members of the black community than he is by members of the Police Department. He is a spokesman for the blacks, giving voice to their long-standing complaints...."

Blacks meanwhile were setting fires all across town, and lying in ambush for police and firefighters. State and city officers were repeatedly pinned down or struck by bullets. Some of these injured officers, like Henry Schaad, were relatives or close friends of prominent town fathers. On Sunday night, July 20, 1969, for example, Officer William Hose, son of Public Safety Director Jacob Hose, narrowly escaped death. An armor-piercing round blasted through the quarter-inch-thick metal plate on the armored car in which young Hose was riding. The round struck Officer Hose on his bulletproof vest, above the heart, bruising his chest.

Police immediately suspected Sherman Spells had at least witnessed the shooting of Officer Schaad. More than thirty years later Spells would officially be named as an eyewitness to the Schaad shooting. Spells' name can reasonably be expected to be found among the list of "5 youths who might be responsible for the shooting of Officer Henry Schaad," mentioned by Captain McCaffery.

Two days after Captain McCaffery wrote his note, on Monday afternoon, July 21, 1969, Sherman Spells and his brother James arrived on Newberry Street in a light-colored Cadillac. By this time the Newberry Street Boys had been throwing firebombs of their own. Someone had even firebombed the office of the Gazette and Daily, presumably angered over the paper's sympathies to blacks.

About four thirty in the afternoon, the Spells brothers walked up to Bobby Messersmith's porch and demanded Bobby and his gang stop firebombing their mother's house. Or they would be back.

The Messersmiths sent out word across town that they needed help. The Spells brothers were coming back and they had to be ready. Police officers were asked to help ambush Sherman Spells. There must have been a lot of smiling between the cops and the boys. At almost nine that night, one of the boys waiting in ambush walked up to state trooper Gerald Roberts and his partner at the barricade and told them to turn their backs when the shooting started.

The shooting the young man told them about was the ambush awaiting an unsuspecting Lillie Belle Allen and her family.

# PART THREE:
## Detective
## Tom Chatman's
## dilemma

# 1
## Family's odyssey continues

Immediately after Lillie Belle Allen was shot in the botched ambush, and after the police at the barricade ran off, Reverend Mosley and his family hurried from Newberry Street in their decimated Cadillac. Rear window shot out. Tire shot flat. Car bullet-hole peppered, people inside salted with shattered glass. The terrorized family drove through the night on the bare rim to Hattie and Murray's house, five blocks away on Pershing Avenue. Hattie drove, hunched over the wheel, the rim screeching on the street.

Back at the house, thirteen-year-old Gladys, left behind to watch the kids, heard the sound of the screeching rim on the road. Even before the car pulled up. Hattie parked at curbside and the four adults hurried into the house. Gladys saw their hair glittered with broken glass. The girl was told the adults had to go to the hospital, that her sister had been shot. Keep the babies quiet, she was told. Should she hear any gunshots, get everybody down on the floor. With that the adults left. The children were upset. The smallest, Toby, wouldn't stop crying. Fearing the men who shot her sister would hear the baby, Gladys stuck a sock in Toby's mouth. She could only hope the adults would get back soon.

They headed out through the rioting city in Rev. Mosley's car, steering for the hospital, to learn of Lillie's fate. They left Murray Dickson's Cadillac in front of the house, parked at curbside. The detective squad wouldn't get around to examining the Cadillac for another three days.

Not far from the hospital, while the family drove, rioting black youth erected a barricade around the Crispus Attucks community center. Police, using the armored cars, rolled over the barriers. Firebombs flew and gunshots rang throughout the night. It sounded like a war zone. Structures burned in every district, north, south, east and west, while snipers' bullets whizzed nearby, making it impossible for fire-fighters, fearing ambush, to get close. Police supervisors refused to send men into some neighborhoods, saying it would be murder. At spots of worst danger, policemen volunteered.

Lillie Belle was admitted to the emergency room of York Hospital at 9:30pm with a gunshot wound to her right chest. The pumpkin ball had ripped apart her vital organs, including her lungs and liver, before exiting her back. Fragments of the exploding pumpkin ball remained in her chest. Not only was Lillie alive upon arrival at the hospital, one surgeon noted, she was *conscious*. York Hospital records state, "Information from the Emergency Room Record reveals the blood pressure was 70/20, heart rate 120/minute. Attending surgeon states that the patient was conscious."

Doctors fought to save her life. They ordered a blood type. She was given a tetanus shot. An IV was administered, and a tracheotomy performed. At 9:40pm, chest x-rays were taken on the way to the Intensive Care Unit. Around 10pm, records state, Lillie became "unresponsive" and an emergency "team (was) called."

The next handwritten entry notes that the " Pt (patient) became unresponsive in ICU and began respiratory difficulty." They put her on a ventilator and tried to message her heart, but the gunshot wound was too great. She "never became responsive," the doctor noted. At last, "Cardiac monitor revealed a straight line and the (patient) was pronounced dead." The pronouncement of Lillie's death was marked as "9:30 PM EST," which is at odds with the notations that she was still alive in the Intensive Care Unit at 10 pm, and had only been admitted at nine-thirty.

The Mosley's meanwhile arrived at York Hospital. The reverend received treatment for a gash in his arm suffered by flying glass. The hospital staff interviewed him and his family. Soon thereafter they were met by three York police officers, Detective Sgt. Harold McIlvain, Detective William Harro, and Officer S. Pauline Musser. Musser was one of the few women on the force in those days. They kept Musser around to interview women, for crimes like rape, I'm told. All three officers, today, are dead.

The detectives took statements from the family. Interesting, as I noted, that the detectives chose the hospital as the place of the interview, and not the scene of the crime. The resulting statements read almost like debriefings. After more than thirty years, they've lost none of their drama.

# 2

# "There were some people on a porch and a trooper there too."

In the hospital, still unaware of her daughter's fate, the minister's wife told the two York police detectives something they didn't want to hear. Beatrice Mosley had been sitting in the center backseat of the Cadillac with a clear view of the road. She was watching the road and could sometimes be a backseat driver, as when she told her daughter to stop at the light at Philadelphia and Newberry. Watching the road as they drove down Newberry Street, the minister's wife saw at least one police officer mixed with the kids waiting to ambush Sherman and James Spells.

Beatrice, unfortunately for the cops, seemed to have a pretty sharp memory.

Here is a transcription of their interview at the hospital:

"State your name and address?" the police asked.

"Beatrice Mosley, 117 Horroy Street, Aiken, South Carolina," she replied.

"Will you tell what you know about this shooting?"

"We had been fishing and we decided to go out to Fields Department Store to get some food, and we were going up Newberry Street and Hattie Dickson, my daughter, was driving the car, and we saw some people sitting on a porch, on the right hand, and as we came up to railroad there looked like a trooper standing there, and Hattie said, 'Oh Lord, they are going to shoot,' and Lillie told her not to stop, and she said she was going to turn around and go back, and Lillie told her to keep going, and there was a cement pole there and Lillie told her to be careful because she was going to hit it, and Hattie said she wasn't going to hit it, and Hattie was sorta excited, and then Lillie said she would drive, and Lillie jumped out of the car and started to the front of the car, and that's when the shooting started and

Lillie dropped to the ground, and then I opened the door and looked out to see if she was just laying down to keep out of the gunfire, and then I saw the blood and I said, 'Oh Lord, Lillie's been shot,' and then I closed the door and got down in the seat and they just kept on shooting and shooting, and then a police officer finally came up and wanted to know if anyone else was hurt and we said no, and he said to keep down, and then the big truck came and the ambulance and we came to the hospital."

Note that Beatrice says an officer came up to the car *before* the arrival of the armored car. Who was this officer?

As I write this, the police report in front of me contains only a transcription of the words. It notates neither the emotions nor the expressions of those in the conversation. The detectives next ask:

"As you were going up to the railroad who all did you see?"

Here one detects antagonism on the part of the detectives. Beatrice seems to detect it too.

"There were some people on a porch and a trooper there too."

This last part she must have emphasized so that they'd understand her, and understand her well. She wasn't backing down.

The detectives must've squinted. They were pros at this statement game. She was just a minister's wife.

"Did you see anyone fire any shots?"

"I didn't see nobody fire a shot, but they just kept firing and firing, but I had my head down in the car and I didn't see nobody."

"Where were you sitting in the car?"

"I was in the middle, in the back seat, and my husband was on the right side and Lillie was on the left side in the back with me."

"Lillie was sitting right behind the driver?"

"Yes."

"You were right on the railroad tracks when the shooting started?"

"Yes."

"Is there anything else you can think of?"

"No, not right now."

The detectives were still uncomfortable.

"Now this trooper you saw, was this a police officer?"

Lillie's mother shook her head yes.

"It was a man with a gun standing there, and there was a bunch of them down by the railroad too."

The detectives seem unhappy. They outright try to put words in her mouth. They asked in a leading fashion:

"You aren't saying that this trooper was the one that did the shooting — or are you saying this?"

Beatrice tried to convey that, when the shooting began, her back was to the shooters, and her head was down.

"Oh no, I don't know who did the shooting. I didn't see anyone *shoot.*"

"Is this statement true and correct to the best of your knowledge?"

"Yes."

They took statements from the other three. Hattie had seen almost as much as her mother. She complained about the officers at the barricade, saying, "we were going up to Newberry Street and I saw several police officers standing there, and I don't know why they didn't tell us that there was trouble in that area, and then we turned right and just as I was coming up over the railroad tracks I saw a guy with a gun in his hand and I said, 'Oh Lord they are going to shoot!' and the rest said that nobody was going to shoot, and I started to turn the car around they were yelling that I was going to hit a cement pole there and then the car got stalled and Lillie said she would drive and she jumped out and started front and that's when the shooting started, and Lillie dropped to the ground, and then I heard Mom yell, 'Lillie Belle's been shot!'"

The police asked Hattie, "Did you see anyone around the railroad tracks at that time?"

Hattie told them, "When we were coming over the railroad tracks there was this guy on a motorcycle sitting there and he had on a white helmet, and there was a guy standing there with him and he had a gun in his hand, but his back was turned, but it looked like he was trying to put his motorcycle up on the sidewalk."

"Did you see anyone in the area?" they asked Hattie's husband, Murray Dickson.

"There was this guy that got down behind a car that was parked on the other side of the tracks."

"What was he doing?"

"There was a whole bunch of them."

"Do you recall what any of them looked like?"

"One was heavy and had on a white shirt, all of them were white," Murray replied.

Rev. Mosley told detectives he hadn't been paying attention until the shooting started.

"Did you see any shots being fired?" they asked him.

"No, I didn't see anyone or any shots at all, but there was a lot of shooting and we just got down and hoped and prayed."

The detectives told them they could go, but requested the family come down to headquarters in the morning. Beatrice told Detective McIlvain she wouldn't leave unless they had "some protection" for the journey back to Hattie's house. McIlvain arranged a police escort.

Before they left the hospital, a doctor came out and told them Lillie Belle had passed away.

That night, when the family got back to Hattie's house, Beatrice put her arm around Lillie Belle's daughter, Debra, and said her mother was gone.

The grownups sat up for some time discussing the incident. Their minds kept returning to the policemen they saw mingling with the shooters. All those police standing nearby on the corner, allowing them to go by. Why hadn't they come to help? Certainly they had to have heard the shooting. Certainly everyone in the neighborhood had heard. What was going on here? They certainly hadn't been too reassured by the detectives, who seemed upset when Beatrice pushed the point about witnessing a policeman at the murder scene. It was too much to comprehend.

This town was no good and come daybreak, Jim Mosley said, they were all leaving.

Reverend Mosley was a thin, slight man, five-foot-nine, about 160 pounds. At last he went upstairs to try to sleep. Outside, down in the street, he heard a truck stop in front of the house. A sudden loud gunshot ripped loose. Worried about the children, someone switched off the lights, and Rev. Mosley hurried downstairs. He crawled with the children through the dark on hands and knees, upstairs to a second-floor bedroom. "We sat on the floor the remainder of the night," he later remembered. It was unbearably hot, but Beatrice wouldn't let them open a window.

## 3
## Tom Chatman's dilemma

Even as Rev. Mosley and his family tried to take cover on the floor, Officer Cybil Pauline Musser, at police headquarters, finished typing the family's first statements to detectives. On Beatrice's statement Musser noted that she finished typing the transcription at 4am, on the morning of July 22, 1969.

As they sat that morning reading Beatrice Mosley's statement, each detective's stomach must've turned. The minister's wife had seen cops mixed up with the white street gang. Here was trouble, and lots of it. Now their own department, and the state police, were mixed up in murder. Even as Sgt. Schaad's kid lay dying on that respirator. If they weren't careful this minister's family was going to land more policemen in a real mess. This riot would never die down.

Available documents make it easy to see what happened next. Rather, what didn't happen next. In the hours after Lillie's murder, a cover-up was already in the works, even as Lillie Belle's family had already discerned quite a few things amiss. And more things would be amiss.

The detectives certainly weren't falling all over each other to get to the bottom of Lillie Belle's massacre. Furthermore, someone in the department early on made a deliberate decision not to ask for an inquest, and to deny any family request for an inquest. No use having too many people asking too many questions. This obviously had to be a decision made by a high-ranking official.

A family of a murder victim can always ask for an inquest. But not this time. No inquest, the family would be told, until an arrest was made. And no arrests could be made, until there was an investigation.

And what about the "investigation?" York city detectives would wait a few more days before anyone got around to looking at the shot-up Cadillac. They'd do everything slow, if they did anything at all. They'd work jointly with the state police, passing the ball endlessly back and forth.

To deal with the family, they assigned one of their few black officers, Sergeant Tom Chatman. That very day, Tuesday, July 22, one of the other six black officers, Chip Woodyard, resigned from the ninety-eight-man force, charging the department was corrupted by racism, bigotry and a double-standard of justice for whites and blacks.

It's odd and curious that Tom Chatman is assigned the case, when Officer Wayne Ruppert's family home, at 121 N. Newberry Street, is a few doors down from the murder scene. Ruppert was even placed at the murder scene by James Frey, known as Fireman Jim. The 1969 Polk City Directory lists Wayne Ruppert as "Lieutenant York Police Department." The 1970 Polk Directory lists Wayne Ruppert as "detective city police." Why wasn't Officer Ruppert assigned to this case?

Detective Ruppert knew the boys on the block, and the neighbors. He could have gotten people to talk. He could have brought much to the investigation. Instead, Chatman was assigned. Did police supervisors expect the black detective would mollify the Mosleys? Or did they for some reason not want the Mosleys to see Lieutenant Wayne Ruppert?

Though police certainly knew the identity of the assailants, there also would be no police line-up. In this case, a "police line-up" would have to include cops in the line-up. The family also was not allowed to even view pictures of the obvious suspects, the Newberry Street Boys, or the Messersmiths, whose house was beside the murder scene.

The day after the shooting, Rev. Mosley and his family were directed to a York funeral home to make arrangements for the return of Lillie's body to South Carolina. Afterwards, someone left a message for them to see detectives at police headquarters. There they met Detective Sergeant Tom Chatman.

Sgt. Chatman was a tall, large-structured man. Chatman knew he was in a rough spot. He also knew where his loyalties lay. One of only a handful of black cops in a corrupt and racist force, he had to put food on his own table. Worse things could happen to him than just losing his job. Too bad about the Mosleys. He knew it could just as easily happen to him.

Chatman tried to reassure the family that the investigation into Lillie's death would continue. I met him once years ago, after he'd become chief of police. He's very affable.

Chatman read Beatrice's statement. He obviously didn't want to go there, the family saw. Perhaps they'd been mistaken. No, they'd seen a policeman. The uniformed cop was standing with the gang that shot at the car. At least one policeman, maybe two policeman. A city policeman, a state trooper, the family wasn't sure. Worse, they suspected police at the nearby barricade had set them up for an ambush. What had this been about? the family wanted to know.

Chatman listened to them. He looked Rev. Mosley and Beatrice in the face. Detective Chatman didn't seem to have any answers. He didn't even seem to want to ask the right questions. They immediately distrusted Detective Chatman. There seemed to be things he wasn't telling the reverend and his wife. One thing for sure: they could tell he wasn't interested in investigating police involvement in Lillie's murder. He floated one flimsy excuse after another.

Records show that Chatman took another statement from the Mosleys. The statement has vanished.

Rev. Mosley inquired about the inquest. Another detective blurted out there'd be no inquest. "An unknown individual said that no inquest could be held until an arrest was made," Rev. Mosley later complained. An inquest often involves a jury, an investigation by independent people.

No inquest until there was an arrest. But no arrests could be made until there were suspects, detectives told them. But for some reason they were having trouble finding suspects. It was a runaround. The York police by this time were experts at runaround. It's a dance very similar to the mayor's sidestep.

They said they didn't know who did the shooting. They were working on it though, Chatman tried to assure them. The family didn't buy any of it. As far as they could tell, the cops hadn't even bothered to check the crime secene or Bubba's Cadillac. Plain and simple, the family didn't trust Chatman, didn't believe the detective was telling the truth. Something was wrong here, and they were beginning to understand what it was.

The Mosleys began to see the black and white facts. Because state and local police in York, Pennsylvania, had been involved, there could *never* be an honest state and local police investigation in York, Pennsylvania.

Hearts heavy, the Mosleys and their two motherless grandchildren started home for South Carolina. They reached Aiken the next morning and straightaway set about making arrangements for Lillie's burial the following Sunday.

They considered their options. What could they do? It had become abundantly clear that York police weren't conducting a real investigation. They were running a cover-up. Police in York weren't going to do a damn thing. They were involved in the murder. They couldn't be trusted. Where could they turn for help?

# 4

## Police belatedly examine Bubba's Cadillac

Sometime after the Mosleys started home for South Carolina, an unknown person or persons made a crucial decision in the murder investigation of Lillie Belle Allen. The investigation became a *joint* investigation involving both the York and Pennsylvania State Police Departments.

Chatman would explain to the FBI that his department would not make a separate investigation. Instead, he was working with Sergeant John Creavey of the Pennsylvania State Police. No reports would be made by his department, Chatman would tell the feds.

The decision to make this a joint investigation had to have been a high-level decision. I am told that once York Mayor John Snyder asked Pennsylvania Governor Ray Shafer for state police assistance, the state police automatically had procedural jurisdiction. The state police are asked in, the state police take over. So why now was there a "joint investigation" with the York police department? Why were local and state police suddenly thick as thieves?

All these actions must be viewed in context. York at that moment was a war zone. The evening before Lillie Belle was shot, state police spokesman James Cox blamed "militant whites and militant blacks" as responsible for what a local newspaper described as "the near state of siege that has fallen upon the city after dark."

People were being shot. This was combat. York police shoulder most of the blame for fanning the flames of riot in the preceding years. Now it had blown up in their faces, and they were in the trenches with the state police, unable to regain control.

Three days after the murder, the state and city police finally got around to examining Bubba Dickson's bullet-riddled Cadillac, still parked in front of the Dickson's house on Pershing Avenue.

Detective Chatman, state police Sergeant John Creavey, and state police Corporal Donald Weiksner, of Troop H, in Harrisburg, examined the Cadillac.

They walked around the car and looked through it. Chatman took pictures. They found the rear window shot out. The area around the trunk had taken the most hits. Sgt. Creavey removed the backseat and found two bullet holes in the rear of the seat, concealing a spent bullet, and some lead fragments. All told, they counted nine visible bullet holes.

Police did not impound Murray's Cadillac as evidence. Later Murray would scrap the Fleetwood. It presumably was crushed, decades ago. More crucial evidence discounted or destroyed.

That afternoon, Sgt. John Creavey types an initial crime report. Creavey types his report on a standard Pennsylvania State Police Initial Crime Report form. The date and time the crime was discovered, Sgt. Creavey types, is 9:15pm on "21 July 69." The date and time investigators arrived to investigate is typed as 3pm on "24 July 69," three days later.

Sgt. Creavey misspells Lillie Belle's middle name in the blank for victim's name. He spells it Lillie Bell Allen. The state police would continue to omit the "e" from her middle name in every report they filed for more than a month.

Sgt Creavey's Initial Crime Report notes that the murder site, "was the scene of a confrontation between White and Negro youths on 17 July 69. The area is predominantly white. As a result of the gang fight the Police Department sealed off the area where the fight began. Barriers were erected at Kings Mill Road and S. Penn St., Newberry and Princess Sts., S. Penn and King Sts., Hartley and Princess Sts., College and Grantley Sts., and College and Oak Lane."

Creavey makes no mention that the "barrier" in question was manned by state and local police. A curious omission. He also omits any mention of the family having seen one or two policemen among the shooters.

He does note that the bullet fragment taken from Lillie Belle's body was "tentatively identified as a part of a shotgun slug."

Creavey concludes, "The area of the crime scene will be canvassed to ascertain any or all information concerning this crime and possible identity of the person (s) responsible. At the time of this writing the area is still considered a peak tension situation with emotions running high."

This first report ends with the words, "INVESTIGATION CONTINUED."

Reading this report years later I smile at the phrase "the crime scene will be canvassed to ascertain any or all information concerning this crime and possible identity of the person (s) responsible." The cops already knew who was responsible. And they certainly weren't interested in "any and all" information. In fact, they would wait thirty years to canvas the area for any pesky physical evidence, such as bullets.

This investigation was fatally flawed from the start, and placed on a bad foundation. Sgt. Creavey and his fellow "investigators" in the city and state police had already decided not to investigate police involvement in this crime. A conscious decision to strip the police from the scene of the crime had already been made.

The victims of this crime identified suspicious police behavior at two separate locations. The police at the barricade allowed them through to the ambush. The victims witnessed at least one or two police officers mixed among the shooters. The family's car was attacked in plain sight of police, who mysteriously vanished.

A professional investigation of this crime should have begun at the beginning. Such an investigation would begin with the police at the barricade, the gateway to the crime. There are at least five central sets of questions that should be answered about the local and state cops at the barrier, questions that to this day authorities have refused to adequately answer. Let's call these the Five Central Questions:

1. What are the names of all the officers at the barricade, and in the immediate vicinity of N. Newberry Street? Police, to this day, try to keep the identities of Troopers Linker, Marchowski, Roberts,

Rendish, and city policemen Zeager and Ruppert, and possibly others, secret. (Zeager says other officers may have been present, including, perhaps, Trooper Rick Dressler; Roberts remembers a "roving" patrol of state and local police in the area.) Who were their supervisors?

2. That evening at least twenty-five boys, and maybe more than one hundred boys, were running around Newberry Street with guns and Molotov cocktails, in plain sight of, and with the consent or even encouragement of, police at the barricade, and, presumably, police supervisors. What understanding or rules of operation had been reached between the police at the barricade and the kids headquartered down the street at the Messersmith house? Were the police and their supervisors complicit with the arming of the street gang, and did the police and the kids have a coordinated plan?

3. Which officer broadcast the alert that a Cadillac had "run the barricade," that Patrolman Charlie Robertson says he heard, and why was this alert broadcast? It seems likely that this broadcast was made over the city police radio band, as it was the call heard by Patrolmen Robertson in the armored car.

4. When the very loud blasts of the shooting started some seconds following the police radio alert — certainly within seconds of the car having passed the barricade — why hadn't the police at the barricade gone the few feet down the street to help the family, which was being attacked within their sight? Witnesses in fact saw the police watching the assault. The officers themselves report they hid behind their cruisers.

5. Where did the police who were stationed at the barricade go once the shooting started? Did they leave the scene of the crime? Were any of them interviewed by other police? What was the involvement of their supervisors in these and other activities? At what point did they resume their duties at the barricade? Did police allow members of the gang to leave the scene of the murder?

Any honest investigator would ask these and other questions. Without the answers to these questions, no serious investigation of this crime can be said to have been conducted, or contemplated. Period. Anyone — police official, prosecutor, judge or newspaper editor — who stands in the way of these obvious questions must be viewed with suspicion. There's an obvious, ongoing cover-up.

Keep in mind the chronology of the various police reports, and witness statements. State and local police not only overlook crucial evidence, they outright lie about it.

Several days after our reluctant sleuths deliver the bullet fragments to the state police crime laboratory in Harrisburg, the crime laboratory Firearms Examiner, E.H. Crowthers, issued a report, dated July 28, 1969.

Microscopic examination of a fragment taken from Lillie's body, as Creavey had guessed in his report, "showed it to be a portion of a discharged shotgun rifled slug." A pumpkin ball.

The bullet found in the car turned out to be "a portion of a caliber .30 bullet bearing six grooves with a right hand twist," Crowthers reports. "This exhibit was NOT discharged from a caliber .303 British Enfield rifle." (Emphasis Crowthers.) It's not clear the significance of the ".303 British Enfield rifle."

Firearms examiner Crowthers concludes by noting that the evidentiary bullet fragments will remain in his custody. Sgt Creavey mysteriously omitted a state police Evidence Room Number from his intitial report. Thirty years later, someone would get around to looking for the bullet fragments, but they had been lost long ago.

The slug that killed Lillie Belle Allen is like life itself. Where it came from, where it went, a mystery.

# 5

## Police search Messersmith home

Some hours after Bubba Dickson's Cadillac was examined, police and National Guard, in the company of York County District Attorney John Rauhauser, finally got around to searching John Messersmith's house for guns.

Someone at last decided enough was enough. All this gunplay was landing everyone, including police, in trouble.

The powers-that-be wanted the Messersmiths' guns. City and state police were aware of the existence of the Messersmiths' arsenal before Lillie's murder, as they also were aware that Bobby Messersmith was a public menace. Things may or may not have turned out differently had Bobby, with police blessing, killed Sherman Spells, like he was supposed to.

The search of the Messersmiths's house began at 8pm. Teams of police and fifty-three National Guardsmen descended on Newberry and Gay Streets. DA Rauhauser stood in front of the Messersmiths', asking for calm. Over a bullhorn he told residents the searches were legal.

Three houses in the N. Newberry Street-area were entered and searched. As the fifty-three National Guardsmen stood outside, twelve state troopers and nine city police officers, in three teams, searched the houses.

A spokesman for the state police, James Cox, described the searches as "very gentlemanly." Cox told reporters the searches were "very quiet, conducted in a very gentlemanly manner by all parties, including residents."

Two of the searches came up with no weapons. One of the places searched, according to police documents, was the plumbing business of seventy-year-old William Boyer, who had been seen by police in proceeding days walking around the neighborhood with guns. The search of Boyer's place, and a second residence, yielded no weapons.

At John Messersmith's house, police found, as expected, an arsenal. In an upstairs closet police discovered four shotguns, six rifles, a handgun, ammunition and an assortment of knives. Police carted off the weapons. They even took away the Messersmiths' letter opener, a linoleum knife, and a Boy Scout hatchet. Messersmith obviously believed in the Boy Scout motto: Be prepared.

The town newspaper, the York Gazette and Daily, reported the weapons seizure by noting, "A Negro woman was killed Monday night by a rifle shot at the intersection of North Newberry and Gay Avenue."

The paper then went on to report the search and seizure without mentioning the Messersmiths by name. The next day's issue of the newspaper reports, "A white male resident at the house in which the guns and ammunition were found last night was brought to city hall for questioning but was later released, police said. They added that the guns will be processed, as will be weapons previously confiscated, to determine if they were used in recent shootings."

It's interesting it wasn't reported which Messersmith police questioned that night. I can find no written reports of this interrogation. It's not a small matter, when you think about it. What did this Messersmith and city police have to say to each other the night of July 25? Did they ask about Lillie Belle? Did police quiz Bobby or John? Did he mention police involvement in the murder? Does it matter which Messersmith they took downtown and looked in the eye?

Who blinked, that's the question.

What transpired that night between the police and the unknown Messersmith sealed a lot of fate, and could explain a lot. For more than three decades Bobby Messersmith has denied firing the pumpkin ball into Lillie Belle. He says he was on his daddy's porch when the Cadillac arrived, and he ran away. What the police from July 24, 1969 on have been looking for from Bobby Messersmith is a nice clean admission of guilt, which Bobby has never given. It's a standoff that will protect Bobby Messersmith from charges of murder for thirty years.

John Messersmith held dark secrets involving his operation of fortress Messersmith. He'd take those secrets with him to his grave when he died of a heart attack and advanced lung cancer in 1985.

The police damn well knew Bobby Messersmith shot Lillie Belle Allen. Police witnessed the murder from behind their cruisers.

The police knew they could not use the testimony of their own men who witnessed the murder. It would implicate those same policemen and probably higher city officials in Lillie's murder.

Hadn't more than just one person killed Lillie Belle Allen? Was it just he who pulled the trigger who should pay for the crime? There was the confused mob, buzzing in front of the Messersmiths' all night. The mob had scared Hattie, and caused her to veer off the road. Hadn't they played a hand?

The police therefore need a nice clean confession from Bobby Messersmith, which he will never give. Without a confession, the police can't risk charging Bobby with Lillie's death. It's too risky.

Still, the police had the stronger hand. They had a trump card to play against Bobby Messersmith. There was the matter of the other shooting in the neighborhood.

Four days before Lillie Allen had been shot, Bobby Messersmith had fired a rifled shotgun slug at Taka Nii Sweeney and John Washington. The shooting occurred following the rumble between black and white youth on N. Newberry Street.

The police would collar Bobby Messersmith for this attempted murder. A much less serious crime than the murder of Lillie Belle, but they still had Bobby, and his father, by the short hairs on that one. A bargaining chip. And now, in the bargain, they also had all the Messersmiths' guns.

All the guns, it would turn out, but one.

Some months after the police raid on their Newberry Street residence, John and Bobby Messersmith jointly filed court documents seeking the return of weapons confiscated from their home the night of July 24, 1969. The inventory makes illuminating reading. Listed are items no York city gentlemen would presumably be caught dead without in a race riot. The list reads as follows:

.22 Caliber SL&LP Marlin – Model 81-G Gunfield Products.

Bolt Action

12-Gauge Shotgun – Single Barrel – Break – Topper Model 158, Harrington Richardson, Inn.

O.F. Mossberg & Sons, Inc., Model 151 M-C, .22 Long Rifle - Single Bolt with Sling.

Rifle with Scope – Lever Action – Marlin Firearms – Model 336 R.C., Cal. 30-30 Serial AA10620

12-Gauge Pump Shotgun, Ithaca Model 37 Feather Light

.22 Caliber Single Shot Bolt Ranger, Model #34 – Initials on Stock "B.M."

Shutgun – pump action – Remington Wingmaster, Model 870, Serial #12 241 32 V

Shotgun – Break Action – Springfield Make – Single Barrel – 12-Gauge 1929 Model

Rifle with 4x32 scope, Bolt Action, Foreign Make #138421 L.M. Dicksouy

Pistol, Foreign Make

23, 32-30 Winchester (100 Grain Soft Point Bullets) Peters (in one box)

50, 32-20 Winchester (100 Grain Lead) Peters – One Full Box

50, 32-20 Winchester (100 Grain Lead) Peters – One Full Box

2 Full Boxes of 20 shells each - 303 British – Remington

17, 303 British shells – Remington (in one box)

1 Full Box – 303 British Winchester Super Speed Power Point (20 shells)

2 Full Boxes 30-30 Winchester – Peters (20 in box)

1 Full Box 30-30 Winchester – Remington (20 in Box)

2 Boxes (25 each) 12 Gauge 2-3/4 Magnum – Full Piston – Peters

4 Boxes (25 each) 12 Gauge Assorted Shot – In Peters Boxes

9 Loose Assorted 12 Gauge Shotgun Shells – Found Loose in Box

1, 16-Gauge Shotgun Shell – Found loose in box

1, 303 British – Found loose in box

1, 753 Rifle – Found loose in box

1, 30-30 L.P. – Found loose in box

Canvass (sic) gun case (which was empty)

1 Large Wooden Handle Knife with 13 inch blade

1 Hunting Knife with 8 inch blade
1 Letter opener type knife with 6 inch blade
1 Rifle sling
1 Scout Hatchet (in leather case)
1 Linoleum Knife
1 Hunting Knife – 3-1/2 inch blade in case
1 Hunting Knife – 3 inch blade in case
1 Pocket Knife – 2 blade, 3-1/2 inch and 2 inch blades
1 Small Pocket Knife – 2 blade
43 Live rounds of .22 Super X (long)
10, .22 long with a diamond trade mark on case
4, .22 long Peters
2, .22 short with XR on case
1, .22 short with U on case
1 Super X .22 Long – in one box
5 Long Rifle and 12 long in one box
45 Super X .22 Long – in one box
1 Full box of 50 Long Rifle - .22 long – Western Expert
42, .22 Short – Peters – in one box
50, .22 Short – Peters (1 Full Box)
41, .22 Long Rifle – Expert – in one box
38, .22 Long Rifle – Expert – in one box
1 Loaded Clip with 6 live .22 Long Rifle

# 6

## State and local police search high and low for suspects

The day after they took away the Messersmiths' guns and went through Murray Dickson's Cadillac, the Pennsylvania State Police and the York Police Department finally got around to conducting what were their first documented interviews of civilians concerning Lillie's murder.

Police begin to record page after page of eyewitness reports to the murder. A murder which for three decades police would publicly say they had no witnesses, and no suspects.

Eighteen-year-old Russell Leroy Wantz, Jr., of 145 N. Newberry St., a self-employed vending machine operator, was the first to be officially interviewed. Wantz was asked to come down to the local state police barracks. He was interviewed in the presence of Sgt. John Creavey, Cpl. Donald Weiksner, and Detective Thomas Chatman. Wantz's statement reads as follows:

"I was standing out on the front porch at 137 N. Newberry St. when the shooting went on. This is the home of my aunt and uncle, Jake and Lottie Berkheimer. My mother (Helen Wantz) was on the porch with us. I saw the grey Cadillac come up Newberry St. There were four or five occupants in the car. The car was heading north. It was around 9 PM. The cigar store across the street was closed. The car attempted to make a U turn on the railroad tracks. When they did this, they backed up toward the kids. The kids were over on the east side of Newberry St. There were about twenty-five in the group. I saw a woman get out of the rear left door of the Cadillac. She no more got out of the car and closed the door when there were shots fired. She was falling then. The people inside of the car tried to pull her inside of the car. There was more gunfire. There was continuous gunfire until the armored car arrived. No one went near the car until after the armored car left. Then some of the kids went over to where the car was and looked around the tracks and the road. There was shooting from both sides of the street.

"There were no shots fired from the Cadillac. I didn't see anyone with a gun at the Cadillac."

Following this interview, Sgt. John Creavey, wrote, signed and filed a Pennsylvania State Police Supplement Report dated *"25 July 69."*

The interview with Russell Wantz is fascinating to Yorkers for a variety of reasons. Wantz at the time serviced the gumball machines in York. Putting in them gumballs, taking out them coins. In this period young Wantz also began a close, lifelong friendship with York police Detective Russell Schaad. In the years ahead, Wantz would instill in the bereaved father a love of coin collecting. The two became inseparable. People remember them together all the time, talking about coins. Wantz would hang out all the time in the detective bureau. "The detective bureau was Wantz's second home in that period," a retired detective told me. In 1974, on his marriage license, Wantz would list his occupation as "Deputy Sheriff." He would work as a police officer in Mount Wolf and Yoe. The York Daily Record would chattily report in 2000 that Wantz knew both Russell Schaad and his son Henry "from way back. Wantz grew up on Newberry Street in York and Russ Schaad grew up just a few blocks away on North Street." Years later, when Schaad left the York police force to open a private detective firm, the Schaad Detective Agency, Wantz followed along. When Schaad finally passed away of a heart attack in 1977, Wantz took over the agency.

So, on the ground, witnessing Lillie's murder, we have a close friend of Det. Schaad and his mortally wounded son, Henry.

It's fascinating that Wantz was the first documented interview. Who told Sgt. Creavey to interview Wantz? Had Schaad put Creavey onto Wantz? What had Schaad learned, and when, from the young bubble gum vender who with time would become like an adoptive son? Russell Wantz, the eyewitness on Newberry Street.

The next day, Saturday, July 26, 1969, Creavey, Chatman and

Weiksner took two more witness statements at the York state police barracks.

Richard Eugene Eisensmith, age forty, of 332 Smyser St., an AMF employee, told the officers that at the time of the ambush "he was at his home inside. He heard three shotgun blasts and then several rifle shots. The shooting went on for at least a full minute." Eisensmith added, "After the shooting stopped I walked down to the scene and saw the car across the railroad tracks. It was a grey Cadillac and was at an angle facing towards Gay St. The Police were there and I didn't stay around." From Creavey's report, it's not clear which police "were there."

Chester Bechtel Smith, age fifty-one, of 306 W. North St., an employee of the Yorktowne Hotel, gave police this vivid account:
"It was about nine or quarter after. I heard small arms fire like a .22. I flew down to the corner of North and Newberry to see what was going on. I was about 75 to 100 feet from where the Cadillac was setting. The front end of the car was on the railroad tracks facing west. The back end of the car was on Newberry St. It was almost straight up the tracks as if it was going up the tracks. I ducked down on my knees at the stone wall. The guys across the street (Newberry St.) were shooting at the car. They were on the east side of Newberry St. It was the 200 block. The house seems to be the gang's hang-out. They were shooting at this car and I could see the car quiver everytime it was hit. I heard one of the guys yell, 'I got one of them.' The last shot fired was into the tires because I heard the air swoosh out. They must have fired at least 15 rounds and I know the car was hit about ten times at least."

Chester Smith's statement shows that the police were aware, early on, that the gang's "hang-out" was the Messersmith house, and that one of the gang yelled, "I got one of them." It could not have been very difficult at this point to round up suspects. But the police still made no arrests. Add this to Wantz's statement, and it's clear police knew who shot Lillie.

Following the interviews of Eisensmith and Smith, Sgt. John

Creavey wrote, signed and filed a Pennsylvania State Police Supplement Report documenting both interviews on a single report sheet, dated *"26 July 69."*

# 7

# Lillie Belle is buried

Funeral services for Lillie Belle Allen were held the next afternoon, Sunday, July 27, 1969, in Aiken, South Carolina, at the Cumberland AME church, where Lillie had been a member. Rev. A.W. Holman, church pastor, officiated. Afterwards, Lillie was laid to rest in the Pine Lawn memorial garden, Aiken's black cemetery, in a small plot in the back. Today it is windblown and overgrown, while the nearby white cemetery is neatly kept.

Word already had begun to spread among the Mosley family and friends that the police had had a hand in Lillie's murder. There was only one thing to do, Lillie's family was told. City and state police in Pennsylvania weren't going to do anything; they were involved in the murder. The family shouldn't fool themselves about the level of police and court corruption in York, Pennsylvania. The federal government must be brought in. They had to go to the FBI. And they'd better go to the FBI office in Columbia, South Carolina, not in Pennsylvania.

The Mosleys' son, Benjamin, who the family had planned to visit in Brooklyn, New York, didn't want to stop there. He advocated applying more heat by getting the United State Department of Justice's Civil Rights Division involved. A federal statute empowered the Civil Rights Division to investigate murders like Lillie's, involving public officials or police. While his parents contacted the FBI, Benjamin would work on the Justice Department.

The very next day, Monday, July 28, 1969, Jim and Beatrice Mosley drove the sixty or so miles to Columbia, the state capitol of South Carolina. In the FBI office late that afternoon they gave statements to two FBI special agents, George Ross and Dick Oyler.

Rev. Mosley's statement is four pages long. Statements given to the FBI are transcribed on a government form numbered "FD-302," and hence are referred to in the trade as 302s. Rev. Mosley's 302 reads, in part, "We arrived at a traffic light in York, Pa. and there were benches partially blocking the road. There were also approximately 15-20 police officers at the street corner. They did not stop the car."

The statement goes on to describe the attack, and the subsequent suspicious encounters with the York police detectives. Each encounter with the detectives made Rev. Mosley more suspicious.

Reverend Mosley rolled up his left sleeve and showed the agent the half-inch wound on his upper arm he'd received from flying glass.

Beatrice Mosley's statement to the FBI is as clear as can be. Beatrice's chatty 302 reads in part, "we approached an intersection where there were several troopers, armed with rifles and wearing helmets. I do not know if these men were from the York Police Department, Pennsylvania State Police or which department, but they were dressed (in) bluish-gray police type uniforms.

"...As we approached the railroad crossing... we observed one of the troopers raise his rifle and point it in our general direction. This act frightened Hattie and she said, 'Oh Lord mama, these people are going to start shooting.'"

Beatrice concludes her statement by adding, "We came to the FBI Office in Columbia, S.C. today in order to tell our story for whatever assistance it might be. We are also concerned over the outcome of the investigation in York, Pa., why it happened and any other information that can be made available to us. We were not sure what we could do about this situation, but thought perhaps the FBI could help us."

Retired special agent George Ross still lives, in 2002, in Columbia, South Carolina. Sixty-eight years old, he now performs contract work for the military and the FBI. Background checks, that sort of thing.

I was excited to find him, to talk to a man who had once looked into James Mosley's eyes and heard his story.

He expressed surprise to hear from me, as he had recently been following the case in South Carolina's newspapers. There'd been several write-ups, he said, since the 2001 arrest of a former York policeman in connection with Lillie Allen's murder. The case now seemed fascinating to him, he said, particularly as the family had apparently long ago said police were involved, and now a cop had been arrested.

Unfortunately, he told me, he has no recollection taking of Rev. Mosley's 302. He expressed surprise to hear that Lillie Belle Allen's father, thirty-three years before, had sat in front of him and told his story. He seemed apologetic, slightly embarrassed, though intrigued.

He seemed to agree with my suspicion that more cops might be involved. A cop had been arrested, but had they bagged the right cop?

He apologized again for not remembering the case.

But, had he transcribed the 302, he offered, he probably forwarded it to FBI headquarters in Washington DC, to the Philadelphia bureau, and the Justice Department.

# 8

# Another witness implicates police

On Wednesday, July 29, 1969, Pennsylvania state police Sgt. John Creavey, in the company of York police detective Tom Chatman, visited forty-nine-year-old Harold Loss at his place of employment, York Shipley, a local boiler and heating business. At the time, York Shipley was one of the top-five boiler manufacturers in the world. York Shipley was bought and sold twice. The company is still located on the eastern side of town, near Rt. 30. I'm told Harold Loss (pronounced Lose, rhyming with dose) worked for many years at Shipley as a boiler tester. He's remembered as short, stocky and smoking a pipe. He died around 1980.

In 1969, Loss's supervisor at York Shipley was a black man named Bill Myers, whose family had been one of the first to move into a white neighborhood in York. During the riots, the Myers family had to be protected by National Guard. Loss had some knowledge and sensitivity about what blacks had to endure in York. Loss also turns out to be a pivotal witness, in that he saw policeman at the nearby barricade, watching but doing nothing, while Lillie Belle was murdered.

The night of the murder, Harold Loss had been sitting on the porch of the Second Hand Store at 127. N. Newberry Street, halfway between the police barricade and the railroad tracks. He'd been visiting an acquaintance, John Nelson, owner of the store. Loss lived some miles away, on Carlisle Road. It's not clear from documents how police found Loss, or whether Loss himself had phoned the police.

Following the interview, Sgt. John Creavey filed a Pennsylvania State Police Supplement Report dated *"30 July 69,"* which reads as follows:

"Harold Eugene Loss, W-M age 49, 1925 Carlisle Rd. York, Pa.

(employed at York Shipley).

"I was sitting on the porch of the Second Hand Store 127 N. Newberry St. John Nelson who operates the store was there too. It was about 9 or 9:15 PM. We saw this Cadillac go up past us. There were about four people in the car. The two up front were colored. They got on the tracks and it looked as if they tried to turn around. Before they turned I heard a shot. Then I saw a woman get out of the car. She was wearing a blue and white striped blouse with two inch stripes. She got out of the car on the driver's side. It wasn't a second until she got shot. She fell right down and never got up. I heard a lot of high power rifle and small .22 fire. The woman in the car (Cadillac) didn't shoot.

"I believe there were four officers at the corner of W. Philadelphia and N. Newberry Sts. during the shooting."

Creavey's report concludes, "The above subject was interviewed at his place of employment by Det. Sgt. Thomas V. Chatman and the writer. Mr. Nelson the owner of the store to be interviewed. INVESTIGATION CONTINUED."

Loss's interview is significant for several reasons. As we'll see, the police would soon lie about having interviewed Loss and writing this report.

We can surmise a few more things from this report. If Loss was able to see that Lillie had been wearing "a blue and white striped blouse with two inch stripes," he certainly could also plainly see her murderers. He probably was also aware that kids with guns were running up and down the block telling the neighbors to any moment expect the Spells brothers' Cadillac. From his vantage point, halfway between the barricade and the railroad tracks, Loss also saw the cops, how they interacted with the gang, and how they had done nothing to aide the Mosley family.

Most significantly, and no doubt about it, Harold Loss here is pointing police investigators up the block to the their fellow officers standing at the barricade. This certainly was a problem for Sgt. Creavey. Sgt. Creavey didn't want to look, or couldn't look, in that direction.

The barricade at the corner of Newberry and Philadelphia would turn out to be a kind of black hole, or cop trap, for policemen investigating this crime. Otherwise good cops like Creavey kept getting sucked into the black hole, unable to investigate or implicate their fellow officers, or their departments. This continues to this day.

In Harold Loss's mind, and in the mind of any independent investigator, the police here should be reasonably suspected of complicity with the white gang. In fact, *the police are inexorably entangled in this crime.* It would become the challenge of Sgt. Creavey and a succession of other state and local police officers to attempt to keep the police out of the investigation. It couldn't be done, and they'd be forced to kill the investigation to protect their officers and their departments, and probably their own careers and jobs.

For reasons that become apparent, the state police would shortly outright lie to the FBI and the U.S. Justice Department about having written this and other reports.

# 9
## "A crowd of whites accompanied by one or more police officers"

One day after Sgt. Creavey and Detective Chapman interviewed Harold Loss, on Thursday, July 31, 1969, Lillie Belle's brother, Benjamin Mosley, managed to shake things up even more. He creates a real problem for the state and local police by contacting the Civil Rights Division of the U.S. Department of Justice.

The Civil Rights Division is responsible for prosecuting crimes involving public officials and police officers. It was, and remains, the family's best shot at bringing Lillie's murderers to justice.

On the phone to the Civil Rights Division, Benjamin Mosley described how family members had seen police officers mixed in with the crowd shooting at their car.

The Justice Department is unable to investigate. It relies on the FBI. The Civil Rights Division offficially asks the FBI to get involved.

Jerris Leonard, Assistant Attorney General, Civil Rights Division, in a memo dated August 1, 1969, written to J. Edgar Hoover, Director of the FBI, relates the story given by Mosley:

"On July 31, 1969, Benjamin Mosely (sic) of 816 Lincoln Place, Brooklyn, New York... contacted this office and stated that his sister, the victim, was killed on July 21, 1969, while traveling through York, Pennsylvania," the memorandum begins. "...Persons in the car related to Mr. Mosely that as they drove along Newbury (sic) in or toward a white section of the city, they came to a railroad track. On the far side of the railway was a crowd of whites accompanied by one or more police officers. Mrs. Dixon (sic) attempted to turn the car around and while she did so the whites fired on the car."

The Civil Rights Division lawyer now asks the FBI to investigate.

"Please interview the occupants of the car, including Mrs. Haddy Dixon, 334 S. Pershing Avenue, York, Pa., and Rev. and Mrs. James

Mosley... to determine if any of them saw police officers in the crowd of accompanying those persons who fired on the car.

"Should these person substantiate the report of the complaint, please conduct a preliminary investigation.

"In addition, please advise us as to what, if any, investigation has been made by state or local authorities, and the results thereof."

By this time, of course, Jim and Beatrice Mosley had already given their statements to the FBI — at the office in Columbia, South Carolina. We know what they said: they had seen police officers at the scene of the shooting. They had already, in the spirit of the memo, substantiated the account.

The last paragraph of this memorandum, asking the FBI to "advise us as to what, if any, investigation has been made by state and local authorities, and the results thereof," would turn out to be a very interesting request, one that does not seem to have been honored with any honesty or integrity.

# 10

## Another man witnesses police at corner

On Saturday, August 2, 1969, state police Sgt. John Creavey and another state police detective interviewed John Nelson, age forty-six, owner of the second-hand furniture store where boiler inspector Harold Loss had been sitting during the murder. Nelson's store, J&H Used Furniture, located at 127 N. Newberry, was located between the barricade and the railroad tracks, a few doors down from Officer Wayne Ruppert's mother's house.

John Nelson's statement reads, "It was around 9 PM just turning dark. There were police officers up on the corner at the church (W. Philadelphia and N. Newberry Otterbein United Methodist). I saw a gun metal grey Cadillac go up by (North on N. Newberry). There was a lot of shooting. I wouldn't know anything else about it. I was standing in the doorway. I believe I was eating a sandwich at the time. Mr. Loss was outside on the porch."

Following this interview, Sgt. John Creavey, wrote, signed and filed a Pennsylvania State Police Supplement Report dated *"2 August 69."*

## 11
### FBI interviews Hattie and Bubba Dickson

Two days later, the following Monday, August 4, 1969, FBI special agents Norman Hendricks and John William Daane, directed by the Justice Department's Civil Rights Division, pay a visit to Hattie and Bubba Dickson. Hendricks and Daane were stationed in York.

Hattie's FBI 302 recounts the incident. Her statement concludes, "One man in the crowd had on matching pants and shirt and a white helmet. He was pushing a motorcycle onto the sidewalk when I first saw him. This man may have been a policeman due to the matching pants and shirt and helmet."

The statement was "witnessed" by special agents John William Daane and Norman Hendricks.

Bubba Dickson's statement concurs with Hattie's: "One man in the crowd had on matching pants and shirt, grayish in color, and a white helmet. The top of the helmet was white and the bottom a darker color. He was pushing a motorcycle from the street to the sidewalk. Just before the shooting started I saw him walking north on Newberry Street. I felt he may have been a policeman as his matching pants and shirt resembled a uniform."

When I study the statements the four witnesses have given the FBI, I'm struck by the consistency of what they've been saying. They keep talking about a policeman or two among the shooters. They also keep talking about the state and local policemen standing a short distance away, at the corner barricade. They believe the policemen at the nearby barrier are an important part of the ambush, a suspicion they can't put out of their minds. For good reason, as we know from Trooper Roberts.

These Pennsylvania FBI agents don't want to hear about it either. Living and stationed in York, they are colleagues with the local and state police. They downplay Hattie and Bubba's account from the start. The identical phrase, "may have been a policeman," is used in both 302s. The phrase is obviously not Hattie and Bubba's, in their own words, and waters down what they saw.

They saw *a cop*. At least one, maybe two. Beatrice time and again said she saw a *Pennsylvania state trooper*. The minister's wife made no bones about it, and told anyone who would listen. This church lady was a real problem for police.

Daane died in the mid-1970s. Former special agent Norman Hendricks is now retired in Williamsport, Pennsylvania. I wondered about his impressions of Hattie and Murray when he took their statements.

Hendricks, unfortunately, like retired agent George Ross, says he has no recollection whatsoever of any involvement in the case. He expressed surprise when I told him his name was on Hattie and Bubba's 302s, that he was listed as having witnessed the statements.

"I don't remember interviewing that woman," he told me. "I don't remember doing anything with that case. There wasn't any case as far as I know."

Though Hendricks professed not to remember anything about Lillie's murder investigation, he remains remarkably lucid concerning other details from the riots. He told me his job in York for two years had been to monitor the disorders and report back to Washington.

"Tempers were volatile in the community," he told me, and the FBI in Washington wanted to be kept abreast. "I'd send them updates on the situation, the size of the thing, where it was going, and so on." He had an office on the second floor of the York post office, downtown, he said. He'd worked with Special Agent John William Daane, who everyone called Bill. Hendricks told me he lived at the time in York, and had regular professional and even social contacts with York and state police, particularly, he said, on the supervisory level.

Daane was his supervisor, he added, the RA, or resident agent.

When the 1969 riots began, Hendricks remembers, Daane was

on vacation, and didn't get back until, "a day or two after the riots were over."

He says they were very busy, dealing with many incidents, riot related and not. But as for the murder of a young mother in which police were implicated, he says he has, "Not a faint memory of it even. Not at all."

Hendricks does remember, however, the shooting of Officer Henry Schaad. He used to work with Schaad's father, Detective Russell Schaad, he told me. He remembers that the killing of young Henry left the father "very sad."

"Russell Schaad had a hard time with it," Hendricks told me. "My impression was he was very sad. His son was a young fellow, taken out of life. It was evident what had happened."

Hendricks even remembers attending Henry Schaad's funeral.

"There were lots of people at the funeral. Lots of police, people in town, the chief of police I know was there. Everyone was very sad." Hendricks went on to speak glowingly of Detective Tom Chatman, who Hendricks described as a colleague with whom he regularly and closely worked. When I began to ask questions about Chatman, Hendricks seemed to ice over and concluded our talk.

# 12
## State and local police lie to the FBI

The very same day FBI special agents Bill Daane and Norman Hendricks interviewed Hattie and Bubba Dickson, on Monday August 4, 1969 the agents also interviewed state police Sgt. John Creavey and York Police Detective Thomas Chatman. This was in keeping with the Civil Rights Division's August 1, 1969 request that the FBI "please advise us as to what, if any, investigation has been made by state or local authorities, and the results thereof."

The interview with state police Sgt. Creavey set the pattern of events to come. FBI agents seemed only too happy to help out in the deception and the stonewalling.

Sgt. Creavey's statement to the FBI begins, "Sergeant John Creavey, Pennsylvania State Police, furnished the following information when interviewed:

"As a result of the recent racial disturbances in York, Pa., he is presently assigned to investigate some of the more serious matters that took place during the disturbances. One of the matters he is investigating is the murder of Lillie Belle Allen which happened on July 21, 1969. This investigation is being conducted under PSP Incident #H7-67357. To date, *no report has been written* in this matter and it is still under investigation." (Emphasis mine.)

This of course was an outright lie. Sgt. Creavey had already written and filed *five* reports, all of which he did not wish to share with the Civil Rights Division.

The Pennsylvania State Police Initial Crime Report had been written, signed and filed by Sgt. Creavey on July 24, 1969, more than a week earlier. This was the report in which Creavey describes Lillie's murder and the belated inspection of Bubba Dickson's Cadillac by himself, Chatman and Cpl. Weiksner, and makes note of the initial statements given by the family to York police.

On July 25, July 26, July 30 and August 2, 1969, Sgt. Creavey had likewise written, signed and filed the Pennsylvania State Police Supplement Reports of the interviews with, respectively, Russ Wantz; Richard Eisensmith and Chester Smith; Harold Loss; and John Nelson. Loss and Nelson had volunteered there were "four officers at the corner of W. Philadelphia and N. Newberry during the shooting," in plain sight of the murder. Creavey had typed these reports before he knew of the Civil Rights Division's interest.

Here the Civil Rights Division was specifically requesting information concerning police involvement in the crime, and Creavey lies about having a written report and possible evidence that could have substantiated the Mosleys' claim. This is obstruction of justice.

They want to keep the Civil Rights Division out of this case, and to keep the policemen involved in Lillie's murder out of harm's way. They'll do whatever they have to. Unfortunately for the state and local cops, the Civil Rights Division would turn out to be persistent. The state and local police would be forced to lie early, and lie often.

So out of the gate the cops are lying about the case. Their credibility concerning everything to come must be called into question.

In his statement to the feds, Creavey continues, "The gunfire was allegedly caused by a gang of white youths from the North Newberry Street area who had a confrontation with a gang of Negro youths on July 17, 1969."

This of course was the incident touched off by the twelve-year-old playing with the lighter fluid.

Creavey's statement continues, "At this point in the investigation, he has not interviewed any of the other persons who were in the (Dickson's) vehicle but has concentrated on attempting to learn the identities of the individuals who were in the white gang firing on the stalled vehicle. This investigation has developed the fact that on July 20, 1969, an automobile containing Negroes had driven down North Newberry Street and as it reached the area of the Western Maryland

Railroad tracks, the trunk of the vehicle had suddenly opened and some Negroes in the trunk had sprayed the area with gunfire as the vehicle sped off. He understands that some white persons were injured by this gunfire; however, he does not know their identities.

"Sergeant Creavey believes that this incident had the residents of the North Newberry Street area rather jumpy and when another vehicle occupied by Negroes turned around at the tracks and a Negro woman got out of the vehicle, the gang in the area believed they would be shot at from the trunk of the vehicle. He bases this part on the fact that the majority of the shots hitting the car hit it in the right rear, particularly in the area of the trunk."

When one thinks about this amazing statement, one realizes how much the cops already know at this early date. Creavey knows about the incident involving the shooter in the trunk on July 20. He knows this incident involved "the gang in the area," the Newberry Street Boys. He certainly knows the identities of the gang, though he doesn't yet know which boy had earlier been hurt by the gunfire from the trunk. He knows these same gang members — the Newberry Street Boys — mistakenly shot Lillie the next day, and how it happened. *He knows everything.* He knows the suspects, the motive, the screw up, the opportunity, the fatal incident. He has been told this by the police in the area — no doubt by the cops at the barricade, who understood and witnessed the entire crazy scenario. Or perhaps York policemen Wayne Ruppert filled him in, or another cop who'd been standing around. Suddenly Creavey's entire "investigation" seems like a farce. It's actually a cover-up. They also know that cops are involved.

Creavey's statement concludes by negating allegations of police involvement: "His investigation has determined that there were no city or state policeman in the immediate area where the vehicle was shot at and the closest officers were at the intersection of North Newberry and West Philadelphia Streets. Also, all PSP (Pennsylvania State Police) on riot duty in York, Pa., at the time were issued and wearing crash-type helmets, light blue in color. Most of the policemen after the first day or two of the disturbances, wore bullet proof vests as a protection against the sniper fire which they were constantly running into."

The main argument the cops would use to refute claims that Lillie's family had seen a policeman mixed among the gang was that the family hadn't seen a bulletproof vest on the officer near the tracks.

But the cops, allied with the white street gang, didn't need bulletproof vests on N. Newberry Street. Certainly Officer Wayne Ruppert didn't wear a bulletproof vest while visiting his mother.

They also refute the eyewitnesses by saying that Lillie's family had seen a white helmet, not a "light blue" helmet. This was dusk going into night, and one's eyes could easily have trouble distinguishing light blue from white in such low-light conditions, particularly in a car going down the street into a gun-toting gang. Plain and simple, the cops are using whatever excuse they can cook up to refute the eyewitnesses and kill any investigation of fellow police officers.

It's amazing at first blush that this explanation of Creavey's gets past the prosecutors. The real story here is that Lillie Belle's family doesn't have the clout, nor the money, to make the system do the right thing. They still don't.

Contrary to retired agent Hendrick's feeble recollection, the record shows that Hendricks and his partner next interviewed York police detective Thomas Chatman. Chatman's August 4, 1969 statement to the FBI is just as telling.

Sgt. Chatman's statement reads, in part, "A racial disturbance commenced in York, Pa., on July 17, 1969. This was mainly a disturbance between a group of Negroes and a group of white individuals. As a result of the gang incidents, the police department attempted to seal off two areas of town." One of which, he says, was Newberry Street.

In his statement, Chatman, like Creavey, denies that any reports are being made by his department. Already Chatman isn't telling the truth. His department has already written the reports of the family's statements taken by city police at the hospital, and Chatman himself has taken statements from James and Beatrice Mosley, which have vanished.

Chatman's FBI statement goes on to defend the police by mentioning the same canard about the vests and the light-blue helmets: "Sergeant Chatman stated that all officers of the department are issued light blue crash-type helmets which they were wearing during the disturbance. Also, most officers were wearing bullet-proof vests as protection against sniper fire which was constantly being aimed at them."

It seems that both police departments had jointly cooked up a cover story, and they were sticking to it.

This much is clear: the state and local police were refusing to investigate police involvement in Lillie's murder, and they both were lying to the Justice Department.

The next day, they got a boost in their attempted cover-up when local FBI agent Bill Daane discussed the eyewitness reports of police involvement with local assistant U.S. attorney for the middle district of Pennsylvania, Carlon O'Malley.

Daane reported on August 5, 1969, O'Malley "stated that in his opinion there was no need for further investigation. From the facts developed, the only thing that indicated a law enforcement officer was present in the white gang responsible for the shooting of Lillie Belle Allen was that an individual wearing matching grayish pants and shirt and was wearing a helmet. This individual was not wearing a bullet proof vest as were the officers on the nearby corner and his helmet was different from that of either the PSP or the York City Police. Furthermore, this individual was not observed to be taking any action with the gang but when last observed, was actually walking away from the vehicle in which the victim was riding and had his back to the vehicle."

If this was one of the city or state policemen on roving patrol, mixed in with the gang, of course he was walking away. He had foreknowledge of the planned ambush of the Spells brothers and he was getting the hell out of there, and doing nothing to help the family, like the cops at the "nearby corner," who at the same moment, having allowed the Cadillac to pass, were about to watch from behind their cruisers while the shooting started, and then run off, while the terrorized family prayed for help.

While the assistant U.S. attorney for the middle district of Pennsylvania shrugged off investigating police involvement in the murder, those officers weren't off the hook yet. The local U.S. attorney's office had nothing to do with the Civil Rights Division's investigation. Down South, the local U.S. attorneys often fought the Civil Rights Division in Washington, I'd learn. That's what was happening here. O'Malley's demurrer simply meant that the cops involved in Lillie's murder were being given a pass by their colleagues, the local FBI agents and the local federal prosecutor.

The Civil Rights Division was much more persistent, and its meddling in this police killing would be much more of a problem.

# 13

## Police report first murder suspects in August 1969

The same day the assistant U.S. attorney in Pennsylvania decided not to investigate the state and local police, August 5, 1969, Sgt. Creavey and Detective Chatman conducted an important interview with a neighbor near N. Newberry Street. Annabel Mae Kline, age 57, of 304 W. North Street, a nurse at the Lutheran Home, gave detectives several pieces of information. She told Creavey and Chatman that she had witnessed three young men — apparently James and Sherman Spells, and Bobby Messersmith — arguing on the Messersmiths' porch on the afternoon Lillie Belle was murdered. Bobby Messersmith had been holding a rifle or shotgun, she related, while he argued with the two blacks.

Kline had witnessed the Spells brothers warning Bobby Messersmith not to firebomb their mother's house again, or they'd be back. Of course, the police at the barricade, and the neighborhood (and much of the city) knew about this confrontation and warning, though now the detectives had a witness.

Kline went on to give additional details that could hurt the police, and again suggested police foreknowledge of the planned murder.

"After supper," Kline's police statement continues, "I went out to North & Newberry Sts. It was between 7-8 PM. The gang of kids were congregating. They usually got together every evening at this time. I went back to my yard and sat down. I saw three fellows with guns on the roof at 231 N. Newberry, one of them was hanging on the chimney. This was about 8-8:30 PM. I went into the house and called the City Police. I told them there were snipers on the roof. I believe I told them 233 N. Newberry. I had the wrong number. I don't know whether the police came or not."

This was about the time that John Messersmith was passing out weapons and assigning armed kids to posts on the roofs, alleyways and windows, warning all that the Spells' Cadillac was coming, and telling kids that he was listening to the police scanner for the tip-off that the Cadillac had reached the barricade. It was probably about the same time state trooper Gerald Roberts, standing at the barricade with his partner, encountered the white youth who had come up to them and instructed the two state troopers to turn their backs when the expected Cadillac arrived and everything would be okay, that the troopers wouldn't be shot.

So here the police found a witness who says the city police had been warned about the snipers on the Messersmiths' and a neighbor's roof shortly before the ambush. Had anyone responded to Kline's tip-off to police? There are a few tantalizing clues. Thirty years later, Stephan Noonan, one of the kids in the street that night, told prosecutors that police had arrived at the Messersmiths' before the shooting and, in the words of a circa-2000 county detective's document, the "officer told them at Bobby's to stay inside with guns." Noonan would also tell investigators he'd seen a police cruiser at the Messermiths' shortly before the shooting.

Was this the trooper that Beatrice Mosley had seen mixed in with the gang of kids? Or had Beatrice Mosley seen one of the "roving" state and York policemen that retired Trooper Roberts says moved around the neighborhood, and who returned to the barricade "from time to time?"

The only reliable characteristic about police during the York riots is that they were totally unreliable and unprofessional. The night before, on Sunday, July 20, 1969, the Newberry Street Boys had repeatedly firebombed the home of a black couple, Mr. and Mrs. Frank Meyers, on adjoining Cottage Hill Road, with foreknowledge of police. The Meyers were the only blacks in the neighborhood. They lived in a row house next door to a white man, Clifton Kohler, of 286 Cottage Hill Road. Evidence was developed in the previously mentioned 1970 federal civil rights trial that Clifton Kohler on July 20, 1969, shortly after 10pm, "reported to City Hall that a member of the white group assembled at the bridge had threatened to firebomb his home and Kohler was told by a person answering the telephone, 'What are we supposed to do about it?'" The 1970 federal judge's findings of fact relates, "Thirty minutes later the Kohler and Meyers homes were struck with a firebomb and then riddled with gunfire. These incidents were reported to police by Mr. Kohler, but he was told that there was nothing that could be done about it. Later in the morning further shots were fired and Mrs. Meyers was cut by flying glass."

In any event, Annabel Kline went on to tell Sgt. Creavey and Det. Chatman that she heard the attack on Lillie Belle Allen. "They started shooting at five minutes to nine. I came into the house and looked at my watch. It sounded like there were ten guns shot at one time. Then there was one or two shots afterwards. They didn't shoot too long. It sounded like one big blast from a fort and it was all over."

By the time they interviewed Annabel Mae Kline in early August 1969, the Pennsylvania state police knew that the federal government's Civil Rights Division was looking over their shoulder, haunting them with the very real possibility that murder charges could. be filed against their officers. The state police by this time finally got around to adding more men to the case. The police have just been informed *they are under investigation for murder;* they now must massage the system to ensure they aren't *charged with murder.*

To give appearances that they give a rat's ass about Lillie Belle Allen, but really to protect their own skins, state police supervisors throw more manpower at the case. A case where they already know the solution. State police detective Corporal Kenneth Markel is suddenly added to the crack team of Sgt. Creavey, Cpl. Weiksner, Det. Cronin, and city detective Chatman. Ah, the Keystone Cops.

On August 6, 1969 state police detective Arthur Cronin hit the streets and single-handedly interviewed *twelve* Newberry Street neighbors. Det. Cronin interviews more people on this one day than all the others had interviewed in the preceding fifteen days since the murder. This is the same day FBI special agent Bill Daane asked assistant U. S. attorney Carlon O'Malley whether the state and city police themselves should be investigated. The Civil Rights Division certainly seems to have gotten someone worried at state police headquarters. If only for appearances sake, now the cops were finally starting to beat on doors, and wear down their shoe leather. If only they could find some clues, some witnesses—.

In August 2000 Trooper Keith Stone wrote a Pennsylvania State Police General Investigation Report explaining Cronin's presence on the scene in 1969. After thirty years even the state police had lost track of who did what and why, and a trooper had to write a report about it, reminiscent of the Pentagon Papers. Cronin, Trooper Stone writes, "was a supervisor sent down from PSP DHQ in 1969 to supervise the investigations during the riots." So the big boys at departmental headquarters sent Cronin to follow the heart of darkness several hundred feet up Newberry Street from the railroad tracks to the black hole at the barricade. He was an errand boy, sent by grocery clerks, to collect an overdue bill. He'd go bad on Newberry Street, like the others before and after him.

Cronin's interviews were largely non-productive, but interesting, and telling. They seem to document the cover story that the neighbors don't want to talk. Rather, there's something about Cronin's manner that makes the neighbors not want to talk. Something about Sgt. Creavey's personality, on the other hand, makes people open up and talk to him.

That day Cronin mostly concentrates on the 200 block of Newberry St. He seems to have knocked on nearly every door but the Messersmiths, at 229 N. Newberry. Why not 229? We can suppose it was because the territory-protecting Messersmith brood for a change wasn't at home, that they were perhaps away designing the space shuttle for NASA, or working on the first micro-processor chip with Andy Grove. But that's unlikely. Cronin obviously didn't knock on the Messersmiths' door because the police *already* know the Messersmiths are prime suspects in the murder. Det. Cronin is canvassing to learn which of their neighbors is willing to walk the plank and talk, since the police won't. But Det. Cronin doesn't do a very good job at making people feel comfortable. The cops don't instill much confidence in these neighbors. They don't feel protected in police presence.

Next door to the Messersmiths, at 227 N. Newberry, seventy-four-year Macie Yingling tells Cronin she had gone to visit her daughter during the "disturbance" and that she was not at home during the shooting.

Two doors down, at the row home on the other side of the Messersmiths', at 231 N. Newberry, Cronin next enjoys a tête-à-tête with Richard Shaffer, age forty-three. Evidence would be developed that next-door neighbor John Messersmith had stationed boys with rifles on Shaffer's roof, and that the Shaffers had hosted some of the street gang in their home. But Cronin couldn't get Shaffer to talk. Cronin's report reads that Richard Shaffer, "stated the he was not working during the week of 21 Jul 69. He stated on the evening of 21 Jul 69 he was on the front porch of his home with his wife and eight year old son. He stated that when he heard the shooting he went into the house without seeing who was doing the shooting. Mr. Shaffer stated he did not know that any persons were up on the roof of his home during the shooting with guns as previously given by reliable witnesses. It is aparent (sic) that Mr. Shaffer knows some of the persons doing the shooting at the Allen woman but for reasons of his own, he refuses to state any persons."

Cronin's spelling isn't stellar, his grammar is lazy, and his reports, in general, lack the rat-a-tat-tat literary punch of Sgt. Creavey's. He keeps referring to Lillie Belle as "the Allen woman." That troublesome, troublesome Allen woman, who just won't die and go away. What's interesting about this entry is that here Cronin mentions "reliable *witnesses*," plural, who he writes already have told police that snipers were stationed on Shaffer's roof. Though such reports would be written and filed by police later, only a single *written* report mentioning snipers on the roof of 331 N. Newberry to date had been filed — that of Annabel Kline, the day before. The police we can glean were talking to many people whose names had not made it on to written reports. Cops, maybe?

Cronin's August 6, 1969 Supplement Report lists the other ten neighbors he interviewed that day. Nobody seemed to have much to say much to Cronin.

Verna Keller, seventy-four, of 226 N. Newberry, "who wears a hearing aid, stated she went to bed early in the evening and did not hear the shooting." Her son, Harold Keller, "upon being interviewed stated that he was working 3:00 PM to 11:00 PM at the time of the shooting."

Vickie Doukounas, of 207 N. Newberry, "Greek origin, has one of her children interpret for her. She stated that on the night the Allen woman was shot, she and her family were not at home."

Orr Monroe, age fifty-five, of 213 N. Newberry, "stated he was in his livingroom, during the evening of 21 Jul 69 and heard the shooting but did not see anything and did not look out."

Gus Liazis, of 215 N. Newberry, "was working the night of the shooting at the Famous Resturant (sic) and his family heard the shooting but no one looked out."

Nelson Conner, age seventy-one, of 223 N. Newberry, "stated the night the Allen woman was shot he was standing inside his front door and looking down the street. He stated he saw the car come up the street and the driver attempted to turn the car around at the railroad tracks, when the shooting came from all along the 200 block of Newberry St. He stated he did not see the woman get out of the car and that he feels that the shooting was uncalled for. He stated he doesn't know who did the shooting or who was carrying rifles during this period."

Mrs. Stella Sier, 233 N. Newberry, "stated that she was on vacation for two months in N. Mexico with her husband and children during the disturbances in York."

Arthur Morris, 156 N. Newberry, "(owner and operator of North-end Cigar Store) stated his store was hit with bricks and stones at or about 11:15 PM on 17 July 69 by a group of Negro youths, at which time the store was closed. The store was closed and he was not in the area on 21 Jul 69 when the Allen woman was killed at the rail road crossing, located near the front of his store. There was a rifle bullet shot through the glass door of his store at the time of this incident."

Mrs. Gloria Myers, age thirty-two, of 302 Smyers St., "stated she has lived at this address since October '68 and on the night the Allen woman was shot, she was in her home and stayed there. Prior to the shooting she saw boys on the street but does not know their names and did not see any with weapons.

Robert Downey, age forty-three, of 314 Gay St., "stated stated (sic) he was sitting of (sic) the front porch of his home on the eveing (sic) of 21 Jul 69 with his wife. He observed a cadillac being driven north on Newberry St., the car was going slow and looked to be making a U turn at the railroad crossing. He stated as the car was turning the shooting started and he believed some of the shooting came from the cadillac. He stated he did not see anyone with a gun prior to the shooting and after the shooting stayed in the house." This is the first report the police would file stating Lillie Belle or one of her family had fired a gun — which is untrue.

Det. Cronin notes at the bottom of his report, "It is obvious to this reporting officer, that the persons interviewed and the general feeling in the area, is the shooting was justified and to justify this by rumor, are attempting to create the feeling the persons in the cadillac fired first."

The same day state police detective Arthur Cronin so deftly interrogated twelve neighbors and wrote his report, blaming the neighbors for their non-cooperation, newly assigned state police Corporal Kenneth Markel also ventured out to interview five Newberry Street residents. Markel filed a separate Supplement Report. The two were canvassing together, looking high and low for clues. Interestingly, neither Cronin nor Markel knocked on the door of 121 N. Newberry, to interview Officer Wayne Ruppert's family. Why?

Instead, Cpl. Markel charges into the tank like a well-heeled state trooper, saluting smartly, the strap of his ranger hat no doubt pulled snugly under his nose.

Markel's crisply typed report begins, "On the date of this report the undersigned officer proceeded to the 200 Block of North Newberry Street, York, Penna, for the purpose of interviewing the residents of this area to determine if there were any witnesses to this captioned crime." Note how they already seem to be tacking the tack that witnesses are hard to come by. Since he was looking high and low for witnesses, one wonders why Markel doesn't interview the cops who saw it all from their hiding places behind their cruisers at the barricade. He then goes on to describe the six neighbors who, by and large, profess to have seen no evil.

Ida Belle St. Clair, W-F-71 (white, female, age seventy-one), 245 North Newberry St. "Occuptation, grocery store owner and operator. Mrs. St. Clair stated that she was in her store and didn't see anything."

Miss Vickie Brooks, W-F-15, 245 North Newberry St, "student, stated that she was sitting with her parents, Gary and Josephine Brooks and a sister and a brother, Scotty and Brenda. The shooting started and we all ducked into the house. We didn't see who shot, but there were alot of kids from all over York, who we didn't know."

Anna Mae Wolf, W-F-40, 243 north Newberry St., "housewife. Stated, 'I didn't see nothing.'"

Avis D. Glatfelter, W-F-58, 239 North Newberry St., "housewife, stated, 'I was on the porch, I saw the car coming up the street and it turned as if to turn around on the railroad tracks. I heard shots and I ran into the house. I saw a lot of kids with guns, but I don't know who they are."

Eva Noss, W-F-70, 237 north Newberry St., "housewife, stated, 'I was inside the house and didn't see anything. When the shooting started I pulled down the blinds and shut and locked the door."

The most haunting story heard by Cpl. Markel was told him by Nancy McAuley, a thirty-seven-year-old housewife living at 237 Newberry St. McAuley explained that she and her husband weren't home the night of the shooting, but were staying at her house in nearby Red Lion. The day after the shooting McAuley returned to town and was in Ida Belle St. Clair's neighborhood grocery store when she'd had a poignant encounter with the son of a policeman. "The next day a young man came into St. Clair's Grocery store. He appeared visibly shaken and stated that he was sick over the whole affair and that he hated himself. He left the store without another word."

Decades later, on the circa-2000 grand jury witness list, investigators add that McAuley, "was in store day after- heard young boy, the son of a cop, say it was too bad what happened to the woman (Lilli) (sic) — (now) doesn't specifically recall hearing that even though her '69 statement says it.

Cpl. Markel's report makes no mention that the "young man" McAuley is talking about is the son of a cop, presumably the son of Newberry Street neighbor Lt. Wayne Ruppert. His first day out, Cpl. Markel has fallen into the tank. He adds fig leafs of his own.

Thirty-one years later, one Newberry Street resident, Glen

Monday, would help explain the neighbor's attitude toward the police. At the time of the murder, Monday was an eleven-year-old member of the Newberry Street Boys. In 1969, he lived at 41 S. Newberry, on the other side of Philadelphia Street.

Glen Monday, on August 21, 2000, met with investigators working for the county DA's office. County Detective Rodney George recorded the conversation as follows: "The first thing (Monday) remembered about the riots was that a couple of days or so before the woman was shot, he was on N. Newberry Street by Gay Street when a car came up Newberry Street. The car was driven by a young black male and there may have been at least one other black male with him. This driver of the car stopped the car in the middle of the street. The other subject got out of the back seat. The driver opened the trunk of the car and got out a shotgun. When this occurred, one of the older guys that he was with yelled to get down. Monday fell to the ground and he could hear the shotgun pellets hitting above his head. He stated that the guys got back into their car and drove away. Monday stated that this incident was not provoked by anyone on Newberry Street in any way and that he heard the last name of Spells mentioned as the guys who shot at them."

George continues, "Monday stated that after the incident the Newberry Street Boys had meetings in Farquar Park. These were organized by James Messersmith who according to Monday was the leader of the Newberry Street Boys. Monday stated that when the riots started the difference in the meetings was that members of the Girarders and Swampers were also invited. Normally these groups would be at odds with each other but at this time the message to them was that they all had to stick together and protect themselves. Monday stated it was not against all blacks, just the ones that came into the neighborhood and started trouble. Monday stated that he remembered some police officers being at the meetings.

"Monday stated that he was at his house the night that the woman was shot on Newberry Street. The next day he went up to Newberry Street and heard about the woman getting shot. He stated that the talk was that the car came up Newberry Street and the woman got out of the car. When she did she got shot.

Glen Monday then tells investigators, "he thinks that the police were partially responsible for the woman being killed because they were at the intersection of Philadelphia and Newberry Street and should have stopped her from going down Newberry Street. Monday remembers that he and his young brother were stopped by the police at that same intersection and were not allowed into the area only days before the woman was killed. He stated that they put him and his brother in a police car and took them home."

Monday's statement goes a long way to explain the neighborhood distrust of the cops. Everyone on the block knew that the cops for days had sealed their street, except for the night Lillie was shot, when they had let the wrong Cadillac through. And now the cops were coming around wanting the neighbors to point the finger at anyone and everyone but the cops.

The police were there and knew what happened. A mob of kids had been running around with guns under the noses of the police. Why were the police now asking the neighbors to stick their necks out, when the cops wouldn't?

The same day state troopers Cronin and Markel were looking high and low for clues, Monday August 11, 1969, Sgt. Creavey was back in the saddle and writing a report of an interview he'd taken while accompanied by Det. Chatman. This interview also underscored the neighbors' distrust and suspicion of the police.

William Boyer, age seventy, ran a plumbing business at the rear of 300 Smyser Street, overlooking Newberry. Boyer's place had been searched for weapons on July 24. Boyer told Creavey and Chatman that on Monday, July 21, he had been "standing in the doorway of his shop (rear) which faces N. Newberry St., west side. It was between 8:30 and 9 PM.

"I saw the whole thing," Boyer went on. "I saw the car coming up Newberry St. The car made a turn. U Turn. She got over too far and the front wheels were off the pavement and on the tracks. (RR tracks). Whoever was driving choked the car and it stopped. I think the driver was confused.

"There were about seventy-five kids over there on the corner (northeast corner of Newberry). Kids seventeen, eighteen years old running around with guns in broad daylight. Soon as the car stopped they all started shooting. Nobody in that car fired at all. Nobody down the street fired, all the shooting came from across the street from where I was. It's hard to tell how many were shooting.

"There must have been fifteen guns floating around over there. I saw someone fall out of the car on the left side, the driver's side. To tell you the truth, I didn't see any people in that car. They all ducked down. Mr. Conners, across the street, saw me standing in the doorway. I don't think he saw the shooting. The shooting came from up the street farther.

"I don't know how the kids saw who was in the car. I couldn't see who was in the car. I don't know why the police didn't chase them kids off the street."

Doh! Again, the finger pointed back to police. Seventy-five kids, running around in broad daylight with guns, with the acquiescence of police.

The cops saw if they were going to get anywhere they had to at least attempt to steer attention away from their fellow officers at the barricade, and stick it on the kids. Hopefully it wouldn't keep bouncing back on them.

On August 11, 1969, Cpl. Weiksner finally got around to typing and filing a report of five interviews he'd conducted on August 1st, 2nd and the 6th. Four of the interviews were of young men, ages eighteen to twenty-two. The interviews are significant for several reasons. For the first time, state police documents show they identified by name some of the young men who fired at the car. They show the state police identified two of the suspects days *before* Creavey and Chatman falsely told the FBI on August 4 they had no suspects, and further lied to the feds about not having written any reports.

On August 1, 1969, Gary Richard King, age nineteen, told Cpl. Weiksner he had been sitting on the porch of the Slick home the night of the murder. King said he watched as the Cadillac attempted to make the turn at the railroad tracks.

"I heard someone say 'whitety-whitey' and then I heard two shots and then it sounded like a war," King told Weiksner. "I didn't see anyone shooting but it seemed the shooting came from Bob Messersmith's house." At last, the police reports mention Bobby Messersmith. King continues, "I noticed Bob Messersmith on the balcony of his house and three other people. These three had guns but I didn't know any of them. One of them had on a blue jacket with 'Yorklyn' printed on it. One of the guns sounded like a cannon."

William Charles Ritter, age eighteen, also known as Sam Ritter, told Cpl. Weiksner on August 2, 1969 that he had been sitting on the porch of the Slick family home at nearby 426 West Gay St. "The shooting started about 9:30 PM and I ducked behind a truck," Ritter said. "I seen the Cadillac stop on the railroad tracks at North Newberry Street and Gay Street. I then heard a lot of shooting. Someone was also shooting from on North Penn Street towards the car. I don't know who did the shooting."

Thirty years later, William Ritter would tell a grand jury that he had been one of the boys shooting from the Penn Street bridge, and that he thought he'd emptied a clip of six bullets from a .22 rifle he aimed at the car. He would be one of nine indicted in 2001 for Lillie Belle's murder.

# 14
## "All hell broke loose"

By the middle of August 1969, Sgt. John Creavey interviews Hattie and Murray Dickson. This time the couple is interviewed on behalf the Pennsylvania State Police. Creavey files a Supplement Report that conspicuously refuses to even mention either of the two having witnessed a "trooper" mixed in with the shooters. The cops at the barricade remain a real problem. It's hard to tell the story of the ten second ride down Newberry Street without starting at the church corner where the officers are standing and watching. Hattie naturally expects safe passage, not a planned ambush, nor a riot scene, when they pass the cops on the corner.

Creavey in his reports here appears to begin referring to police as "the guys," particularly when witnesses are referring to police officers Creavey doesn't want mentioned in the report.

Still, Creavey is a good writer, with a fine ear for his subjects' dialogue.

Bubba Dickson tells him about the intersection of Newberry and Philadelphia. Dickson says, "We went down Pershing to Philadelphia. There was a trooper car and an armored car. The troopers had vests and guns, shotguns, they saw us but didn't say a word.... We turned right at the Y (YMCA) and went up Newberry St. My wife, Hattie was driving. As we went over the tracks, I saw a guy with a gun on the right side of the street. It looked like he was wearing a white T shirt and dungarees. There was a fellow putting a motorcycle off the street on to the sidewalk. He was near the guy with the gun. It looked as if he was talking to him. My wife started to turn. She tried to make a circle. We thought she was going to hit the pole, and she stopped. The car was on the tracks. Lillie Bell (sic) said 'Let me get it out of here.' She opened the door and stepped out. She was sitting behind my wife, Hattie.

"When she stepped out the shooting started. There was one shot fired. We thought she ducked down. Mom opened the door and said, 'Oh Lillie Bell (sic) is hit. Hattie got out and she came back and I pulled her in the car.

"They started shooting again. All hell broke loose."

Hattie Dickson tells Sgt. Creavey, "We had been fishing all day Monday. We left the York Reservoir at about twenty-five of nine. We came down to the store — a little fruit stand. We bought milk, ice cream and cookies. My dad asked if the food was high. I said yes, but we shop at (the) J.M. Fields store. We came home and I took the stuff in the house. My dad went to the bathroom. We came out and my car wouldn't start. Dad wanted to take his car. We got our car started.

"We went up Pershing Ave. to Philadelphia. I turned my signal on when I saw the policemen at Newberry and Philadelphia. My mom said, 'Don't you see the light?' I was looking at the policemen and nearly run it. I stopped at the light and then turned up Newberry. Just as I was going over the railroad I saw the guys with guns. I got so scared I started to turn around. They wanted me to go straight ahead (persons in the car). When I turned I had my head layed over (ducking down). They said stop you are going to hit the pole. My foot was on the brake but the car was moving. I stopped. I didn't cut the car off (ignition). Lillie said, 'Stop the car and I'll take the wheel.' When I stopped she got out of the back and went to open the front door (my door). There was a shot fired. I put the car in park and pushed my door open and got out. Lillie was lying at the door. I could see her insides hanging out and her head was toward the front of the car. I got out and started up the railroad track and I saw the car lights were on. I came back to the car to turn the lights out. I started to get into the car and wasn't completely inside and a second shot was fired. My husband pulled me back into the car down on the seat. There was more shots fired."

The issue of the cops at the barricade nags Sgt. Creavey. So much so that he and Detective Chatman pay a visit to the office of the York City Engineer to check out the scale maps of the area. They measure the distance from the barricade to the railroad tracks.

On August 15, 1969, the day after interviewing the Dicksons, Sgt. Creavey files a brief Supplement Report.

"Investigation was continued to approximate distances in this case," Creavey writes. "The distance from Philadelphia St. north on N. Newberry St. to the Western Maryland Railroad tracks on which the victim's car was stopped is 525 feet." Then, for reasons unknown, since there was no barricade north of the tracks, Creavey notes, "The distance from North St. at N. Newberry south to the railroad tracks to where the car was stopped is 381 feet." About a tenth of a mile from the barricade to the tracks.

This report, like every state police report filed since the crime, continues to misspell Lillie Belle's middle name as "Bell." Three weeks after the murder Creavey still didn't care enough about Lillie to get her name right.

# 15
## Ammo on the bed

Almost one month after Lillie's death, the state police add another investigator to the case. They have regrouped. Now they have decided to forget altogether the cops involved and focus full tilt on identifying members of the white street gang.

Corporal Ron Dixon is the new trooper on the case, this time with a mission not to look up Newberry Street toward the barricade. On August 20, 1969, Cpl. Dixon pays a visit to one Stephan Noonan, age eighteen, at the boy's job at the Bon-Ton Department Store, on the square in downtown York.

The resulting report filed by Cpl. Dixon vividly describes the confusion on the street before the shooting. Noonan explains that word had gone out across the city that a Cadillac full of black troublemakers was expected that evening on Newberry. Noonan was a member of the Yorklyn Gang, and he explains how word buzzed through his gang that afternoon. The cops have hit on a strategy of flushing out one of the gangs, the Yorklyns. Strangely, this gang is probably farthest removed from the Newberry Street Boys, who the cops know are at the center of the crime.

Soon lots names of boys, mostly high school students or recent graduates, begin spilling off the pages of the state police reports.

Stephen Noonan, Cpl. Dixon reports, "furnished the following statement: On 21 July 1969, at about 8:30 PM, upon completion of football practice at West York high School, he and an acquaintance, Joe Kluyber, departed from the school grounds in his automobile. At this time Kluyber requested to be taken to N. Newberry Street, indicating there was going to be trouble with the coloreds. He advised that he would drive him there, however, he wouldn't remain himself.

"At about 8:45 PM, they arrived and parked in front of 209 N. Newberry Street, facing north along the east side, approximately twenty to thirty yards north of the railroad tracks. There was a group consisting of approximately twenty-five to thirty white youths, congregating at that location. He estimated that about five of the boys appeared to be armed, at least two of them with hand guns, however, he couldn't be certain as there was much confusion.

"The boys, some of whom he knew, were in the fourteen through twenty age bracket. They then alighted from the automobile and began talking to some of their friends in the group. He remembers talking to the following persons: Tom Smith, W-M, Hayshire; Bill Conway, W-M, Yorklyn; Gary Fink, W-M, Hayshire; Jim Rummel, W-M, Hayshire; Ben Mathis, W-M, Yorklyn; Gordon Snyder, W-M, Pleasureville; Darryl Kauffman, W-M, Emigsville; and Gary Holtzapple, W-M, Hayshire.

"He further stated that they all attended Central High School and believed that three of them, Mathis, Rummel, and Holtzapple are presently attending. The group including himself have become acquaintances through attending school and residing in the same neighborhood. In that they usually travel in a group they are more or less affiliated with the title 'The Yorklyn Gang.'

"While in their company he observed that one of the boys, Tom Smith, was armed with a rifle, which he removed from the rear seat of his automobile, parked in front of his vehicle. He believed the rifle had been concealed under a blanket and when Smith removed it he had to assemble the various pieces as it was broke down. Smith at this time advised that it was a .30-.30 calibre (sic) rifle.

"The boys in the entire group were talking about problems with the colored people coming into the neighborhood on previous occasions and stated they were ready to get them (the colored people), if they came looking for trouble. At about 9:00 PM, he decided to move his automobile to another location and drove north along N. Newberry Street. He then parked the vehicle near the park in the 400 block.

"He then walked along N. Newberry Street on the east side, pausing occasionally to converse with people sitting on their porches. Suddenly he heard several boys in the crowd shouting that, 'The niggers are coming!'

"He then observed a grey colored Cadillac traveling north along N. Newberry Street. The crowd of boys began scattering throughout the immediate area, some of them entering homes situated along the east side of N. Newberry Street.

"The Cadillac then swerved sharply to the left and stopped broadside across N. Newberry Street, facing in a westerly direction and the headlights were turned off. Suddenly one of the occupants in the Cadillac alighted from the left side.

"It appeared to be a colored woman and she turned facing north along N. Newberry Street, waving both her arms in the air.

"At this time he heard three gunshots and immediately dove to the ground, however he did observe the woman standing near the Cadillac slightly stagger backwards before she fell to the ground.

"He then immediately crawled between a passage separating two row homes and continued to look south along Newberry Street. At this time approximately fifteen to twenty more gunshots were fired in rapid succession. The shots sounded like shotguns and rifles being fired and he observed muzzle flashes coming from homes and parked vehicles along the east side of the street.

"Suddenly someone began shouting that a police armored car was approaching the area and groups of boys began scattering in all directions throughout the neighborhood. He then began running north along the east side of Newberry Street towards his automobile.

"At this time Kluyber and Roger Kinard, W-M, Yorklyn, who he didn't observe earlier, also joined him. As they were approaching his car Tom Smith came running by holding his rifle. He asked Smith at this time how many shots had he fired. He replied one and he departed. He further stated that he then drove Kluyber and Kinard to their homes and dropped them off. He then arrived at his home at about 10:10 PM.

"Shortly thereafter Kluyber, Mathis, and Rummel arrived at his home and requested him to accompany them back to the N. Newberry Street neighborhood. They also requested him to bring along any firearms that he might have. However, he refused to accompany them and they departed in Rummel's automobile. He later learned that Kluyber had been arrested by police and charged with firearm violations.

"He further related that sometime during the week of 27 July and 2 Aug 69, in the early evening hours, he stopped at a drive-in restaurant known as Craig's. At this time he observed Tom Smith there and struck up a conversation with him regarding the shooting and murder of the colored woman.

"At this time Smith related to him that he had fired only one shot at the Cadillac. Smith appeared to be very nervous at this time and emphasized that the woman had already been hit before he fired his rifle. He further stated that he believed Smith was accompanied by the following boys on the night of the fatal shooting: Gary Fink, Gordon Snyder, and Darryl Kauffman, however, he couldn't be positive. He was also fairly certain that Smith was armed with his father's rifle.

"He further related that he was not too familiar with the Newberry Street neighborhood and wasn't acquainted with the people over there. He was unable to identify any of the other boys in the group, however, he was of the opinion that Kluyber and Tom Smith were familiar with the boys, possibly the group known as 'The Newberry Street Boy.'

"He was unable to furnish any additional information at this time as to aid in this investigation, however, he indicated that if it was absolutely necessary for him to appear in court to clear the case, he would do so."

More than thirty years later, according to prosecution documents, Stephan Noonan would tell grand jury in 2000 that about the time he arrived at the Messersmiths, at about 8:45 (within minutes of Lillie's arrival), "he saw a police car at Bobby's and officer told them at Bobby's to stay inside with guns." This perhaps significant detail is missing from Cpl. Dixon's report.

Though Tom Smith was implicated by Noonan in 1969, authorities wouldn't indict Tom Smith until 2001.

For thirty-one years, police instead would lie and tell the community they had no suspects, and that witnesses weren't coming forward.

The very next day, August 20, 1969, at the York state police barracks, Cpl. Donald Weiksner interviewed at least four of the boys mentioned by Noonan.

Joseph Kluyber, eighteen, of York, told Weiksner that he and Noonan had left football practice together and reached Newberry Street, he thought, around 8 PM. Kluyber said when the shooting started he was standing about twenty-five yards north of the tracks, on the east side of the street (which would place him near the Messersmiths').

Kluyber said he "started to walk close to the building in a northerly direction on Newberry Street. He stated that while the shooting was going on, he seen one Greg Neff, a member of the 'Girarder Gang,' fire a shot from a second floor window in the direction of the car. He further stated that he seen Neff before the shooting at the same window with a long-barrelled gun. He stated that he knows Neff, but not on a personal basis. He added that following the shooting he and Noonan left the area and returned to the Yorklyn area. He added that later that evening he and a boy by the name of Searer left his home with two guns and returned to York and were arrested for a game violation and curfew violation by York City Police, for carrying the guns and also being out after curfew."

A week later, on August 27, 1969, state police documents show, Kluyber returned to the barracks and told Cpl. Weiksner that "upon reviewing the seriousness of the case, retracted his statement of seeing Greg Neff in the area. He stated that he heard Neff was in the area but did not see him."

William Conway, seventeen, arrived at the York State Police Barracks with his father. The younger Conway said he hadn't been in the area of Newberry Street on July 21, as reported by Noonan, but had been working for his father, who ran a janitorial service. His father vouched for his alibi. William Conway told Cpl. Weiksner that there were about forty members of the Yorklyn Gang, and that his older brother, John, age twenty, was the current president.

Gary Fink told Cpl. Weiksner that he had left Newberry Street at 8:45 PM, shortly before Lillie's arrival. He hadn't seen any kids with guns, he said. He remembered talking with two reporters from the Baltimore Sun, one a Negro, before he left. On the west side of

Newberry Street he observed "an older man with a gun," but Weiksner doesn't get him to elaborate.

Roger Kinard told Cpl. Weiksner he'd been dropped off at Newberry Street by two other boys, who went their way. "He stated he mingled with a large group of boys near the railroad tracks," Weiksner writes, "and while standing there a group of three boys carrying rifles came down to his group."

Prosecution documents written three decades later note that Kinard saw Bobby Messersmith, saw the car arrive, and then heard someone yell, "Get 'em Neff!" Kinard says he ducked before the shooting but afterwards saw Tom Smith carrying away a gun in parts. He also saw Marvin Kohlbus, Noonan, Tom Smith and Bobby Messersmith's brother, Artie.

Bob Treattino told Cpl. Weiksner that he had arrived at Newberry Street that evening at 6:30pm, with Tom Smith, Gary Fink and Gary Holtzapple. Traettino reported he had loaned Smith his rifle for groundhog hunting, and he saw the gun in Smith's car.

"He stated that he seen a bunch of guys standing around the Messersmith house," Weiksner writes. "He stated he seen the Cadillac come up the street and turn on the railroad tracks. He stated that when the shooting started he jumped into a house. He added that following the shooting he sat around and later he left with Smith in Smith's car. He stated at this time the rifle was in two pieces and laying in the back. He stated he did not see Smith with the assembled gun during the shooting. He stated that later that evening he heard Smith say that he fired at the car and believed he shot out the window of the Cadillac."

Cpl. Weiksner notes, "The above mentioned weapon, a 30.30 Harrington and Richardson rifle was turned over to Detective Arthur Cronin, PSP, Harrisburg. This weapon is to be turned over to the Crime Laboratory for ballistics tests."

Thirty years later, Traettino would tell a grand jury that he'd witnessed a number of people arrive and dump ammunition on a bed in the Messersmiths' house that night. In the year 2001, Greg Neff would be indicted for Lillie Belle's murder.

# 16

## Police arrest Bobby Messersmith for earlier shooting

Friday, August 22, 1969, wasn't a good day for Bobby Messersmith. That was the day police came with a warrant for his arrest for a shooting. Not for the shooting of Lillie Belle Allen. He wouldn't be indicted for the shooting of Lillie Belle for another thirty-two years.

On this day Bobby was pinched for the lesser crime of attempted murder. Police accused Messersmith of shooting Taka Nii Sweeney and John Washington four days before Lillie's murder. This had been the shooting that had helped spark the riots.

The criminal complaint reads, "August 22, 1969, Defendant arrested, Complaint read to Defendant. Defendant informed of his Constitutional Rights and Right to Remain Silent. Defendant in default of bail is committed to jail." Bail was set at ten thousand dollars.

The complaint specifically reads that Messersmith "did… assault the aforesaid victims with a shotgun using a projectile known as a *rifled slug which was fired from a shotgun* in the hands of the accused." Emphasis mine.

Here the cops were arresting Bobby Messersmith for a shooting involving a rifled shotgun slug — a pumpkin ball. It was the same type of slug police knew had killed Lillie Allen.

You can't say here was a case of the left hand not knowing what the right hand was doing. The accusing officer on the Sweeney-Washington criminal complaint was Harold McIlvain, the same detective who had taken the Mosley's statements at the hospital the night Lillie Belle was shot. The statement in which Beatrice had said she'd seen cops all over the murder scene.

The officer who arrested Bobby Messersmith for attempted murder of Sweeney and Washington was state police Cpl. Kenneth Markel. The same Cpl. Markel who was working on the Lillie Belle Allen investigation.

Now police had arrested Bobby Messersmith for a lesser offence, when they knew full well he'd killed Lillie Belle with the same weapon.

Records indicate Bobby sat in county jail for four days, until August 26, 1969, when bail was arranged. The following Thursday, August 28, Bobby Messersmith and his attorney, Norman Petow, appeared in county court and pled not guilty to the charge of attempted murder.

Messersmith was released, pending trial.

# 17

## "His constitutional rights were explained to him"

While Bobby Messersmith cooled his heels in jail, the York state police barracks hosted a steady stream of boys explaining their whereabouts and activities on the night of July 21, 1969. Each boy dropped the names of more boys, broadening the dragnet. Once most of these boys started talking, they kept talking. Police soon found themselves swimming in a broadening river of useful information. And that river kept flowing to the door of Bobby Messersmith, and his father, John. But police for some reason didn't want to go there, not for this crime.

Police interviews open a window into the world of the young men of York of the time, hanging out in school yards, gas stations and corners, hunting, football practice, talking to the guys, hiding guns in Mustangs, at drive-ins trading stories of murder. There were stories of laments and recriminations concerning the young mother they'd all accidentally killed on Newberry Street.

Jay Kohr, eighteen, of York, on August 22, 1969, told Cpl. Weiksner on the night of Lillie's murder he'd left Newberry Street by 9pm, "because he didn't want to get picked up for curfew violation. At the time while he was on Newberry Street he stated he didn't see anyone with guns." After leaving Newberry Street he'd gone to Paul's Atlantic gas station and stayed until closing time at 10:30pm. "I think I brought Gary Holtzapple and Robert Dennis back with me. I remembered seeing Steve Gunarich, Bob Traettino, Darrell Kauffman, Jim Rummel, Tom Smith, Gordon Snyder and Tom Keeney on Newberry Street that evening." Snyder, Keeney, Gunarich and Fink left when he did, he told police. He added, "later Tom Smith and Bob Traettino stopped at the station. At the time no one stated that anyone of our gang had any guns in the area. Sometime later that evening either Tom Smith or someone at the gas station said Tom Smith fired one shot at the car."

Steve Gunarich, fifteen, of York, told Cpl. Weiksner he departed Newberry Street before 9pm, to go to the Atlantic gas station. Gunarich said that at about 9:30 or 10pm Tom Smith, Bob Traettino and Gary Holtzapple came to the station and "Smith stated he fired one shot at the Cadillac and thought he shot out the rear window." Smith showed him the gun the next day, he said. While on Newberry Street, he told Cpl. Weiksner, he saw "Bob Messersmith sitting on his porch on North Newberry Street holding a 12-gauge shotgun."

Gary Holtzapple, seventeen, of York, on August 25, 1969, recounted to Cpl. Weiksner that he'd begun the evening in question at 6:30pm, "in the area of the Hayshire School. He was with Tom Smith, Bob Traettino and Darrell Kauffman. They decided to go to the area of North Newberry Street and at this time he heard there was a gun taped under the hood of Tom Smith's Ford Mustang." The boys concealed guns to avoid police searches at roadblocks, such as the one at Philadelphia and Newberry. Cpl. Weiksner's report continues that Holtzapple next "went to Paul's Atlantic station located on North George Street Extended and at this time he left for Newberry Street accompanied by Smith, Darrell Kauffman and a Gordon Snyder.

"They arrived at Newberry Street at approximately 1915 hrs. (7:15 pm) the evening of the 21st. Holtzapple stated he got out of the car in the area of the railroad tracks and Smith parked the car up the hill on Newberry Street. He stated he was sitting on the east side of Newberry Street about two doors south of the Messersmith residence when the Cadillac came north on Newberry Street. He stated as the car came to the railroad tracks it turned sideways on the tracks and someone got out."

He quotes Holtzapple: "I heard some shots and I ran between the homes. After the shooting was over I went into one of the homes in the area and I met John Duke, whom I know. I came out of the house and sat and talked with Bob Traettino. We went up Newberry Street and we met Tom Smith at his car and we left the area.

"We drove to Paul's Atlantic Station in Hayshire. Just prior to leaving the area of Newberry Street, someone in the group asked where the rifle was and someone said it's under the back seat. At the station later, someone also said that Tom Smith fired a shot at the car and he thought he knocked out the back window.

"Tom left the station to pick up his dad and I left and went home for the night."

The next day, August 26, 1969, Cpl. Weiksner chatted with Ben Mathis, who explained he'd gone to Newberry Street in Jim Rummel's 1961 Austin-Healey Sprite.

Mathis began by mentioning two names that keep echoing in the dark heart of the story: Bobby Messersmith and Greg Neff.

"Rummel parked the car on Newberry Street near Farquar Park and they walked down Newberry Street and talked to a bunch of kids at the cigar store," Cpl. Weiksner relates.

Mathis then walked to a point on the west side of Newberry Street, between the Messersmiths' house and the railroad tracks, and sat. He watched Bob Messersmith, Greg Neff and six or seven other boys walking around with guns. Messersmith had a long-barreled gun but Mathis couldn't say whether it was a rifle or a shotgun. Messersmith was carrying the same gun before and after the shooting.

Two boys, at least, were on the roof with guns. One boy was stationed on the Messersmiths' roof and another on the roof just north, the house of Richard Shaffer, at 231 Newberry.

Mathis remembered it this way: The Cadillac came up Newberry Street, turned out its lights, and then turned broadside on the railroad tracks.

He heard a shot and then a lot of shots. He saw gunfire from all around the Messersmiths' house. Boys leaned out the second floor windows, firing rifles, and others were firing from the roof.

He took off running up an alley between two homes, running with Jim Rummel and Marvin Kohlbus. A streetlight had been shot out above them and they ran farther up the alley.

After some time passed Mathis walked back to Newberry Street. The armored car was at the Cadillac, but the ambulance hadn't yet arrived.

He saw Bobby Messersmith standing with a gun outside his

house. Cpl. Weiksner makes it a point to note that Bobby Messersmith was standing alone. Weiksner deliberately ignored the strange fact that here Bobby is standing a few feet away from the crime scene, holding a smoking shotgun, while *four* York city officers in the armored car ignore him. The state police at this juncture make a conscious effort to snip and edit the police completely from the story.

While Mathis stood in front of the Messersmiths' house, a crowd gathered. One of the boys said he "got one," but Mathis professed not knowing who made the remark. Shortly afterward, Mathis said, he left Newberry Street with Jim Rummel.

Jim Rummel, for his part, told police in 1969 that he had arrived on Newberry Street with Ben Mathis. He saw Lillie's car arrive, but hid, he told police at the time. At the scene he saw Kluyber, Mathis, Kauffman, John Duke, Tom Smith, Gary Fink and Gordon Snyder.

Thirty years later Rummel told investigators he'd witnessed a lot of people with guns and much activity around the Messersmith house that night. Today he says he saw Bobby Messersmith fire a shotgun at Lillie right before the group started shooting, a fact which he says police neglected to extract from him at the time.

The police and prosecutors would not prosecute this case for thirty-two years. Police to this day tell the victim's family, the public, the FBI, the U.S. Justice Department, that no suspects in the crime could be found in 1969. To this day they outright lie about not having identified suspects from the first day of Lillie's murder.

Police documents in fact show that on August 27, 1969, only five weeks after Lillie's murder, police felt they had enough evidence on one of the boys, Tom Smith, to officially inform Smith that he was a *suspect* and read him his rights. Other suspects in the widening dragnet, especially Bob Messersmith, weren't far behind.

Cpl. Weiksner writes a state police Supplement Report dated August 27, 1969, recording that Tom Smith "was interviewed at the York sub-station on 27 Aug 69. He was informed that he was a suspect in this case and his constitutional rights were explained to him and (he) signed a waiver form."

(Miranda rights, demanded by the U.S. Supreme Court in June 1966, are read to *suspects* questioned by police. In explaining his opinion in the Miranda case, Chief Justice Earl Warren praised police "when their services are honorably performed." But when police abandon fair methods, Warren said, "they can become as great a menace to society as any criminal we have.") As we'll see, police read Miranda rights to several suspects in the Lillie Belle Allen case, as required by the Supreme Court for all suspects, though for years afterward police and prosecutors would lie to the public and even the U.S. Justice Department and say no suspects had ever been identified.

Having been read his Miranda rights, Tom Smith dropped some dimes on Bob Traettino. He said he'd met Traettino and two other boys at the Hayshire School before going to Newberry Street. He admits to having had Traettino's rifle, but not the barrel. He says Traettino brought the barrel, and Smith hid it behind the grill of his father's car, while the other parts were placed on the backseat. Someone brought to school a brown paper bag containing ten rounds of ammunition and the bag was placed in the glove compartment.

The four boys drove to Newberry Street, arriving at about 7:30pm. He parked in front of the Messersmiths', and assembled the rifle. The ammunition went into his jacket pocket. By this time he was out of the car. One of the boys standing on the Messersmiths' porch yelled that all the guns were to go into the house, Smith said. Smith, contrary to what others told police, says he handed the rifle and his jacket to the boy on the porch.

Smith said he mingled with a large group of boys in front of the Messersmiths'. Shortly after 9pm he heard a yell from someone down the street. "Colored coming up!"

He  said he was behind a parked car and watched as the grey Cadillac came up the hill and turned at the railroad track. He saw a woman get out of the left side of the car and a shot rang out. He heard the woman scream and then a second later there was lots of shooting, which he said came from the Messersmiths'. He denied firing. He told police he didn't see who was shooting, nor, he said, did he see anyone walking around with guns.

After the shooting he went into a house next to the

Messersmiths', Richard Shaffer's, where he "observed several girls, two older women and a man." About fifteen minutes after the shooting he and three other boys returned to his car, which he had moved before the shooting. "He does not remember who brought the rifle to the car, but he remembers saying he did not want to carry it." He tells police Traettino, Kauffman and Holtzapple had carried the gun to the car in sections. He couldn't recall how the ammunition got back into the glove compartment, but remembers seeing it there. Several days later, he says, he got his jacket back.

He told police he didn't recall saying to anyone that he had shot out the rear window of the car after the woman fell.

Having taken Smith's statement, police placed the Miranda-ized suspect in a squad car and drove him to Newberry Street. Standing in the street with police at his side, Tom Smith pointed his finger at the Messersmiths' house. That's the place where the guns and ammunition had been brought, he tells the cops. He pointed next door, to Richard Shaffer's house, as the home he had gone inside after the shooting. Some block party.

The police weren't done with Tom Smith for the day. Back at the barracks they confronted Smith with Bob Traettino. Traettino repeated in front of Smith that on the way home he'd heard Smith say he'd fired one shot. Traettino then corroborated Smith's account that Traettino had carried the butt of the rifle to Smith's car, though Traettino couldn't recall who had handed him the butt, Cpl. Weiksner notes.

Seems like they had some suspects after all. in fact, seems like a pretty good case. But charges for some reason would be slightly delayed, for thirty-two years, until the next millennium. Tom Smith would be indicted in 2001. He would be one of ten men eventually indicted.

In front of the grand jury in 2000, Tom Smith dropped a few more dimes, this time on police. Prosecution documents in 2000 mentions that Smith now says he went to a Farquar Park rally attended by police officers, some time before Lillie was shot. At the rally, Smith says, he heard police officers instruct the boys to protect themselves. This information of course never makes it into Cpl. Weiksner's August 28, 1969 Supplement Report.

# 18

Police discover how to spell Lillie Belle's name

Two days after Bobby Messersmith was bailed from the slammer for the attempted murder of Sweeney and Washington, the state police host another get-together with a Newberry Street Boy at the local barracks. This time they chat with Chauncey Gladfelter, eighteen years old, living at nearby Parkway Boulevard, and working at your friendly neighborhood Coca Cola bottling plant.

The state police Supplement Report dated August 28, 1969, detailing Gladfelter's interview, is remarkable for several reasons. Our crack team of five state police investigators finally spells Lillie Belle Allen's name correctly, adding a second "e" to her middle name. In the five weeks since her death, the state police until this date have consistently misspelled her name in reports as "Lillie Bell Allen."

The half-page report detailing Chauncey Gladfelter's police interview kicks off by advising us, "Information had been received that this subject was at the scene of the crime during the period of time in question." The police do not here tell us who has fingered Gladfelter. Could it be one of the neighbors who watched the kids running around with guns all day? More likely, I think, Gladfelter was identified by one of the cops who witnessed the murder.

The police here report that Gladfelter had been stationed at the rear balcony of the Messersmiths' house, certainly placed there by John Messersmith.

The Supplement Report reads: "Gladfelter stated on date of 21 Jul 69, prior to the shots being fired, he was in and out of the Messersmith house throughout the day and early evening. He stated that just prior to the shooting he had been requested to go to the rear balcony of the Messersmith home and watch for any colored person sneaking into the Newberry Street area from the colored communities.

He stated that there was another boy with him on the balcony with a .22 Cal. rifle, however he doesn't know his name.

"He further stated that (when) he first heard the shots being fired he ran to the second floor of the Messersmith home and into the 2nd floor front bedroom. There were two boys with .22 cal. rifles at the front two bedroom windows and he heard one of the boys fire a shot. He does not know either of these boys. He then ran downstairs, at which time the shooting had stopped.

"Upon arrival downstairs he observed Bob Messersmith and his father, Mr. John Messersmith, seated at the kitchen table and with shotguns propped against the wall. In the front room there were about ten boys standing around, however none of them had weapons in their possession. There was a number of rifles and shotguns in the living room, on the floor, and propped against the wall.

"He did observe Greg Neff in the living room and Mark Barr, aka Gabriel Mark Barr. Mark Barr is in the Air Force and was home on leave at the time of the shooting."

The report concludes with the following: "It should be noted that Gladfelter is a member of the Newberry Street Boys and was very evasive in his answers to questions posed by interviewing officers. It is apparent that Gladfelter is friendly with the Messersmith family and does not want to place himself in the position to offend any of the Messersmiths or any of the Newberry Street gang."

This admonition, that we must keep in mind individual loyalties to member posses, strikes me as equally applicable to the state and city police, who we must view with equal suspicion in this case, when it comes to their loyalty to members of their own posse — fellow police officers who have witnessed or participated in Lillie's murder.

Gladfelter's interview, the report tells us, was conducted by Cpl. Kenneth Markel, "in the presence of Det. Arthur Cronin."

It was the same Cpl. Markel who, five days earlier, had arrested Bobby Messersmith for the attempted murder by rifled slug of Taka Sweeney and John Washington.

Thirty-two years later, in 2001, Chauncey Gladfelter would be indicted for the murder of Lillie Belle Allen. One of the boys mentioned by Gladfelter, Greg Neff, would also face indictment in 2001 with Gladfelter, Bobby Messersmith, and six others.

Seems like they had another suspect and another witness.

In the year 2000, York County prosecutors would discover that Gabriel Mark Barr cheated the exceedingly fine-grinding wheels of American justice by dying of a stroke in 1999.

# 19

# Newberry Street Boy told he's a murder suspect

Back in 1969 Gabriel Mark Barr was still a very much alive and healthy twenty year old, on active duty as a cook with the United States Air Force. It would turn out that at the time of Lillie's murder Barr was absent without leave from the Air Force.

The day after Chauncey Gladfelter implicated Mark Barr, our intrepid investigators Cpl. Kenneth Markel and Cpl. Donald Weiksner take themselves to a York used car lot to collect more information on murder suspect Gabriel Mark Barr.

The Newberry Street Boys by this time were suffering the slings and arrows of outrageous fortune. Once they were the self-proclaimed hero-protectors of the neighborhood. Now it seemed the whole town scowled at them. In their famous encounter with Lillie Allen, the heavily armed young men had blown away an unarmed mother of two. Guilt, recriminations and derision now floated around. Some of the Newberry Street Boys sought to deflect criticism by suggesting, quite falsely, that Lillie Belle had been armed when she got out of the Cadillac.

This talk of the town led state police investigators on August 29, 1969, to a used car lot owned by Arthur Murphy, age forty, of York. Arthur Murphy co-owned the San Carlos Supper Club, also in York. Gabriel Barr's daddy, Mark Barr, worked as a bartender at San Carlos. Barr couldn't stop bragging about his son, which irritated others at the bar, and prompted Murphy to inform police.

Arthur Murphy told state police Cpls. Markel and Weiksner that bartender Mark Barr kept "bragging about his son, Gabriel Mark Barr, being involved in the shooting of the Allen woman."

The state police report goes on to explain that Murphy told them, "The elder Barr stated that he had supplied his son with a

30/30 cal. rifle and that the son was on Newberry St. at the time the victim was killed. The father informed Murphy that the son stated the Allen woman came out of the automobile with a gun and fired at the whites on Newberry St. Murphy informed the elder Barr that this was not true and that his son was lying."

This caused the younger Barr to indignantly telephone Murphy at the used car lot. While a car salesman, Dick Marchico, listened on the extension, Gabriel Barr castigated Murphy for contradicting the story Barr had told his father. Gabriel Barr told Murphy, "We had over fifty guns and were on the roofs and in the windows of the homes and the nigger woman did have a gun and did fire first." Murphy told Barr he was a liar.

Police soon learned Gabriel Barr was by this time awash in other troubles. The supplement report notes, "Information had previously been received that Gabriel Mark Barr… was a member of the United States Air Force and was absent without leave at the time of the crime. It was also learned that this subject was born in Belfast, Ireland and is not a citizen of the United States."

Cpl. Markel next contacted York Air Force Recruiter Sgt. Earl Lambert. Lambert told police that Gabriel Barr "enlisted in the air force on March 17, 1969 and had completed both basic training and training at cook's school. After completion of the cooking school he was given a military leave which was to have expired on day of 14 July 69." So Barr was already AWOL when the riots started on July 17. It seemed more important to Barr to fight alongside the Messersmiths in York, than with the Air Force in Vietnam.

"Barr failed to report for duty as he was assigned at Chanute Air Force Base, (in) Illinois," the report continues. "The base is approximately 100 miles south-east of Chicago, Ill." It turns out that on August 15, 1969 Barr had finally gotten around to reporting to the York Air Force recruiting office, telling Sgt. Lambert that his parents were giving him the necessary funds to return to Chanute Air Force Base and that he would be leaving the next day, August 16.

Almost ten days later, on August 25, 1969, Sgt. Lambert told police, he got a phone call from the duty sergeant at Chanute, who informed Sgt. Lambert that Barr had just arrived. Barr, now seriously

AWOL, falsely told the duty sergeant at Chanute that he had "turned himself in" to the York recruiter. Lambert told the duty sergeant that wasn't true.

Sgt. Lambert then gave police an interesting tidbit of information. The duty sergeant at Chanute told Lambert that, for some reason, upon his arrival at Chanute, Barr requested that he be allowed to talk with a Catholic priest before being placed under arrest for his AWOL. Lambert couldn't say whether the request for a priest had been granted. He told the state police that the Air Force punishment for such AWOLs usually was fairly mild, that the offender usually is given company commander's discipline and is restricted to base.

And there was one more thing, the York recruiter told Cpl. Markel. When Gabriel Barr had come to his office on August 15 he appeared to be sincere and very nervous.

Barr told the recruiter he got a girl in trouble. One can only wonder whether he'd gotten someone pregnant, or whether he'd shot a girl in the back of a car.

Armed with this information, two of our intrepid sleuths, Det. Art Cronin and Sgt. John Creavey, on September 3, 1969, took themselves across state lines to Chanute Air Force Base, in Illinois. There they met face to face with Gabriel Barr, read him his Miranda rights, and asked for his statement concerning the murder of Lillie Belle Allen.

At Chanute Air Force Base, already under restriction for his AWOL, Gabriel Barr told Creavey and Cronin that he would talk. Thirty-one years after talking with Creavey and Cronin, Barr's statement would help drive another man, Don Altland, to commit suicide.

# 20
## Dead men *do* tell tales

"I want to warn you that you have an absolute right to remain silent and that anything you do say can and will be used against you in a court of law," begins the transcript of Gabriel Mark Barr's September 3, 1969 statement to state police. The Miranda rights continue, advising him that he may speak to an attorney and, if he can't afford one, "one will be appointed to represent you without charge before any questioning if you so desire." Another suspect requiring Miranda protection.

Barr acknowledges that he understands his rights as a *suspect,* and that he wishes to make a statement. It's a little after four in the afternoon. Sgt Creavey is taking dictation. Creavey's unusually good ear for dialogue makes the statement a good read. The cops begin questioning Barr, talking to the young airman using military times:

Q: How far did you go in school?

A: I graduated from William Penn Senior High, York, Pennsylvania.

Q: Are you or have you been a member of the Newberry Street Boys?

A: Yes.

Q: Will you tell us in your own words and to the best of your knowledge what happened on North Newberry Street, York, Pa., on the evening of 21 July 69 at or about 2115 hours (9:15 pm)?

A: I went to the Messersmith house at about 1700 hours (5 pm). I believe it is 229 N. Newberry St. I seen Bob in the cellar and he said that the colored people were coming up N. Newberry Street and burn it out. I brought my father's .22 rifle with me. During the early evening I was out on the street. There were a lot of boys there. Right before dark I went to the roof of the Messersmith home, along with Donald Altland. I was at the lower roof at the back of the house. I heard someone yell, "They're black!" and someone else yelled, "Gettum Neff!" At this point I heard one shot and seconds later I heard a barrage of shots. I went up to the front roof to see what was happening and I could see the back of a light Cadillac broadside on the railroad tracks. I could see the tail lights and part of the trunk. I didn't see any shots hit the car. The firing lasted about one minute.

Q: Did you actually see anyone shoot?

A: No.

Q: Do you know of anyone that actually shot?

A: Yes, I heard this shot and I turned around and I see Donnie Altland holding a rifle in the direction of the car. I think it was a .30-30. By that time they stopped shooting and we both came down off the high part of the roof. I asked Donnie did he shoot and he said, "Yes, once." Then he told me that he couldn't see very good but he thought he hit the back of the car.

Q: Who owned the rifle that Donnie Altland had?

A: Bob Messersmith, I think.

Q: Did anyone use your rifle that you had brought over to the Messersmiths'?

A: No, not as far as I know.

Q: Who else was up on the roof that night?

A: Dick Wales, who is now in the army, "Fireman Jim," and "Dave," I don't know his last name.

Q: Did any of these persons you named do any shooting from the roof?

A: Yes, Donald Altland and I am not sure that "Fireman Jim" did any shooting or not.

Q: How long did you stay on the roof after the shooting?

A: About five minutes until after they drove the car up the street (Cadillac).

Q: Then what did you do and what did you see?

A: I came off the roof into the second floor of the Messersmith house from the balcony. I seen people in the front window of the second floor. Some of them were sitting and laying on the beds. There were guns (rifles and shotguns) by the front window. The rifles were

.22s. There were fellows at the window in the front bedroom but I don't remember who they were. I then went downstairs and looked into the kitchen. Bob or Mike Messersmith was sitting at the kitchen table. In the living room I seen Greg Neff, Rick Knouse, Dick Wales and "Dave." There were others there who I can't remember at this time. There were some rifles and shotguns propped up against the walls downstairs.

Q: What did you do next?

A: I walked down to the tracks where the car had been to see if there was any blood. I saw the blood and I came back up to the Messersmiths'. I went back up to the roof with Donnie Altland and Fireman Jim was up there too. I stayed up there until Jim Messersmith came home. Me and him walked across the street to see the guy with the two-way radio to see if anything happened to the lady who was shot. We started to walk back across the street when the guy said the lady died. After that me and Jim went back up on the roof. We were up there talking and Jim was mad about the people running in and out of his house. We were up there for about an hour and then we came down. I layed on the couch and fell asleep.

Q: Mark, do you know who fired the first shot?

A: I don't know, but I heard it was Bob Messersmith or Greg Neff.

Q: Do you know of your own knowledge who did any of the shooting?

A: I didn't see anyone else shoot other than Donnie Altland. I just heard the shot.

Q: When you heard Donald Altland shoot, where was he situated and where was the rifle pointed?

A: He was situated on the north side of a chimney of 225 N. Newberry with the rifle aimed south in the direction of the car, the Cadillac on the tracks.

Gabriel Mark Barr's statement is a little more than two typewritten pages long, mostly single-spaced. Barr signs the bottom of each page, and Sgt Creavey and Det. Cronin sign as witnesses.

Barr's statement is interesting and important for any number of reasons. He mentions that he and Jim Messersmith "walked across the street to see the *guy with the two-way radio* to see if anything happened to the lady who was shot. We started to walk back across the street when the guy said the lady died."

The "guy with the two-radio" certainly is a policeman, uniformed or plain clothed, as only a police officer can *transmit* on the police band. Was this officer also there before the attack, broadcasting that the Cadillac had run the "barricade?" Was this the officer who had made the broadcast that was heard by Officer Robertson over his police radio? Was this one of the officers on the "roving patrol" mentioned by retired state trooper Gerald Roberts? Was this one of the troopers that Beatrice Mosley saw?

Also important, Barr mentions the names of several boys the police wouldn't get around to interviewing for thirty years. Donnie Altland, Dick Wales, Rick Knouse, Greg Neff, "Fireman Jim."

Rick Knouse, finally interviewed in October 2000, told investigators "a whole group" of cops had been instigating the kids on Newberry Street to shoot blacks. "It was not just (Officer Charles Robertson). It was a crew of police down there." Knouse would also say that John Messersmith barked orders to the kids to guard different areas, because the Cadillac was coming.

"It was like a order," Knouse says. "You go here. You, you, you and you go down here and look for, wait for this Cadillac cause it's on the way. And I think that (had) something to do with the police scanner...."

Police never questioned Dick Wales. On February 1, 1974, almost five years after Lillie's death, Wales placed a .22 caliber revolver to his right temple and pulled the trigger. He died at age twenty-two.

Investigators in 2000 would finally track down the boy known as "Fireman Jim." He would be identified as James Frey. In 1969 James Frey and his wife lived at 256 Cottage Hill Road, just around the corner from Newberry Street and the family home of York police Lt. Wayne Ruppert.

In the year 2000, when investigators finally got around to tracking down and interviewing James Frey, he recalled that Officer Wayne Ruppert "shortly after" Lillie's murder told the boys they "did the right thing."

I'm told Wayne Ruppert, who would later become chief of York city police, was in his early days a beat motorcycle cop.

Which begs the question, who *was* the policeman pushing the motorcycle, and talking to the kids, who Beatrice Mosley witnessed seconds before the attack?

The police in 1969 (and in 2000) would never follow up on many of the leads given by Gabriel Barr. Barr as I say would die of a stroke in 1999. On April 10, 2000 investigators would finally confront Donald Altland regarding information obtained from Barr thirty-one years earlier. Donnie Altland, by then a 51-year-old wastewater treatment worker, that day learned that dead men sometimes do tell tales.

Fortunately for Altland, Gabriel Mark Barr was dead, and his statement would most likely be declared inadmissible in court, and could not have been used against Don Altland. Unfortunately, investigators never bothered explaining this to Altland.

The next day, April 11, 2000, Donnie Altland would leave behind two tape recordings, one for his family, the other for police. Then he would place a gun to his head and shoot himself along the banks of the Susquehanna River.

# 21

"Well, we got one"

September 3, 1969, was a big travel day for the state police in the Allen murder investigation. The same day Sgt. John Creavey and Det. Art Cronin traveled to Illinois to interview Gabriel Mark Barr, state police Cpl. Donald Weiksner and Trooper Dale Allen took themselves to Fort Dix army camp in New Jersey to interview another boy, John Stephen Duke, age eighteen.

Police had been told about John Duke's presence at the murder by two boys they'd earlier interviewed, Gary Holtzapple and Jim Rummel.

Cpl. Weiksner's Supplement Report of John Duke's police interview tells us that in September 1969 Duke is "presently in the United States Army stationed at Fort Dix, New Jersey."

The report reads that John Duke "stated that on 21 Jul 69 he went to the North Newberry street area with a Doug Leber from East Prospect, Penna., in Leber's car, a 1963 or 1964 White Chevrolet. They arrived in the area at about 1900 hrs. (7pm) and Leber parked the car in the area of Farquar Park and he and Leber went to the Messersmith home.

"He stated he was on the Messersmiths' front porch for about two hours. He stated he seen the Cadillac come up the street and someone yelled, 'Everyone off the street who doesn't have guns.' He stated he doesn't know who shouted this warning, but it sounded as if it came from the area of the corner near the railroad tracks.

"He stated he ran from the Messersmith porch into a passageway between the Messersmith home and an adjacent home into the Messersmith home's back yard and laid down. He stated he heard four or five quick shots as he was in the passageway and while he was laying down he heard about twelve more shots.

"He further stated after the shooting he got up (and) went to the front porch of the Messersmith house and seen several boys with long barreled guns, among them Bob Messersmith, Greg Neff, and further stated that he believes Bob Messersmith had some type of shotgun.

"He stated that when he got to the front of the Messersmith home the Cadillac was gone from the scene. He stated he hung around the Messersmith home the rest of the evening until the following morning and left with Doug Leber and Marv Kohlbus, both members of the Yorklyn Gang. He also added that when he emerged from the Messersmith back yard to the front of the home he seen a Joe Diaczun and Artie Messersmith and another boy with guns in the second floor window of the Messersmith home.

"He also stated that he heard four or five other boys say that Bob Messersmith fired the first shot at the car, and heard Bob Messersmith state, 'Well, we got one.'

"He stated that while he spent the evening in the Messersmith home, the entire group of about fifteen boys talked about the riots and very little about the shooting. He stated that the three Messersmiths were there, including Bob, Artie and Mike, Greg Neff, who left about 0100 hrs. (1am) the morning of the 22nd of July, Joe Diaczun and several others whom he does not know.

"He stated that when most of the boys left they took their guns with them. He also stated that he seen a Tom Smith, a member of the Yorklyn gang, with a gun on Newberry Street before the shooting with a .30 caliber rifle, but when he came from the back yard after the shooting he seen Smith, but with no rifle at this time. At this time Smith told Duke that he fired at the body of the car.

"Duke also stated that although some of the boys who left the Messersmith home took their guns with them, there were several of them who left their guns in the Messersmith home so that they would not have to carry their guns with them into the area the next night.

"He also stated he seen a Rick Knouse, a member of the Girarder gang, with a gun after the shooting was over and also stated that as he recalls when he came from the back yard into the street he seen Joe Diaczun at the middle window of the second floor of the Messersmith home and Artie Messersmith at the end window nearer to the railroad tracks and the other window was occupied by a boy he does not know.

Duke further stated that although he was in the area he did not have a gun and he did not shoot at any time."

This interview with John Duke provides many leads and much potential court testimony. Aside from Duke's important statement about boys witnessing Bob Messersmith having "fired the first shot at the car," Duke provides other clues. New names keep popping up. Joe Diaczun's name comes up, as does the name Rick Knouse, and others. The cops are closing in. It's illuminating to see what the state police do, and don't do, with these leads.

The next evening, September 5, 1969, at 8:45 pm, Trooper Dale Allen hosts Joe Diaczun at the York state police barracks. Diaczun, contradicting John Duke, denies at he was the murder scene. Diaczun lives around the corner from the railroad tracks on Newberry Street, at 249 W. Philadelphia Street, within sight of the barricade.

Joe Diaczun tells Trooper Allen, "On the day the Allen woman was shot I left the house at 11:00 AM and I went to the North End Cigar Store on Newberry Street. I stayed there awhile and then I went to shoot basketball, after that I went up to Art Messersmith and then he and I went back to the cigar store. After I stayed around the store for a while I went home. I stayed at home all night and watched television. I guess it must have been around 7:00 PM when I went home. I wasn't near the Messersmith home at all that night."

Trooper Allen next interviews Joe Diaczun's mother, Helen Diaczun, who tells the police "her son was at home all evening. She stated that they were sitting out on the front steps and saw a car with several colored people turn up Newberry Street, she said that her son never left the house that evening."

Believe it or not, Helen Diaczun's interview will be for some reason the last recorded state police interview in the Lillie Allen murder investigation for thirty-one years. It is totally fitting, almost poetic, that in this last interview Helen Diaczun mentions seeing the Cadillac rounding the corner into ambush. One more set of eyes witnessing the wrong car making the wrong turn in front of the police at the barricade.

At the bottom of the Diaczun's interview sheet Trooper Allen types, "Investigation continued." In reality, the investigation is over, as far as the state and York police, and county prosecutors, are concerned. An abrupt ending to an increasingly fruitful investigation.

Thirty-one years later, someone would finally get around to interviewing Rick Knouse, who was implicated by John Duke. Knouse would end up telling investigators in the year 2000 that an entire "gang" of police had been prompting the boys to shoot blacks, that some officers had handed out ammunition to the boys, and that he thought someone in the Messersmith household had been listening to a police scanner so as to hear a broadcast heads-up when the expected carload of blacks turned up Newberry Street.

In 2001, Rick Knouse, and eight others, would be indicted for the murder of Lillie Belle Allen. Another would indicted in 2002. By that time, John Messersmith would be dead some fifteen years.

Why had the state and local police in September 1969, so suddenly and inexplicably stopped an active investigation just beginning to bear fruit? Leads and evidence jump out at them.

It's important to remember this: in early September 1969, the white gang members weren't the only parties under investigation for the murder of Lillie Belle Allen.

There were *two* active investigations.

In the second investigation, the state and local police were suspects in the murder. These police departments were subjects of an investigation by the Criminal Section of the Civil Rights Division of the United States Department of Justice.

To arrest the boys would mean to arrest some cops. No matter how they sliced or diced it, too many cops kept turning up at the murder scene as witnesses, cheerleaders, or passive bystanders in the botched plot to ambush Sherman and James Spells. Cops were all over the place. These cops might have interesting things to say about their supervisors. Or city administrators.

The Civil Rights Division of the U.S. Department of Justice has a Criminal Section that prosecutes criminal violations of various federal civil rights laws. Does Lillie's murder fall under the purview of the Civil Rights Division? Let's see.

In 1969 there was no internet. Today we can read about the Civil Rights Division on its web page. "A criminal violation requires the use or threat of force," the Civil Rights Division tells the public. The use of force applies to Lillie's murder.

The Civil Rights Division states on its web page, "The Criminal Section is a trial section whose attorneys frequently prosecute cases of national significance involving the deprivation of personal liberties which either cannot be, or are not, sufficiently addressed by state or local authorities." State and local authorities, as we've seen, are unable to properly address Lillie's case.

The web pages continues, "Allegations of official misconduct constitute the majority of all complaints reviewed by the Section. The 'officials' who have been defendants include state and local police officers...." Police officers certainly are involved in Lillie's murder.

"These officials have been charged with using their positions to deprive individuals of constitutional rights, such as the right to be free from unwarranted assaults," the web page continues. Police officers standing at a barricade, allowing a car to pass into a known or suspected ambush, certainly constitutes depriving Lillie and her family of freedom from unwarranted assault. Obeying the orders of armed kids who tell them to turn their backs. Not coming to the family's aid. Not properly investigating the murder. All are serious breaches of public trust given police officers, and prosecutors.

Lillie Belle Allen's murder turns out perhaps to be the one true case the Civil Rights Division was established to pursue. What then went so wrong in Lillie's case?

The original civil rights complaint in Lillie's case was filed by her brother, Benjamin Mosley, and her parents, James and Beatrice Mosley, in the last week of July 1969.

Once a complaint is received, how does the U.S. Justice Department's Civil Rights Division handle it?

Its web page explains, "Complaints setting forth possible violations of the law for which the Department has jurisdiction are forwarded to the FBI for investigation."

Accordingly, Benjamin Mosley's complaint is recorded in a memorandum dated August 1, 1969, from Jerris Leonard, Assistant Attorney General for the Civil Rights Division, to J. Edgar Hoover, Director of the FBI. The memo, written under Jerris Leonard's letterhead, specifically asks, "please advise us to as to what, if any, investigation has been made by state or local authorities and the results thereof."

As we've seen, the FBI agents on the ground were admiring buddies and colleagues of the state and local police in this case. From the beginning these federal agents weren't disposed to helping Lillie's family prosecute the York and state police. Retired FBI agent Norman Hendricks professes to hold these same police officers in high esteem, and he moreover felt personal sympathy for York Detective Russell Schaad, following the fatal shooting of Schaad's son, Henry.

The FBI, and the U.S. Justice Department, depend on the state and local police departments to investigate and report back on a crime involving the *same state and local police departments that would be the subjects of any federal murder investigation.* That's why the investigation was quashed. The Pennsylvania State Police and the York Police Department weren't about to implicate their own men in murder. Their close friends in the local FBI office, by omission or commission, helped with the cover-up.

As was the case at the moment of her murder, no one was there to help Lillie Belle Allen or her family.

Following the filing of the family's complaint, the Civil Rights Division for months kept asking the FBI to provide reports from the state and local police. The police responded by stonewalling and lying to everyone.

These weren't lily white lies. They were dark, arrogant lies. They lied to Lillie's family. They waited days, weeks (and even decades) to examine key evidence. Much of this evidence — the Cadillac, the bullet fragments — was allowed to be destroyed or lost. Disinterested or co-conspiratorial local prosecutors and judges, by omission or commission, allowed this to happen.

From the start, the state and local police were engaged in lying to the federal Justice Department. On August 4, 1969, when the Civil Rights Division first asked to see police reports, Sgt. Creavey told the FBI "no report had been written," when reports had been written.

For one month afterward, in August 1969, the state and local police went through the motions of investigating Lillie's murder, attempting to cleanse police involvement in the crime. The state police in 1969 wrote and filed thirty-three pages of single-spaced reports.

The FBI, citing a request from the Civil Rights Division, kept asking to see these reports. For months police stonewalled the Civil Rights Division, not turning over the reports until October 1969.

The final state police Supplement Report was written and filed on September 10, 1969, by Det. Arthur Cronin. The short, four-line report details Cronin's and Sgt. John Creavey's trip to Chanute Air Force Base to interview Gabriel Mark Barr.

The same day, September 10, 1969, a memorandum from the office of FBI Director J. Edgar Hoover to FBI agents in York, Pennsylvania, notes the Justice Department's Civil Rights Division's "request for a preliminary investigation to include results of investigation made by state or local authorities."

Hoover's memo concludes, "Submit results of investigation by PSP (Pennsylvania State Police) for dissemination to the Department."

In plain English, give us the reports.

A week goes by, and nothing. Another memo is issued from Hoover's office on September 18, 1969. "If results of PSP investigation have not been obtained, (advise us on) your efforts to do so and advise when they will be made available."

The next day, September 19, 1969, York FBI special agent Bill Daane responds to the FBI director, "Constant contact is being maintained with Sergeant John Creavey, Pennsylvania State Police at York, Pa., for a copy of his report in the instant matter. Sergeant Creavey has requested copy of this report from headquarters in Harrisburg, Pa., and will provide as soon as received." Special Agent Daane feels compelled to reassure, "This matter is being followed and report will be forwarded to the Bureau as soon as possible."

Ten more days go by, and nothing. Once again, on September 29, 1969, Hoover's office fires off another memo to the local agents, again asking for the state police reports. They've been asking now for *two full months*. The agents are advised to go over Sgt. Creavey's head, to his state police superiors.

"If the report has not been received to date, immediately contact

Creavey's headquarters at Harrisburg in effort to obtain the report," Special Agent Daane is instructed.

The next day, September 30, 1969, Special Agent Daane replies to Hoover's office, "Contact has been made with the Commissioner, Pennsylvania State Police, who advises copy of report being duplicated and will be made available on 10/2/69, at which time it will be immediately forwarded to the Bureau."

So now the involvement of the *commissioner* of the state police is shown to be required, though no explanation is offered for his department's glaring irregularities in this case. Suffice it to say, the highest levels of the Pennsylvania State Police are now involved.

On October 2, 1969, the state police commissioner at long last coughs up the reports.

Special Agent Daane advises J. Edgar Hoover's office, "On 10/2/69, Captain Roy O. Wellendorf, Headquarters, Pennsylvania State Police, State Capitol, furnished copies of all State Police reports concerning the shooting of Lillie Belle Allen. These reports total 33 pages. These report copies are enclosed."

Handwritten on the bottom of this memo are the words, "cc enc to CRD... 10-7-69." So on October 7, 1969, J. Edgar Hoover's office forwards a copy of the state police reports to the Civil Rights Division (CRD), with a memo stating as much.

The very next day, October 8, 1969, the Mayor of York, John Snyder, suddenly dies. Mayor John Snyder was an unapologetic bigot who bears the lion's share of blame for the race riots in his town, and the criminal behavior of his police department, as administered by his Public Safety Director, Jacob Hose.

Word of the ongoing federal investigation certainly reached York Mayor Snyder. The day after the Civil Rights Division finally receives a laundered and stonewalled set of police reports that might well put members of his police force behind bars, Mayor Snyder drops dead.

Mayor Snyder, 76, died of a massive heart attack and or, "the rupture of one of the main arteries from the heart," said a hospital spokesman. The coroner attributed death to a "ruptured abdominal aneurysm." Something really blew out his plumbing.

Funeral services were held the following Saturday, attended by three hundred people. Give the people what they want, and they'll come out every time.

Snyder's death is widely credited for helping to ease racial tensions in York. A timely death, if ever there was. Never imagine there's no justice.

Now that they have the reports, it's not clear the lawyers in the Civil Rights Division know what to make of them. It's clear the Civil Rights Division isn't satisfied, and continues to hound local and state police, and expects local prosecution in Lillie Belle Allen's case.

"Reference is made to your memorandum dated October 7, 1969," reads a November 21, 1969 memorandum under the letterhead of Civil Rights Division Assistant Attorney General Jerris Leonard, to J. Edgar Hoover. "Please keep this Division advised of any local prosecution arising out of the shooting of Lillie Belle Allen."

Not merely a thorn in the side of local and state police, the Civil Rights Division is a serious threat to any policeman involved in Lillie's murder. The Civil Rights Division is prosecuting policemen around the country, particularly in the South, where police officers in the 1960s regularly cooperate with the Klu Klux Klan in the murder and beatings of blacks and civil rights workers.

Police, more than anyone, know if the investigation of the murder of the "Allen woman" isn't contained the Civil Rights Division will put them in jail.

Three days later, in a memo dated November 24, 1969, the FBI director's office forwards to its Pennsylvania agents the Civil Rights Division's request to keep the division lawyers advised "of any local prosecution arising out of the shooting of Lillie Belle Allen."

The memo instructs agents in Pennsylvania to conduct a limited investigation and to "advise all persons interviewed... at the outset that this investigation is being conducted at the specific request of the Assistant Attorney General in charge of the Civil Rights Division, U.S. Department of Justice, referring to him by name as well as title." The FBI agents are further instructed to continue to follow the case "every thirty days until matter is resolved." A note to this FBI memo reads, "We did a preliminary investigation at request of Department as it was alleged that a 'trooper' had been involved, however, investigation indicated policemen apparently took no part in shooting of victim. (Civil Rights Division) now requests they be advised of any local prosecution arising out of shooting of victim."

On December 1, 1969, FBI Special Agent Bill Daane asked none other than York police Detective Thomas Chatman to advise the Justice Department on the progress of the Lillie Belle Allen murder investigation. By this time the state and local police have done nothing on the investigation for two full months.

Chatman, amazingly, tells the FBI that York and state police have been unable to get any breaks in the case, that they remain in the dark about the identity of Lillie's murderers. It's a flat out lie, told to the United States Justice Department. He also says the investigation is ongoing, which is another lie. They haven't talked to anybody in two months, and they're letting the trail go cold.

Special Agent Daane reports back with the results of his interview of Sgt. Chatman. A December 1, 1969 memo on FBI letterhead reports the following:

"The following is the result of a limited investigation:

"Sergeant Thomas Chatman, York Police Department, York, Pa., was advised on December 1, 1969, that investigation in this matter was at the specific request of Jerris Leonard, Assistant Attorney General, Civil Rights Division, United States Department of Justice.

"Sergeant Chatman advised that his department in conjunction with the Pennsylvania State Police, York, Pa., was still conducting investigation of the incident in which Lillie Belle Allen was shot during the summer of 1969 racial disturbances at York, Pa. He stated that to date, the identity of the person or persons who shot her have not been determined. He stated that he would advise of any breaks in this matter as soon as they might occur."

Sgt. Chatman here tells a deliberate untruth to the FBI. He states, "the identity of the person or persons who shot her have not been determined."

To the contrary, the York and state police by this time have identified in their own reports (which they attempted to suppress) the following *thirty* individuals as being at the Messersmith house the night in question:

Bobby Messersmith, Artie Messersmith, Chauncey Gladfelter, Rick Knouse, Greg Neff, William Charles "Sam" Ritter, Tom Smith, John Messersmith, Stephan Noonan, Joe Kluyber, Bill Conway, Gary Fink, Jim Rummel, Ben Mathis, Gordon Snyder, Darryl Kauffman, Gary Holtzapple, Roger Kinard, Marvin Kohlbus, Bob Treattino, Jay Kohr, Steve Gunarich, Jim Rummel, Tom Keeney, John Duke, Gabriel Mark Barr, Donald Altland, Dick Wales, James Frey aka Fireman Jim, and Doug Leber.

Two of the boys, Tom Smith and Gabriel Mark Barr, *were specifically told they are suspects* by police in August and September 1969 and were read their Miranda rights. Smith would wait thirty-two years to be indicted.

Of these thirty, the first seven boys (Bobby Messersmith, Artie Messersmith, Chauncey Gladfelter, Rick Knouse, Greg Neff, William Charles "Sam" Ritter and Tom Smith) would in the year 2001, thirty-two years later, be indicted for Lillie's murder.

Their indictment three decades later rested primarily on the original state police reports. The state police lied about the existence of these reports from the start and kept them from the Civil Rights Division for months.

By the year 2001, some of the individuals identified in the original reports escaped justice by dying or committing suicide years earlier. These include John Messersmith, Donnie Altland, Dick Wales, and Gabriel Mark Barr. All lived out their lives and were allowed to get away with murder.

The effect of Sgt. Chatman's lie to the FBI is to help these men escape justice, and to obstruct the Civil Rights Division from bringing policemen, and others, involved in Lillie's murder to justice.

Back in 1969 and 1970, the local FBI agents, as instructed, every thirty days continued to ask officials of the York Police Department for the status of the Allen case.

On December 31, 1969, the FBI interviewed Captain Charles McCaffery, chief of the Detective Division of York police.

McCaffery tells the FBI, "it had not been possible to ascertain who might have shot her, and unless a witness comes forth and volunteers information as to who may have shot her, it is going to be nearly impossible to determine just who did shoot her. He said that so far no one among the numerous people questioned on this matter would admit seeing who had fired the shot at Mrs. Allen." Captain McCaffery concludes, "he would be happy to advise of any new developments in this case as they might come up."

McCaffery knows this isn't true, as witnesses have told police they saw Tom Smith and Donnie Altland fire at the car, while others told police either Bobby Messersmith or Greg Neff fired the fatal shot.

About a month later, the FBI interviewed, of all people, Captain Russell Schaad, now chief of York police detectives. Captain Schaad's son, Patrolman Henry Schaad, by now had been dead six months, with no prosecution in that case.

Captain Schaad lies to the FBI, obstructing justice, on February 2, 1970, when he states, "no breaks in this matter have developed which would lead to the identity of the person or persons who shot Mrs. Allen. He advised that he would be happy to advise of any new developments in this matter as they might occur."

And so it would go for the next few months. On March 2, 1970, York Police Chief Leonard Landis told the FBI there were "no new leads" in the case.

On April 2, 1970, Captain Russell Schaad told the FBI, "no suspects for this shooting had been developed," when records clearly show individuals had been informed by police that they were suspects.

On May 5, 1970, York police Chief Leonard Landis told the FBI that he "hoped that eventually some witness would step forward to identify the shooter or shooters in this matter."

Again, on June 4, 1970, Chief Leonard Landis again outright lies to the FBI, and the United States Justice Department, when he tells them, "no suspects had been developed in this case."

The same day, June 4, 1970, J. Edgar Hoover's office instructs the local FBI agents to no longer interview York police officials about the murder of Lillie Belle Allen.

Hoover's memo states that he is advising the Civil Rights Division that the Allen case "will no longer be followed unless specifically requested."

Hoover instructs the Pennsylvania FBI agents, "Close your file."

After lying from the start about the existence of written police reports, after stonewalling for months, after lying time and again and obstructing the administration of justice, the York and Pennsylvania State Police have accomplished what they set out to do.

They no longer are suspects in the murder of Lillie Belle Allen.

Or so they think.

# 23

## York city hall gives Bobby Messersmith a job

At the same time the police were lying and obstructing justice to avoid prosecution for their part in Lillie's murder, many of the same cops were slapping Bobby Messersmith's wrists for his role in the shooting of Taka Nii Sweeney and John Washington.

In August 1969, released from the slammer on bail, Bobby Messersmith presented himself to a minister at a local church. The minister, a Reverend Snyder, would later testify on Bobby's behalf in the Sweeney-Washington case. The neighborhood protector, it seems, was depressed.

"Mr. Messersmith appeared to me in my office at the church in August and I have been counseling with him ever since, your honor," Reverend Snyder would tell York County President Judge George Atkins. "He has been attending church regularly.... In counseling with Robert I have found that of course he was deeply depressed and filled with anxieties and in many conversations that I have had with him he has indicated that he is going to try his very best to be a good citizen in society."

In October 1969, Bobby stood trial on charges of assault with intent to kill, aggravated assault and battery, and assault and battery in the shootings of Sweeney and Washington. The officers testifying against Messersmith in this case included familiar names from the Lillie Belle Allen investigation, including York City officers Harold McIlvain and Thomas Chatman, and state policemen Donald Weiksner and Arthur Cronin. The case was prosecuted by District Attorney John Rauhauser, who at the same time was turning a blind eye and was refusing to prosecute Messersmith for Lillie's killing.

This trial resulted from a cursory police investigation. State police

Cpl. Weiksner on September 4, 1969, typed out a three-paragraph Supplement Report, citing statements from only two witnesses, sixteen-year-old Pamela Klinedinst and fifty-three-year-old Roy Unger, both Messersmith neighbors.

On the evening of July 17, 1969, Pamela Klinedinst's statement reads, "I was in my house, and then my grandmother said she seen a bunch of colored kids run down the street and seen white kids chasing them. I went out on the sidewalk and looked up the street and we looked down the street and see a whole group of people down at the cigar store." Following the melee between the black and white kids at the cigar store, Klinedinst walked home. Shortly afterward she saw Bobby Messersmith and another boy run past Roy Unger's porch. Bobby carried a shotgun, and as he hurried by he stopped to talk with Unger, before disappearing through Unger's backyard.

"Did you hear what Mr. Unger said to the boys or what the boys said to him?" Cpl. Weiksner asked the girl.

"I heard Mr. Unger say something which sounded like 'did you get any?' And Bob said, 'Yes.'"

Roy Unger's statement reveals the police almost immediately had the means to arrest Bobby for the shooting, as Unger had called police after hearing the shot, and had witnessed Bobby running home with a gun. Unger's statement reads that he was returning home at about 11:30pm on July 17, 1969 and "I observed a group of people at the cigar store on Newberry Street. I parked the car and I walked down to the cigar store to inquire what happened. I learned that a group of colored had come by and had smashed the windows in the cigar store. I was standing there talking to a neighbor when someone hollered, 'Here boy come down to the railroad tracks.' I then went to my house. The white and the colored boys then had a stone fight on the tracks. I didn't see the colored but I assume that's who they were fighting. I then went and called City Hall. I went back on my porch and was talking to a neighbor. I was sitting on my front porch and I heard a shot which sounded like to have come from the area of Kane's house at the railroad track at the entrance to the gas plant. Shortly after the shot I saw two boys turn the corner at Grant Street and Cottage Hill Road and turn west past my house. They cut up my steps to my side yard. They did not stop."

"Do you know who these boys were?"

"I know the one. Bob Messersmith."

"Was anything said at this time?"

"Yes, I said what happened and he said, 'I shot.'"

Unger recounted that Bobby and the other boy disappeared through Unger's side yard. About ten minutes later, Unger says, "I noticed Bob and a girl come out of his backyard, which comes to my side yard. When he went by I said, 'Bob what the devil's going on?' and he said, 'I shot at them but the gun jammed,' but at this time I'm not sure what he said. I don't remember whether he said he shot at them but I know he told me his gun jammed."

Weiksner asked, "When you seen Bob Messersmith cutting through your yard did he or the other boy have any type of weapon?"

"He was carrying a large barreled shotgun," Unger replied.

"Was Bob the one you seen carrying the shotgun?"

"Yes."

The cops had less evidence against Bobby in the Sweeney-Washington case than they had against him in the murder of Lillie Belle Allen. Still DA Rauhauser and the cops prosecuted Messersmith for the lesser crime. The parallels between the two cases are interesting. In both episodes, witnesses saw Bobby with a shotgun, saw him shoot, and heard him say afterward he shot.

As in Lillie's murder in 2001, Messersmith in 1969 pled not guilty in the shooting of Sweeney and Washington.

At a hearing for the attempted murder, a neighbor living on Gas Avenue, Robert Sweitzer, testified he was looking out his second-floor window the night of July 17 when he saw two boys come across the railroad track from Newberry Street. One of the boys carried a long-barreled gun. Sweitzer watched the boys cross the railroad bridge then stop under a street light at Gas and Pershing avenues, he estimated about one hundred and fifty feet from his window.

"I seen one boy lift a rifle up to his shoulder," Sweitzer testified. "I saw him fire.... I saw the fire come from it."

Then what happened? DA Rauhauser asked.

"It jammed on him. It must have jammed."

"How do you know that?"

"Well, I seen him try to cock it back and get another shell in it; but he couldn't get it in." With that, one of the boys said, "'It's time to go,' or they wanted to get out of there, because they couldn't get another shot off."

Sweitzer said he got a good look at the one with the gun under the light.

DA Rauhauser asked, "Since that time, have you been asked to review the photographs of a large number of individuals?"

"Yes, sir."

"By the police?"

"Yes, sir."

Sweitzer pointed out Bobby Messersmith as the boy who had fired the gun at Sweeney and Washington.

I wonder why police hadn't allowed Lillie Belle Allen's family to view "photographs of a large number of individuals?"

York police detective George Smith testified at trial about the attack. On the night of July 17, 1969, he'd stopped a group of black boys, among them Taka Nii Sweeney and John Washington, near the corner of Philadelphia and Pershing. It was almost midnight, and the boys were violating curfew. Sweeney was trying to sneak away around the corner, and was out of Smith's sight when the shot was fired. While talking with the other boys Smith heard the shot. At first he thought it was a firecracker, then one of the boys told him to get down. Someone was shooting.

"And this is when one of the boys said that they shot Taka Nii," Det. Smith testified. He went around the corner and found Sweeney bleeding on the ground. "He was lying on his side, I think, and appeared to be in grave pain." Sweeney had been shot in the right side of his back. Det. Smith went to help Sweeney, at which time John Washington told Smith he'd been shot too, in the arm. It was dark, and Det. Smith said he "went to Sweeney's aid. I told him to lie still. I went back to the cruiser to summon help, and I returned back to Mr. Sweeney." Detective Smith testified he could not see who had fired the shot in the darkness.

Sweeney was hospitalized for two weeks.

On October 30, 1969, following two days of testimony, a jury deliberated four hours and twenty minutes and found twenty-year-old Bobby Messersmith guilty of shooting Taka Nii Sweeney and John Washington. He was found not guilty on the intent to kill charge, but guilty of the much lesser offense of aggravated assault and battery. In York County, a jury doesn't think much of black lives.

Bobby was released pending sentencing, and in December he was even given a job by York city government. Following his conviction, Messersmith's attorney petitioned the court on behalf of Bobby and his father, John, for the return of the weapons confiscated on July 24, three days after Lillie's shooting.

District Attorney Rauhauser filed a remarkable document asking the judge not to return the Messersmiths' guns. The city solicitor filed a duplicate brief, on behalf of York Police Chief Leonard Landis, who himself was busy lying to and stonewalling the FBI over the Allen murder.

DA Rauhauser tells the president judge the return of the weapons aren't relevant to any current proceeding before the court, that the guns weren't confiscated due to the Sweeney-Washington shooting. "No representation has been made by the District Attorney, the City or the State Police," as to why the guns had been confiscated, the DA writes. However, he goes on, "A number of serious unresolved criminal offenses remain the subject of investigation by the City and State Police charged with that responsibility, growing out of the same events or series of events which resulted in the charges lodged against Robert N. Messersmith, of which he has heretofore been convicted. The homicide of one person within a short distance of address of said defendant remains unresolved as well as certain lesser offenses, all of which are subject to a continuing and further investigation."

"(U)nder the circumstances," the DA and the chief of police tell the county's top judge, the district attorney "would not deem it appropriate to return said guns. The District Attorney of York County continues to refuse to accept responsibility to advise the voluntary return of said weapons under the circumstances presently existing."

So here District Attorney Rauhauser and the Chief Landis are noting the fact that Lillie Belle Allen had been killed "a short distance" from Bobby's doorstep and, wink, wink, nudge, nudge, Your Honor, we don't think you should give back the guns, because *we* won't be responsible. This filing is strange for several reasons, beyond the obvious. By this time, November 14, the state and city police haven't conducted an interview in the Allen case for two and a half months. Already the police, and DA Rauhauser, have deep-sixed the case. Within two weeks, the FBI would be knocking on Sgt. Chatman's door to ascertain the status of the Allen investigation on behalf of the Civil Rights Division, and Chatman would say, "the identity of the person or persons who shot her have not been determined. He stated that he would advise of any breaks in this matter as soon as they might occur."

Here we see that DA Rauhauser, the chief of police, the president county judge, *everybody,* knows that Bobby Messersmith had a hand in Lillie's murder. But they're not going to do a damn thing about it but lie and not give Bobby and John Messersmith back their guns. They don't care about Lillie, or justice. They only care about their own skins.

On April 27, 1970 Bobby Messersmith was sentenced for the aggravated assault by shotgun and rifled slug involving Sweeney and Washington. At a sentencing hearing, Bobby's attorney, Norman Petow, told Judge Atkins, "I say personally I think Mr. Messersmith is sadly in need of medical and psychiatric evaluation. I am not trying to make an excuse for the prisoner, the defendant I should say, I am saying to the court, if he does not receive this I think society will have imposed a punishment far in excess of mere confinement. I think the young man is not well. I think he needs medical evaluation in the manner prescribed by law.... I believe sincerely this is what is required. I think incarceration for the young man will be completely and utterly injurious to his health. I fear for his sanity, I honestly do." Bobby's lawyer got everyone talking about a suspended sentence, with no jail time. Bobby previously had worked for the city parks department, and Bobby's lawyers states his client had been "guaranteed" a new job with the city. Hell, not only isn't the city not prosecuting Bobby Messersmith for murder, they're giving him work.

By this time, in early 1970, District Attorney Rauhauser's term has expired. He is replaced in the county DA's office by Harold Fitzkee, the former public defender, and soon-to-be owner of one of the town's daily newspapers.

"I believe incarceration is appropriate," Fitzkee tells Judge Atkins.

"If you are so sure of employment," Judge Atkins asks Bobby, "I am curious as to why you have not been working for the last two and a half months."

"They told me in City Hall they would not hire me until after my sentence on account of politics or something," Bobby tells the judge.

"Why did you leave your job in December?" the judge asks.

"Which job are you talking about?"

"The one you quit in December."

"Well, I didn't take to indoor work," Bobby tells the judge. "I just don't get along with indoor work. I worked with the city for three years. I tried these indoor jobs. I just didn't fit to it. I talked to Mr. Gross and Mr. Myers about getting my job back and they said they can almost guarantee it after today."

"It seems to me that before you quit one job because you don't happen to like it, you ought to have something else in view before you quit," the judge tells Bobby. "This case is a serious one. You are extremely fortunate you are not standing here convicted of at least second-degree murder. On the facts as they were brought out at the trial, had this one young man whom you shot, and there appear to be no questions that you did, had he not survived there is no question that the facts that were proven at trial would constitute at least murder in the second degree."

Judge Atkins, like the cops and the prosecutors, proceeds to go light on Bobby Messersmith.

"I did consider this a serious case and I still do," Judge Atkins tells Bobby. "I said then and I again repeat that it is only by sheer good luck that we are not dealing with a homicide. I on the other hand have no inclination to try to make a particular example of this young man or any other defendant that appears before the court. I try to treat cases on the facts as they appear in each individual case.

"I cannot bring myself to conclude that this case should be disposed of without any punishment or without any incarceration," Atkins goes on. "I therefore feel that I shall impose a sentence with a relatively short minimum period so that... he may be eligible for an early parole."

Judge George Atkins thereupon sentences Bobby Messersmith to not less than nine months, and not more than three years in prison, minus time already served.

Bobby's father John petitioned the court to transfer Bobby from prison to a psychiatric care unit. Bobby was mentally disabled, John Messersmith told the court, because of "mental deterioration and inability to undergo confinement."

In May and June 1970, Dr. Emil Herman, a unit director of the Harrisburg State Hospital, evaluated Bobby for the court. Dr. Herman wrote to Judge Atkins on June 1, 1970, telling the judge that Bobby was an angry young man prone to lashing out due to his troubled life on Newberry Street.

"Personal history of this 21-year-old, well-developed, well-nourished man includes traumatic home experiences from early childhood due to the presence of a father, a heavy drinker, who had been abusive to the family throughout the years," Herman's letter states. "... He implies that his troubles usually stem from his lack of ability to control his temper which he believes also applies to the issue at hand."

Dr. Herman continues, "He has been a member of the Newberry Boys, a gang which he considers a social club destined to protect the neighborhood from intruders which had particular significance on occasions of what he opined were racial fights and riots. It was when he felt that 'they' attempted to ransack a friend's store in the neighborhood that he assumed a protective role, took his gun and shot. He believes that he would have never done that hadn't he again lost his temper."

It's in this letter that Dr. Hermann divulges that Bobby Messersmith's "Past conflicts with the Law consisted of indecent assault of a six-year-old girl at the age of fourteen followed by probation and Mental Health Center attendance."

Bobby Messersmith was "emotionally unstable," Dr. Herman concluded, though he was not mentally ill. As such, Judge Atkins decided, Bobby should go to jail.

Bobby Messersmith began his sentence at the Correctional

Diagnostic and Classification Center at Camp Hill on July 10, 1970. *Three months later,* on October 9, 1970, he received parole. On December 12, 1970, Bobby was released from prison.

Lillie Belle Allen by this time had been dead nearly a year and a half.

For years after his shooting, whenever Taka Nii Sweeney was seen riding a mini-bike around York, he'd have a rifle slung across his back.

"We were told by higher-ups in the police department to leave Taka Nii alone and not bother him about the rifle," a retired York policeman tells me. "We were told to leave Taka Nii alone."

Less than two years later, on November 6, 1972, sixteen-year-old Charles Keener found himself walking alone on the 1400 block of Salem Road, on his way to a friend's house. A bearded man in his twenties, wearing a red sweater, pulled up in a light-colored Ford sedan. The man yelled out of the car for Keener to state his name.

Keener gave his name. The driver leveled a shotgun out the window. Keener dove, heard three blasts, and was hit in the left leg and hand by buckshot. The car sped away. Keener managed to walk home, where his mother drove him to the hospital.

The police eventually picked up Bobby Messersmith for this shooting. In August 1973, Bobby Messersmith pled guilty to shooting Keener. He spent six months in Farview State Hospital before doctors declared him fit to serve time. Bobby was sentenced to nine to twenty-three months in jail. He served the minimum.

## 24
## "He lied to the FBI!"

The attorney in charge of the U.S. Department of Justice's Civil Rights Division in 1969 was Jerris Leonard. Today Leonard is in private law practice in Washington DC. In early 2002 I telephoned Leonard and asked if he'd meet and talk with me about the Lillie Belle Allen case.

He expressed an interest to meet, though he confessed the case didn't ring any bells. Could I send information about the case before we met? Already I'd posted on the internet a rudimentary article and several FBI documents concerning Lillie's murder. I e-mailed Leonard the website address, and we made tentative plans to meet in Washington after a week or so.

Meanwhile I read about Leonard on his firm's web page. A Nixon appointee to the Civil Rights Division, under John Mitchell. Served in division from 1969 to '71. From Wisconsin. A clean state (not like Pennsylvania); a good government state, home of crusading reformer Robert LaFollette, Progressive Movement, Madison. Wisconsins pride themselves in their good government with the same moral fervor Pennsylvania politicians wallow in their corruption. Would this guy understand Pennsylvania fix artists?

Leonard, I read on, served in the Wisconsin legislature for twelve years in the late '50s until 1969. Majority leader of the Wisconsin state senate. In 1968, he was an unsuccessful Republican candidate for U.S. Senate.

A day or so before our planned meeting Jerris Leonard called and apologetically told me he'd reviewed the article and documents and still had absolutely no recollection of the case. How could that be? I asked. His name, his letterhead, were all over the FBI and Justice

Department memos of the case.

There'd been thousands of civil rights cases before the division in that era, he said. Hundreds of lawyers had worked under him. He simply had no recollection of the case. He'd worked at the Civil Rights Division in busy days, and had handled the Kent State and Jackson State cases. And 1969 was so long ago—. He wouldn't be much help to me, he said, and suggested there was no point in our meeting, that he'd only waste my time.

I felt saddened. Nobody seemed to know about Lillie or her murder, not even those whose names were printed on her murder papers. Another poor forgotten girl, another poor forgotten death.

Quite the contrary, he could help, I pressed Leonard. He could explain to me how the Civil Rights Division operated in those days. In the back of my mind, emotionally, I wanted a connection with anyone who might have had involvement with Lillie's case. Maybe he could point me in the right direction.

He agreed to meet with me, and on a chilly overcast day in April, 2002 I drove from Pennsylvania to Washington DC.

On Jerris Leonard's office walls hung photos of himself with Nixon, John Mitchell, and others. There was a Norman Rockwell print of a small black girl walking off to school. Leonard stood behind his desk and shook hands. He looked to be somewhere in his seventies, in good health, a golfer, mentally acute, concerned.

We chatted some about Richard Nixon. Leonard had run Nixon's '68 campaign in Wisconsin, he told me. He'd hoped for appointment to head the Criminal Division in Nixon's Justice Department, but previous commitments had prevented him from immediately joining the administration, he explained, so they'd offered him the Civil Rights Division.

He'd met with Nixon about the job and asked what would be expected of him at the Civil Rights Division. Shaking his jowls, leaning forward emphatically in imitation of the president, Leonard said Nixon told him, "Enforce the law, Jerry."

Nixon hoped the fomenting civil rights issue would go away in time for the '72 election, Leonard said he suspected. Civil rights problems were a distraction, and Nixon wanted to get on with other things. We spoke a bit about a few of the admirable achievements of the Nixon administration, and how these were overshadowed by Watergate. The Lillie Belle Allen case took you back in time.

We got down to the purpose of my visit.

I showed him the Justice Department memos concerning the Allen case, most of which mentioned the name "Jerris Leonard." He explained all division correspondence as a matter of course had been sent out under his name. One of the hundreds of attorneys working under him actually handled the case, he said. There were several initials that Leonard said he presumed to be of the attorney handling the case, but he and I couldn't make them out. Similarly, he went on, J. Edgar Hoover probably had never seen any of the documents bearing the address, "Director, FBI."

"Hoover never saw any of this," he told me.

You couldn't help feeling a little worse for Lillie and her parents. The poor girl's case had been lost in obscure corners of the Justice Department.

"Where are the 302s?" he asked. I dug out the FBI interviews, which I'd brought along in a folder. I started to explain the documents, but he stopped me, "I know what they are." He read through them.

Sitting back at his desk, casting a critical eye my way, he asked what evidence had I that any suspects had ever been identified in the murder of Lillie Belle Allen.

From my folder I withdrew the stack of state police reports, thumbing to the September 4, 1969 interview of John Duke. "Well, for example," I told him, "there's this—." I pointed to place in the reports where Duke told police "he heard four or five boys say that Bob Messersmith fired the first shot at the car, and heard Bob Messersmith state 'well we got one.'"

"It goes on and on. There's page after page of suspects identified here—." I started to tell him.

Leonard took the reports. With what can only be described as a look of growing concern, he sat reading the accounts of Lillie's death.

"This is very disturbing," he said, now reading the reports closely.

Clearly, he had to agree with me, police had identified suspects.

Had this case been brought in 1969, he pointed out, the young men identified would certainly have provided police with more leads, more suspects, more arrests.

At last he arrived at statements York police had given the FBI in late 1969 and 1970. Holding aloft the December 1, 1969 statement of detective Thomas Chatman, wherein Chatman states, "the identity of the person or persons who shot her have not been determined," Leonard appeared startled.

*"He lied to the FBI,"* Jerris Leonard gasped.

Taking from his desk a Post-it notes dispenser, Leonard stuck a red flag on the margin of Chatman's FBI statement. He likewise flagged the statement of Captain McCaffery, in which McCaffery said there were no witnesses. When he arrived at Captain Russell Schaad's February 2, 1970, statement, in which Schaad reports "no breaks in this matter," Leonard flagged the page, and asked if this was the Schaad whose son had been killed in the riots.

"Yes, his son Henry was killed," I told Leonard. Applying the red flag, Jerris Leonard frowned. None of this, I saw, looks good to an outsider.

He said when he'd first come to the Justice Department the Civil Rights Division had been organized to look at cases geographically. The South, obviously, was a hotbed for civil rights abuse cases. He'd rearranged the caseload on a task basis, he said, though he was still prone to look for troubled regions of the country. This obscure case in Pennsylvania had slipped under the radar.

Leonard went on to apply red flags to each of the misleading statements given to the FBI by the York police. Seven red flags in all.

The Justice Department relies on the FBI, Leonard explained. If people lie to the FBI, the Justice Department can't do its job.

"What do you mean by marking those pages with the red flags?" I asked. "Do you believe those policemen committed obstruction of justice?"

"There's something there," he said. "It has to be looked at."

Did I realize, he asked me, that there is no statute of limitations in civil rights murders? With a determined look, Jerris Leonard said he thought the Lillie Belle Allen case was probably still open at the Civil Rights Division. Perhaps it should be reactivated, he suggested.

# 25

## "We were the state police!"

I set about interviewing some of the policemen who had worked on the Lillie Belle Allen case. It wasn't easy. All were retired, many were dead, and some were hard to track down. There was another problem, I'd learn.

I found retired state police Sergeant John Creavey living in retirement in Dillsburg, Pennsylvania, outside Harrisburg. I got out of the car and Creavey came out of his house to greet me. He was a neatly groomed. His gray hair was swept back, setting off his steel gray eyes. He had a ready smile. He appeared to me to be in his mid- to late-seventies.

I introduced myself and explained I was working on a book. He seemed surprisingly pleased to see me, and asked me inside. Pictures of grandkids were on display all over the place. There were lots of windows, and Creavey had a pleasant view of the countryside around him.

Standing in his parlor, Creavey said my name sounded familiar. Why was that? he puzzled. I said I'd written a number of book concerning police and court matters in Pennsylvania. Perhaps he'd read The Sins of Our Fathers, I ventured, about old-time mafia and the police in Harrisburg. Yes, he said, he thought he may be familiar with some of my books. But where else had he heard my name?

I said I had the same name as my father, who served several governors. Why yes, the retired trooper said, that's where.

I grew up around the governor's office, I told him. "I learned my alphabet on the governor's desk."

"Then you're one of the family?" he said.

Yes, I allowed, I was one of the family. I'd grown up around state troopers. "They used to come over to the house when I was a kid and give us bullets to horse around with."

He smiled knowingly.

"Some of the finest men I've ever met are Pennsylvania state police troopers," I earnestly told Creavey.

He said he agreed.

I said that's what brought me here. To talk to him about one of his cases, from the old days. Could we sit for a few minutes, so that I could show him some documents? I brought a folder containing Creavey's police reports. I told him I was trying to understand what had happened.

Yes, he said, we should sit down. Where should we sit? he asked. Why not here at the table. He started to take me over. Abruptly he stopped. What were we doing? he asked. We were sitting down, I said. Oh yes. He suggested we sit on the sofa. Fine, I said. We started for the sofa. Then he stopped. What we're we doing? he asked.

I looked at him, at last understanding.

He had Alzheimer's.


I sat with him for a few minutes and we had a nice talk. He remembered much of his life as a trooper. He remembered the York riots. He spoke of being assigned by Harrisburg to go down "to the bottom of the state" and work on the riots.

He had a punchy, nice way of talking that reminded me of his reports.

"We were the state police!" he told me proudly. "We could go any where in the state and arrest 'em! Bing bang boom!" He pointed his fingers like six shooters. "They'd send us down there. There was a bunch of guys taken in. We had it. We did it. It worked out and it was done. Bing bang boom! We'd bust 'em up! We were the state police!"

He remembered quite a few generalities, but had trouble with many specifics. I tried to press him on the Lillie Belle Allen case, which he seemed to remember.

"We had a good outfit and we took over because the local guys—." His train of thought would trail off. I was sitting on the edge of my seat.

The riots, he said, were crazy. It wasn't just uniformed troopers on the scene, he assured me. "Plain clothes state troopers came from all over the state to get in on it," he winked.

Really? I asked.

Oh yeah, he said.

"We were the state police. We could arrest 'em all over the state."

I asked, "Were there any plain clothes troopers on Newberry Street the night Lillie Belle Allen was shot?"

He said he didn't know, but there could've been. Newberry Street was a well-known hotbed, he assured me.

"See, these plain clothes troopers could just go anywhere in the state."

"You mean, without being assigned?"

"Sure. We were the *state* police. They came from all over for the riots in York."

Why had there never been any arrests for the murder of Lillie Belle Allen? I asked. Creavey tried his hardest to concentrate. He tried to tell me something.

"The York Police Department was a strong police department," he told me. He explained that the local police kept getting in the way of the state police in the case.

He started to elaborate, but lost the thought. He apologized for the trouble he was having.

I told him it was all right, and thanked him for the visit. He led me to the door, and I told him to take care.

"I'll be all right," he winked at me, crossing his arms. "Nobody's got me tied up."


From Creavey's house I proceeded to the suburban Harrisburg home of retired state police detective Arthur Cronin. It was a pretty little ranch house with a flag flying out front on a pole. Adults were out on the sidewalk for an evening stroll, while children played in their yards nearby.

The door was cracked open, and I knocked. A man reclined on a sofa inside, watching TV.

"Hello!" he says.

"Art Cronin?"

"That's me! What can I do for you?" He seemed cordial. He appeared slightly heavy, his head boasting a thick, whitening mane.

I told him I was writing a book about the York riots, and his investigation of Lillie Belle Allen's murder.

His demeanor changed. In an unfriendly way he told me to go away, that he didn't want to talk about it.

I yelled in through the screen door that I'd just been to see his old partner, John Creavey.

"Lots of luck there. You didn't get much from Creavey. He has onset of Alzheimer's."

Cronin still reclined on his sofa. I was yelling through his screen door. He was somewhere in his sixties, I thought.

"Why didn't you ever file charges in the Lillie Belle Allen case?" I asked.

He gave me the public line.

"We could never find any suspects." He sounded blasé about it.

"That's not true," I burst back at him. I was getting mad. "You found suspects. You found lots of suspects." I held up his police reports.

He looked suddenly startled. He saw I knew about the lies.

Now I was indignant. He was still reclining on his sofa.

"Were you at the barricade the night Lillie was shot?" I yelled at him through the screen.

"No!" he shot back, even more startled. "I wasn't there! I didn't get into York until several weeks after the incident." Cronin's name actually first appears on police reports beginning August 2, 1969, ten or eleven days after the shooting.

I could see he wanted no part of the business at the barricade. He was about as much use today as he was three decades ago.

# PART FOUR:
## Cracker delights

# 1
## Meet the boss

York, Pennsylvania is a strange and mysterious place. It's often mentioned in the same breath as its two nearby sister cities, Harrisburg and Lancaster. That's misleading. York isn't much like Harrisburg or Lancaster.

Harrisburg, the capitol city, is a government town. Tax revenues always flow into Harrisburg, even in bad times. Harrisburg also enjoys an upscale, transient population. People move in and out of Harrisburg with the change of each governor's administration. It's easier to get a job in Harrisburg. Both political parties are strong in the capitol. It's possible to alienate half the population and still find welcoming hands with the other half. Thanks to the pressroom in the capitol, Harrisburg is a media town. Secrets don't last long in Harrisburg.

Lancaster is the famous agricultural town. It rests on a six-foot bed of some of the most fertile farming soil in the world. It's always been prosperous. God probably lives somewhere in Lancaster County. A Lancaster County farmer doesn't have to punch any man's clock, or kiss any man's ass. He can afford to have his own opinions, and isn't afraid to share them.

York is the poor sister of Harrisburg and Lancaster. It is an industrial town. Think of what that means. It means prosperity comes with volatile business cycles, if it comes at all. Even in good times the pickings can get slim. It means you better be careful about what you say, because if you lose your job, you could lose your house, and your family. All this helps to make York a very class-structured town. Everyone is expected to know his or her place, and stay there. You did what your daddy did. Workingmen beget workingmen, lawyers breed more lawyers. Many of the bearded laborers seem to have been stamped from the same forge. The Republican lawyer or business administrator often has his own decided look.

Every so often someone comes down to York County to try to figure out the place. The public television station in Harrisburg recently sent a writer to York to scout out fine dining opportunities for readers of its monthly magazine. The writer was stumped, and ended up reporting on the downtown farmers' market, politely noting that there doesn't seem to be much native cuisine in York. A running joke in York County is that a restaurant is considered good if it boasts two overriding qualities: the portions must be big, and the prices low. That's a good restaurant.

Many of my friends tell my they don't like to come to York, particularly York city. "I get a bad feeling there," one friend tells me. The city can seem drab, even oppressive. The police definitely can get out of line. In York city, to understand it, you really must go into the neighborhoods. They still feel close-knit. You need to walk around places like West Princess Street, with its white painted houses, where people like to sit out on their stoops. People will tell you they're comfortable in York city.

In York County one should go into the countryside, late at night, to understand. Places like Crossroads, or Rehmeyer's Hollow. There are desolate stretches of country road stitching together far-flung farmhouses among the rolling hills. You are out in the middle of nowhere, with not another soul for miles. Anything strange or foreign is to be feared. Under the moonlight in such forgotten spots you begin to understand the xenophobia that takes root here.

Rehmeyer's Hollow, incidentally, was scene of York County's hitherto most celebrated murder. In 1928, a powwow faith healer named John Blymire took himself in the middle of the night to the house of another powwower, Nelson Rehmeyer. Blymire was convinced he had been hexed, or cursed, by Nelson Rehmeyer. To break the hex, Blymire was instructed to get a lock of Rehmeyer's hair, or a copy of his witching guide, the Pennsylvania German classic *The Long Lost Friend*. Blymire instead beat Rehmeyer to death, taking the cure to the extreme. "Thank God, the witch is dead!" Blymire said over his victim's body. "The witch was dead," Blymire later explained at trial. "The spell was off. I couldn't be hexed no more."

The murder of Lillie Belle Allen seems poised to overtake the hex murder as the area's most infamous killing. Lillie's murder certainly resonates much more deeply in the hearts of today's York countian.

I moved to southern York County in 1995 and soon learned the facts of life about the place. Two workmen were installing plumbing at my house when I heard them talking about "niggers" in town. I asked why they used that word. They gave me a strange look. One asked if I liked blacks. That's saying it charitably. I flinched. I told them I'd grown up in a racially mixed environment in Harrisburg and that I hadn't heard talk like this since I'd left the third grade. They smiled, exchanged good-ol'-boy glances, and went back to work.

At social gatherings in southern York County someone usually starts telling "nigger jokes." You hear this sort of talk high and low.

One day in August 2001 I was for some reason invited to a luncheon to discuss the future of the abandoned Maryland and Pennsylvania Railroad, known as the "Ma and Pa," which snakes through southern York County. At one time, the Ma and Pa tied York to Baltimore. In attendance at the luncheon were neighbors and associates of the Muddy Creek Forks railroad village outside of Red Lion. Also asked to attend were Republican County Chairman John Thompson, who arrived with Christopher Reilly, the president of the York County commissioners. Thompson and I exchanged stories of the old days of Pennsylvania politics. The lunch included sandwiches and a tomato soup favored by Chairman Thompson. The soup was made from a recipe used at the Yorktowne Hotel. Thompson and the county Republican party hang out at the Yorktowne. Talk over lunch turned to politics and the coming election. Commissioner Reilly expressed displeasure with a Democrat who I gathered was running for commissioner. Chairman Thompson suddenly grimaced and said, "We ought to throw him in jail." Thompson's son is a county judge.

Talk at last turned to the Ma and Pa Railroad. Commissioner Reilly told the luncheon that the County of York controlled miles of abandoned rail lines. Reilly announced that he would be willing to turn the railroad lines to the group for a nominal fee, say five dollars, as Reilly said it would save the county hundreds of thousands of dollars in yearly maintenance fees.

One of the group suddenly said, "There's a nigger in the wood-pile." He said one of the private landowners controlling a vital link might not go along with the plan. I flinched. In the 1990s, a York County Democratic chairperson had been forced to resign her post when, at a state committee meeting in Harrisburg, she had used the same phrase. Now here I was at a gathering with the Republican chairman, and the same phrase was being thrown around. I looked at Thompson, who placidly sipped his soup. I spoke up. I said such talk was not appropriate. This was met with derision. "Shut the fuck up, Keisling," someone told me. One of those seated at the table, to rub my face in it, derisively started telling "nigger jokes."

"What's black and yellow, black and yellow, black and yellow?" he asked. Another man seated at the table added, "That reminds me of the southern sheriff who found a runaway from a chain gang drowned in the bottom of a lake, wrapped in chains.'" It made me wonder. What was I doing here? Thompson and Reilly said nothing to stop the joke telling. Thompson, when he wasn't listening to the jokes, placidly sipped his soup.

Once the round of jokes stopped, Commissioner Reilly, a younger man, almost forty, explained that the reopening of the Maryland and Pennsylvania Railroad lines carried its own set of delicate political liabilities. Reilly told the luncheon, "Residents of southern York County come out to our commissioners' meetings and say they don't want the Ma and Pa rail lines reopened because they don't want blacks riding the trains up from Baltimore." He shrugged, as if to say this was the political reality of York County.

They don't want a railroad above ground, they don't want a railroad underground. They don't want a railroad. Period.

Once in need of money, I applied for a temporary job at a York County printing plant. A good opportunity to sharpen my printing skills, I rationalized. I worked at a southern York County printing plant for several weeks, running a commercial press. Some of the pressmen were first rate. They were expert at printing and their presses, and knew everything about that company. The company unfortunately hired a lot of idiots in the front office. They ran around in ties not knowing the first thing about the business, yelling orders sure to cause mayhem. The pressmen would joke endlessly about the front-office goofballs, but only behind their backs. At meetings, the press-men had to pretend they didn't know anything, and always deferred to the morons. This is very common in a York County factory, I'm told.

Few of the workers at the plant would share their opinions about the Lillie Belle Allen murder. They seemed to clam up. "I usually don't talk about things that don't concern me," one young man explained. Some allowed York could be a fairly racist area.

There were no blacks employed permanently at the printing plant where I worked. I asked about this. They had hired a black a year or so ago, I was assured. He kept having car trouble, they said. Then came the day his car quit working altogether and he borrowed small sums of money from a few employees to get his car back on the road. Ten, maybe twelve dollars here and there. But the next day he disap-peared altogether, taking their money with him. The managers called the employment agency and told them not to send "people like that" to the plant in the future. Now the employment agency for the most part just sent whites.

The racism could be even more overt. One evening, while I took a break outside, one of the pressmen pulled up in his Jeep Cherokee. I told him it was a nice car. Out of nowhere, it seemed, he said, "Your blacks like the Grand Cherokee. They like the soft velour seats." What do you mean? I asked. "Your blacks like soft seats." I let it drop. I was glad I hired on for only a few weeks. Why didn't I just walk out? you might wonder. In York County, there's a lot of talk like this, no mat-ter where you go.

As an aside, other problems of the workingman in York are more universal. Someone kept taking a pressman's lunch out of the refriger-ator in the break room. Finally came the day when this pressman dis-covered someone had stolen his much-anticipated ham and cheese hoagie from the refrigerator. It was the last straw. The pressman stormed into his supervisor's office and said enough was enough. He was going to go to the state police and report the sandwich stolen, and ask for an official investigation.

"No, don't do it!" the supervisor pleaded. "I'll buy you a new sandwich!"

The pressman couldn't be assuaged. He drove down to the state police barracks at Leader Heights. He knocked on the window and told the cops his sandwich had been stolen.

One of the troopers bit. It must've been a slow day at the barracks. He courteously asked the angry pressman into the office. The trooper took out a blank police report and proceeded to type what has become known as a MSR. A Missing Sandwich Report. The cop asked for a detailed description of the lost hoagie. Was that on white or whole wheat? Was it baked ham or capicolla? And what about the cheese? Did it have spicy little Spanish onions? Mayo? Oregano? Yes, but no oil. Hmm, the cop got hungry just typing the report.

The trooper dutifully filed the MSR. The next week, one of the newspapers, hungry for news, reprinted the Missing Sandwich Report in the crime section. The printing firm became a laughingstock, and the pressman found himself suspended from his job for two weeks. The cops weren't much help solving that crime. The least they could have done, it seemed to me, was conduct a steak-out.

# 2

## The wrong car used as stalking horse in 1999

Thirty years passed from the night Lillie Belle Allen was killed. A succession of seven York County district attorneys ignored the case. The two most important witnesses — Beatrice Mosley and John Messersmith — died. Both could have testified about the cops. John Messersmith died in 1985. Beatrice and James Mosley died a few months apart in the winter of 1993-94.

The Mosleys went to their graves never knowing answers about their daughter's murder, and the things they had seen that night.

DA John Rauhauser left office in early 1970. Rauhauser went on to become a county judge. While researching this book, I met a retired York City policeman who said he'd been approached in the 1980s by another city officer, John Crisamore. Crisamore told him to stay away from the parking garage of a York City hotel. "Crisamore told me his informant was making regular drops of money and narcotics into the trunk of Judge Rauhauser's car in the parking garage," he whispers to me. Everyone was afraid of Judge Rauhauser and what he might do if anyone blew the whistle on him, the retired cop went on. I've heard the same complaint about other ethically challenged or outright corrupt York County judges. The retired cop told me he left the force when he learned of Judge Rauhauser's role in York County corruption. "When Crisamore told me about the parking garage I resigned from the force," he says. Rauhauser and Crisamore have gone to their reward.

Harold Fitzkee became DA in 1970. Fitzkee claims when he came into office he found no files left by Rauhauser on the Lillie Belle Allen case. Fitzkee says the county prosecutor's office in those days had no resources or investigators to look into the case. Police corruption or involvement in the murder explains why the cops never brought the case to the DA's office. This does not explain why succession district attorneys ignored this sensational murder. Fitzkee in 2001 went on to say, "To the best of my recollection, I never heard of these defendants." Interesting, since Fitzkee prosecuted Bobby Messersmith for the Sweeney-Washington shooting in 1970. It also strains credulity to imagine that in 1970, while the U.S. Justice Department and the FBI kept asking to be kept apprised of any local prosecution in the case, that DA Fitzkee knew nothing of this request.

Next in the batter's box was Donald L. Reihart, who served as district attorney from 1974 to 1977. In 2001 Reihart would say, "The case was not brought to my attention by the police or anybody. It's not that we weren't concerned about (it), we didn't know about it."

Next comes John C. Uhler, York County district attorney from 1978 to 1982. Uhler did not investigate nor prosecute the case. Moreover, Uhler was the county's chief law enforcement officer when crucial evidence in Lillie's murder was lost. In April, 1981 state police Corporal Nelson Roth, stationed in York, requested the state police crime lab send Roth the bullet fragments from both the Allen and Schaad murders. Roth supposedly requested the bullets for reasons of administrative housekeeping. Records show the bullets were sent to Roth. The bullet fragments were never seen again. In 2000 Roth would tell investigators who were looking for the bullets that "he has no recollection of ever receiving this evidence or preparing any reports relative (to) either of these cases...."

Roth could not explain what happened to the bullet that killed Lillie Belle Allen.

District Attorney John Uhler has offered no explanation for this loss of crucial evidence, nor has he assumed proper responsibility for this mishap as chief law enforcement officer. Where does the buck stop? Uhler's role in Lillie Belle's case becomes more troubling in future years.

The unaccountability in the county DA's office continues through the 1980s and 1990s.

J. Christian Ness served as district attorney from 1982 to 1985. Ness, like his predecessors, did not pursue the case. Ness died in October 2001.

Following Ness, Stanley Rebert became district attorney. At the time of Lillie's murder, Rebert told me, he was in law school. Throughout the late 1980s and most of the 1990s, Rebert, like his predecessors, did not pursue the case.

A lawyer once described Stan Rebert to me as a "wildman." Indeed, Rebert cuts an interesting figure. Crippled with MS, he walks around town with the aid of a walking stick adorned with an elaborately carved head. He is quick with a quip. He seems at times almost Strangelovian. He's quite likable. But that doesn't mean he's doing a good job.

Rebert found himself in a variety of ethical and legal troubles in the 1990s. He began to earn a reputation in legal circles for manufacturing and withholding evidence in his cases. A favored technique of Rebert's is to put informants in the same jail cells with those he prosecutes. These informants then are offered deals to testify against their cellmates. It's hard to trust evidence so developed. It's a troubling practice, for a variety of reasons.

This practice led Rebert into trouble with the state's disciplinary board. Rebert was charged with lying to a judge about withholding material from a defense counsel. The case in question had similarities to Lillie Belle Allen's murder. A high-profile case involving the brutal murder of a young woman. Pushing for the death penalty, DA Rebert placed a convicted felon in the suspect's jail cell, hoping to gain an admission. The felon gave Rebert two statements, on two separate occasions. Rebert only turned over one of the statements to defense counsel, leading to the disciplinary charges against him.

District Attorney Rebert asserted that he was under the impression he'd given both statements to defense counsel. On April 1, 1998, the Pennsylvania Supreme Court ruled that Rebert had an obligation to look in his file to determine whether his statements to the judge were true. Rebert was found to have acted with "reckless ignorance" of the facts. Later, the state's controversial disciplinary board would vote to exonerate Stan Rebert, saying his actions had been unintentional. An attorney familiar with the case, *Disciplinary Board v. Rebert,* tells me that District Attorney Rebert spent approximately $50,000 in legal fees defending himself from the charges.

Rebert is fond of quoting a hundred-year-old appellate court decision: "(T)he commonwealth demands no victims. It seeks justice only, equal and impartial justice, and it is as much the duty of the district attorney to see that no innocent man suffers as it is to see that no guilty man escapes." But these are empty platitudes for Stan Rebert.

Rebert was once reprimanded by an appellate court for invoking The Bible and quoting scripture to a jury as justification for capital punishment. The redeeming power of love, the forgiveness of trespasses, the refusal to cast a stone at a condemned woman, in the mind of Stan Rebert, seems to have nothing to do with Jesus's message. Unless, to Rebert's way of thinking, the "love" is committed between a politician and a call girl.

In the 1980s, DA Rebert revealed his true stripes when he yelled at a murder defendant, "I'll fry your ass!"

Now in his fifth term, Republican Stan Rebert has been subject of growing accusations that his office unfairly prosecutes enemies. There are also indications that Rebert protects well-heeled and politically friendly York countians from a variety of criminal charges, such drunk driving, operating sex clubs, prostitution, money-laundering and organized racketeering.

If all that isn't bad enough, the handling of Lillie Belle Allen's case by Rebert and associates is one of the most outrageous instances of prosecutorial misconduct in Pennsylvania history.

By all accounts, the Lillie Belle Allen case would not have been reopened save for the most amazing series of events. One of the policemen working for the York Police Department in the 1969 riots, Charles Robertson, turned to politics.

Charlie Robertson is a strapping man, six-foot-two inches tall, jovial, naturally affable. In his years as a police officer, he became well known for eating breakfast and lunch with what seems like everyone in town. Everyone talks about whether they've had breakfast with Charlie. To this day he eats lunches at city schools, with the kids. He coached Little League ball, and kept tabs on many city youth. He'd turn out to be a natural politician. In 1975, Robertson was elected to the York City School Board, where he served until 1985. In 1994, Democrat Robertson was elected the mayor of York.

What happened next is a classic study not only of prosecutorial misconduct and political skullduggery, but mass hysteria.

In 1999, Democrat Robertson's enemies at the Republican daily newspaper, the York Dispatch, began publishing a series of articles commemorating the 30th anniversary of the great York race riots. With the help of Robertson's political foe on city council, Republican Tom Kelley, York County Republicans would fashion a whispering campaign against Mayor Robertson that would pervert the facts of the murder of Lillie Belle Allen, while protecting the same parties who've been protected for three decades.

It would be nice to write that the reopening of Lillie Belle Allen's murder case was done for all the right, altruistic reasons, and that Lillie's case is finally receiving a full and open hearing. Just the opposite is true. The case was reopened to settle political scores in York County. What began as the story of the wrong car has mutated into the wrong vehicle for a murder prosecution.

There're lots of ironies here. Until 1999, the York Dispatch spent decades actively ignoring the subject of the town riots in general, and Lillie Belle Allen's death in particular. Thirty years is a long time not to give a damn and then suddenly pretend that you do. Precisely when and why the York Dispatch decided to wade into the waters and profess to recognize four-fifths of the world's population as worthy of equality and human rights is an interesting mystery, as well as a source of small-town controversy.

Modern Pennsylvania newsmen have long fondly regarded the afternoon York Dispatch as a gentle, anachronistic, harmless joke. For many years the staunchly Republican newspaper had a policy of printing local news only on the back page. When the nearby Three Mile Island nuclear generating station melted in 1979 and thrust the area into the international spotlight, the Dispatch editors ran the story on the back page. No use getting the readers worked into a lather about a nuclear catastrophe.

The second York daily, the Daily Record, is a different animal, and at times has been professionally well regarded, though its standards have slipped in recent years. The Daily Record was actually one of only of two local publications to warn readers of nagging problems at Three Mile Island *before* the accident. They used to dig. In recent years both the Dispatch and the Daily Record have fallen on hard financial and editorial times. Both papers today are joined at the hip, unhappily married under a joint operating agreement approved by the U.S. Justice Department. They print on the same presses, and share other facilities, per government anti-trust waiver. Their very existence can any time be threatened or even cancelled by an unhappy bureaucrat, or judge. So both papers in recent years have steadfastly towed the party line, which, in York County, comrades, is staunchly Republican. Only York city has remained a Democratic stronghold.

For the Lillie Belle Allen story, and coverage of the riots of the 1960s, the Dispatch had very low standards to uphold. The Dispatch was simply the apologist mouthpiece of the racist officials who fermented the riots. The Daily Record had a higher tradition to uphold, as its forebear, the Gazette and Daily, was a crusading organ for truth and justice in that era. Its reporters were regularly arrested, accosted by police dogs, or beaten. Its offices were firebombed at the height of the riots, apparently by the white supremists known as the Newberry Street Boys.

Reading each paper's back issue coverage of the riots is entertaining and eye-opening. The Gazette and Daily's young staff every day risked life and limb to tell the story of blacks systematically deprived of rights by an unapologetically racist city government.

The York Dispatch, on the other hand, often didn't even send out a reporter to cover major riot events unfolding in its own town. They'd run a wire service report from Harrisburg. The editorial team of the Dispatch seemed to cower in its offices, hoping against hope to be rescued from the black tide, since the county's last Great White Hope, Robert E. Lee, so miserably fell down on the job in nearby Gettysburg in 1863.

More than a century later, the Dispatch in 1968 and 1969 wrote and published priceless paragraphs describing teaming black mobs brandishing weapons, no doubt betraying the great fear of the editors and their rural readership that denizens of the concrete jungle might one day ring their doorbell, date their daughter, ask for dinner or golf at the York Country Club or, worse, a job at dad's firm. These are old-time southern Gothic traditions the Dispatch's editors are vouchsafing, when they're not searching for the misplaced gin bottle.

Beginning in 1999, to mark the 30th anniversary of the great York race riots, both papers began a series of articles that got tongues wagging all over town, and opened a Pandora's box into which both papers now seem afraid to gaze. These sorcerer's apprentices have helped unleash a monster that has placed their backward, corrupt little town fore square in the eye of the world. They have joined forces with the Republican district attorney to finally indict various individuals in the murders of Lillie Belle Allen and Henry Schaad. What might otherwise have been a two-paragraph story has caught world attention because one of those indicted and charged was a York cop at the time of the murder. Better still, he was the current mayor, running for re-election.

Charlie Robertson, one of the cops on Newberry Street that night, was charged as an accessory to commit murder in the death of Lillie Belle. Robertson, you recall, rode in the armored car that responded to the mystery cop's radio call. Rather than pursue politics, Robertson might wish he had run off into obscurity like the other cops that night.

The papers trumpeted that some new evidence had been found on the killings. It's hard to figure out what new evidence they're talking about. Claims of "new evidence" in this case, held over practically from the last ice age, are on their face untrue and dishonest. As we've seen, police had known the identity of the suspects back in *1969,* and had lied about having that knowledge, and had quashed any further investigations and prosecutions. That's the real headline here.

In fact, the only new evidence uncovered by prosecutors since 1999 seems to be one embarrassing account after another of the involvement of large numbers of police officers — other than Charlie Robertson — in the murder of Lillie Belle Allen. The district attorney's staff not only failed to pursue the growing number of leads pointing to widespread police misconduct, they sought to keep this evidence from the public. They were out to get Charlie Robertson. Period.

This is the worst sort of prosecution, for the worst sort of reasons and motivations. Robertson was one of many cops involved that night, but his role seems at the periphery. As the trial approached, the town's newspapers had not demanded the Republican prosecutor widen an investigation that needs to be widened, with a wrecking ball aimed at York County courts and its prosecutor's office, if need be, to get at the truth. The prosecutors know that mounds of evidence show a coordinated and large-scale police cover-up in the Allen murder.

There is an ongoing cover-up at the hands of these reckless and dangerous prosecutors, kissed on by a sleepy lapdog newspaper or two. The essence of the problem is this: a partisan Republican prosecutor has irresponsibly and selectively indicted a Democratic mayor for murder. This same Republican prosecutor is afraid to demand a necessary investigation of the Pennsylvania state police, because the current governor is Republican, and would surely be highly embarrassed.

Instead they would steer the case as a vehicle against Mayor Robertson. Already robbed of so much, Lillie Belle Allen is being taken for a ride by the worst sort of characters in Pennsylvania government.

Once again we're watching the wrong car roll down the street. The worst sort of prosecution for the worst sort of reasons.

# 3

# The Reciprocity Club

The reopening of Lillie Belle Allen's case is credited to an alliance of three men: Tom Kelley, Ray Crenshaw and Stan Hough. Kelley and Crenshaw were members of York city council, while Hough is the editor/publisher of the York Dispatch. The three set out to distort Lillie Belle's murder and use it for their own nefarious ends, namely to destroy the career and reputation of patrolman-become-mayor Charlie Robertson.

In 1995, Tom Kelley, a Republican, decided to run for city council. Kelley was a young assistant district attorney working in Stan Rebert's office, with various duties including the investigation of child abuse cases. He had come to York County from Bryn Mawr, Pennsylvania, a suburb of Philadelphia, having graduated from Dickinson College and the University of Virginia Law School. Knocking on doors in the city of York, Kelley won election to city council, becoming the only Republican on the body. A seat on the York city council is a part-time job, and Kelley held onto his position as assistant prosecutor.

What set Kelley immediately apart on council was his vicious and unrelenting political and personal attacks on Mayor Robertson. When he wasn't calling Robertson a "buffoon," Councilman Kelley was launching attack after attack on every conceivable policy of Robertson's administration. Councilman Kelley even proposed the appointment of an "independent counsel" to investigate Robertson when the mayor vetoed one of Kelley's proposed ordinances. Endless turf feuds. No compromise, no middle ground, no kindnesses, no give-and-take, no scruples, no decency. As John Kennedy succinctly dismissed Richard Nixon, *No class.* Just a lot of yelling and childish nastiness.

Tom Kelley is a demagogue. A politician who appeals to people's prejudices rather than their rationality. In their class-oriented town, Charlie Robertson had commited the ultimate sin of rising above what Kelley perceived to be a cop's place. Robertson could have risen to the post of chief of police, like Tom Chatman or Wayne Ruppert, and that would have been acceptable. But to become mayor, to be the boss, to occupy a station above lawyer/councilman Tom Kelley, that didn't sit right with Kelley's clubhouse sensibilities. In Kelley's mind, Robertson wasn't a mayor, he was a working-class stiff who thought he was better than he was. Kelley the lawyer wanted to teach the cop a lesson, and put him in his place. Using Lillie Belle Allen's case for these ends makes Kelley's actions not only sad, but despicable.

Pennsylvania has seen many unpleasant public screamers before. In the past, a politician attacking a foe had to dig up a political ally to handle the prosecution. Tom Kelley decided to streamline affairs and personally misuse his post and trust as prosecutor to wage criminal war against his political opponent. The Republican ideal: less government.

Ray Crenshaw was a councilman whose jealousy of Charlie Robertson got the best of him, and who dreamed of succeeding Robertson as mayor, by any means necessary. In fact he dreamed too much. Crenshaw sometimes fell asleep at city council meetings, and his snoozing became a fixture on public access cable tv.

Stan Hough just seems to have thought it'd be fun to use his newspaper to unfairly leave Robertson holding the bag. You hear stories about Hough's reporters returning to the newspaper gleefully announcing whatever embarrassing photo or utterance of Robertson they'd just collected.

In the months to come, an exodus of editors and writers from the Dispatch would complain that Hough was in bed with corruption in York County, while his crusade against Robertson was overly personal and vindictive.

Early on, Kelley, Crenshaw and Hough formed a confederacy of dunces to embarrass and humiliate Mayor Robertson by any means possible. Trouble was, the "buffoon" Charlie Robertson turned out to be a much better politician than Kelley and Crenshaw, with the ability to reach and touch people better than Hough. It must have driven them nuts.

By 1999, Kelley, Crenshaw and Hough embarked on a path to fashion Lillie Belle Allen's horrific murder into a weapon to get Charlie Robertson. After all, they reasoned, Robertson was on Newberry Street that night. As prosecutor of the case Kelley thought he knew how to manipulate the facts and the courts to spare the guilty and skewer the target. Kelley's mission would be to steer the case to destroy Robertson, while at the same time misusing the powers of his prosecutor's office to continue the three-decade-old cover-up and protection of the cops who truly share blame.

Crenshaw and Hough, I guess, can apply for forgiveness, since they are petty mugwumps, and act as expected. Kelley, on the other hand, presents a much more challenging picture. Events show him to be an unscrupulous prosecutor willing to sink to great depths to destroy a political opponent. We must wonder what checks and balances, what basic human decencies, are not in place in York County for Tom Kelley to so misuse its criminal justice system.

All of this might never have happened, as I say, if one of Tom Kelley's political friends hadn't been too cheap to pay a hooker more than fifty dollars. On Labor Day weekend of 1996, York state senator Dan Delp set off an amazing series of events that threatened to destroy Stan Rebert's DA's office over a widening sex scandal. Delp's indiscretion itself would be quick, though the fallout would be slow to gather.

For years, secret sex clubs, with ties to organized crime, have thrived in York County, Pennsylvania. Some of these sex clubs are composed of high-ranking York County business, political and legal leaders.

The most socially prominent of these secret sex clubs calls itself, interestingly enough, The Reciprocity Club. In the mid-to late-1990s The Reciprocity Club was made up of second-tier (i.e. younger) York County community leaders. It split from another, stodgier group of older men. Club members include one of the county's top realtors, I'm told, a man with millions of dollars in yearly sales. Another sex club secretly operates in nearby Wrightsville.

Activities of The Reciprocity Club include greased pig events attended by strippers and call girls. A local restaurant was once booked after hours for the greased pig night, featuring a slippery pig running wild through the establishment, chased by the girls, themselves chased by club members. They wrecked the place. The restaurant never had the club back. Other sex activities included golf games where the winner of each hole was awarded a blowjob from a hooker. These boys know how to have fun!

Investigators would eventually hear that Stan Rebert had attended at least one event at a local sex club. An informant told investigators that District Attorney Rebert witnessed a club member openly receiving a blowjob.

This is only the tip, as it were, of the iceberg.

Sex clubs need "girls." For a steady stream of fresh girls, the clubs relied on several York-area "escort services." One of these escort services, Platinum Escorts, was run by David Ness and Richard "Dicky" Parks.

Richard Parks was a York County private investigator with deep, varied, and long-lasting ties to DA Rebert's office. Witnesses would say that Parks used to flash a special DA's office badge. When he wasn't passing himself off as one of Rebert's associates, Parks was a partner in Platinum Escorts. He had other activities on the fringe of the law. He also used to run midnight "sex club" parties at a bar in town.

Dicky Parks worked for several years as an investigator in the law office of Dale Anstine, a prominent York County personal injury lawyer and longtime friend of Stan Rebert. Park's wife worked as a paralegal in Anstine's office. Parks regularly golfed with Anstine and assistant district attorney William H. Graff, the county drug prosecutor.

When Parks applied for a private investigator's license in 1994, assistant DA Graff paid the $200 fee; Graff's name is on a receipt in the clerk of court's office. When Parks was granted his license by York County Judge Joseph Erb in April 1994, Graff's wife, Leah B. Graff, a lawyer in Anstine's office, represented Parks in this proceeding. Rebert himself, raising no objections, represented the commonwealth. Anstine and four others, including two Anstine lawyers and two bankers, testified on Parks' behalf. Parks' application was submitted on Anstine stationery.

Anstine says he terminated Parks' employment in 1996, though he doesn't say why. By 1996 the money must have been rolling, because Parks renewed his private eye license, this time using his own money. In 1997, he would inexplicably file a change-of-address form with the clerk's office. His new address, 4749 Druck Valley Road — a vacant fruit stand.

Dicky Parks, when he wasn't hanging around the DA's office and passing himself off as a private eye, concentrated his talents running Platinum Escorts. "We started it to make money," his escort service partner, David Ness, tells me.

Another local escort service was operated by Larry Keeney, Keeney's wife, and a silent partner said to be high in York County law enforcement circles. Keeney also operated several massage parlors, one on Queen Street in York, one in Wrightsville, and, I'm told, an establishment in Harrisburg.

Investigators over time would come to suspect the payments to these various escort services also served as a money-laundering scheme enabling broader criminal activities. Observers came to suspect that at least some of this cash flowed from the district attorney's office.

York County ranked high in drug confiscation money doled out by the state. Parks friend and sponsor, William Graff, the county drug prosecutor, administers these funds. The money coming into the district attorney's office is well documented. The money flowing out has never been properly accounted for, leading to suspicions it's been used for dark purposes, needful of laundering. Hence the sex clubs and the escort services.

One day approaching Labor Day in 1996 Pennsylvania state Senator Dan Delp asked his friend Dicky Parks for a girl, "an escort."

Dan Delp was the young son of a wealthy York industrialist. The young Delp parlayed his family's fortune into a state senate seat. They say he's more arrogant than Tom Kelley. Delp quickly became the darling and rising star of the Republican leadership in York and at the state capitol in Harrisburg. He was a close friend and favorite of Rebert's, and county Republican chairman John Thompson. Rebert and Delp used to share campaign funds.

The girl Parks would supply to state senator Dan Delp in the end would laughingly report that senator Delp's climactic conjugal time with her had been very brief indeed. Ah these Republican men. The actual act with Senator Delp lasted slightly longer than a certain car ride down Newberry Street. Likewise, the cover-up continues to this day.

David Ness remembers the fateful day in 1996 when he spoke with Dicky Parks about a girl for state senator Delp. "Dick said can I get two girls to go on a boat ride with Dan Delp? I said yeah I'd be able to," Ness remembers. "I talked to two girls and they said they'd do it."

The girls traveled to Harrisburg to meet Delp and one of his legislative aides. They were taken for an outing on a boat. Afterwards Delp and his aide took the girls to Nick Cantone's, a popular sports bar figuring prominently in Harrisburg lore. The bill was charged to Delp's state expense account. One of the girls they took to the bar was only nineteen.

From there it was back to Delp's place, where the escorts spent the night. Somewhere in here the girl received the quick senatorial honors from our esteemed young politician. In the end, one of the young women would sign a fifty-four-page affidavit describing Delp's dwelling and other intimate details. Sex with Delp had been very quick, she attests. While playing kissey face she says Delp's nose suddenly began to bleed. The other girl, she says, engaged in rough sex with the legislative aide, scratching his back, leaving marks. The other girl was drunk and fell asleep.

In the morning the young women were sent on their way with fifty dollars each. They were mad about it, and complained to David Ness. Ness in turn passed on the complaint to Dicky Parks and the legislative aide. The aide quickly produced one hundred and fifty for each girl, in cash, given by way of Parks, Ness says. Parks kicked in another hundred dollars for each girl.

In 1996 and 1997, our friends the troopers in the York state police barracks, and their sidekicks in the York Police Department, began an unsuspecting crackdown of York County escort services and massage parlors. One night, Ness tells me, two undercover troopers wandered into a sex club event, but found themselves outnumbered by men hopped-up on testosterone. They elected to do nothing at that time. Instead, they booked their own event at a local motel. When the girls showed up at the motel with the escort service driver they were busted. They began to talk, angrily saying they had important clients. Before long one of the girls complained she'd been with state senator Dan Delp. She was mad that he'd initially only given her fifty dollars and wanted to teach Delp and his establishment friends a lesson.

Escort service provider Larry Keener by and by was arrested, his bank accounts frozen. Stashed away in the bank accounts, I'm told, investigators found $1.3 to $1.4 million. People wondered about the origin of the unaccountable cash deposits, about the identities of those who may have helped with the untraceable cash sums. At one point, an observer tells me, criminal charges mysteriously were withdrawn against Keener.

After the police crack-down, and girls kept talking. The York Dispatch got wind of the story. A months-long waltz ensued between the Dispatch, which kept digging on the story but was too frightened to publish anything, and Delp, who threatened to sue. The Dispatch came down with a bad case of lawyeritis, which happens when a writer becomes afraid to think and write without first hiring and then incessantly consulting a truth scrubber. The newspaper even hired a detective to help with the sleuthing, a controversial move in the newsroom. Lawyers, detectives: what happened to the reporter? This story is all about lawyers and detectives. Will calling in fresh teams of lawyers and detectives get to the bottom of things? Won't they join the others in the clubhouse?

The Harrisburg Patriot-News learned of the story in a roundabout way. Dicky Parks had been drawn into the scandal by way of Delp, and feared being made the fall guy. He sought help from a high-profile Harrisburg lawyer, who sent him to the Harrisburg Patriot-News. Eventually Parks would hash out a deal with the Patriot. The paper promised not to use his name. Like the Dispatch, the Patriot was at first intimidated by Delp's lawyers. This silent waltz between Senator Delp and two newspapers went on for weeks, months. Finally the Patriot figured out the public should know that Delp had used his office scratch pad to pay for the meals with the prostitutes at Cantone's. The paper finally published an article. In no time at all we were off to the races with a good old-fashioned sex scandal, with the escort service investigation bubbling in the background.

In the end, Delp would be prosecuted for misappropriation of state funds, procuring a nineteen-year-old prostitute and providing alcohol to an under-aged drinker. Before it was over, he'd resign his senate seat; two men would kill themselves (or were helped, some say); and DA Stan Rebert's office would come under suspicion for connections to mob operatives. All this not over some passionate love affair, but a quick roll in the hay for money.

Rebert found himself staring smack into a scandal that had the real potential to end his career, though the public at first had little idea Delp's indiscretions, through Parks, were hotwired to the DA's office. Delp for his part initially denied everything. In public, Rebert became a staunch defender of the beleaguered senator. Stan Rebert famously (and characteristically) defended Delp by jocularly pointing out that all men one way or another pay for sex.

"Dan's only crime was being young and single," Rebert opined. "We all pay for sex." Rebert stuck his foot deeper: "When we marry, we pay for sex by paying the mortgage or the rent, the groceries or the utilities," he offered. It must be pretty wild to change a light bulb in the Rebert household.

Rebert nevertheless knew this was no laughing matter. On Christmas Eve 1996 Rebert felt pressed enough to dash off a holiday letter to the state attorney general, recusing himself from the case, citing the potential for a real or potential conflict of interest.

The wolves were at the door. "The district attorney or some members of his staff had been called 'clients' or friends of Ness," the York Daily Record would come to report. "Rebert has described the accusations as 'baseless.'"

David Ness told me that he and Parks never sent girls to Rebert or his staff, or other country club types, just Senator Delp. There may have been, he allows, "bachelor parties where police were present."

Another participant disputes this, relating that Ness had a cele-brated connection to Rebert's well-heeled friends, by way of attorney Dale Anstine. One day Ness was in an auto accident, and was referred by Dicky Parks to Anstine's firm. Hoping to conserve cash, Ness offered a junior lawyer in the firm sex with one of his girls in return for legal work. Now there's a concept. The lawyer promptly showed up at the escort service. Ness and Parks kept an office at the Tollgate Plaza Mall. It was a small office with a bedroom in the back. The lawyer was introduced to a girl and shown to the bedroom. Ness left the office. The lawyer thought he was alone with the girl, but Ness and Parks had concealed a camera in a fire detector. Pictures of how a lawyer handles a client's case made the rounds.

The *real* provider of girls for the country club set, Ness says, was Larry Keeney. "He had a lot of people high up in the country club cir-cle," Ness told me.

Ness says one of his girls also worked for Keeney. This girl told Parks that a man high in York law enforcement circles, whom she named, bankrolled Keeney. This man has associations with the Schaad Detective Agency, Ness adds.

By this time, the late 1990s, Russell Schaad was long dead, and the Schaad Detective Agency had passed into the hands of Russell Wantz, who by now was a car dealer and collector. Russell Wantz did not return my call to discuss whether someone involved with his detective firm may have been acquainted with sex club supplier Keeney. Sure is a mystery. Maybe someone will have to hire a detec-tive.

With Wantz, our story comes full circle, back to the eighteen year old who started out servicing bubble gum machines, who collected coins, who witnessed Lillie's murder that night on Newberry Street all those years ago. Russell Wantz, the first person interviewed by Sgt. John Creavey in Lillie Belle's case in 1969. The interview which Creavey lied about to the FBI.

The state attorney general's office soon convened a grand jury on the Delp-escort service affair, and the state media in Harrisburg had a field day. This was no longer a sleepy little event in backward York, where anything goes.

Escort service operators Larry Keeney, Steve Parks and Dave Ness, Senator Delp, drug prosecutor William Graff and DA Stan Rebert all found themselves in trouble. Other escort service providers began to come under the spotlight. Many more upper-crust York countians involved in the secret sex clubs might soon find themselves exposed. At the height of the feeding frenzy, one of the escort service providers (perhaps accidentally) gave a membership list of The Reciprocity Club to the York Daily Record.

"The Record didn't understand what it had, and printed an article making passing reference to the list," an observer told me, snickering.

Many prominent York countians were beginning to squirm. That's when the bodies started turning up.

In January 1997, while traveling in Moosic, Pennsylvania to offer court testimony, escort provider Larry Keeney, age forty-nine, was found dead in his locked room, stabbed a single time in the chest. The police suspected foul play, but the coroner ruled suicide.

By this time Keeney and his wife had been charged by the state with promoting prostitution, criminal conspiracy and *money laundering*.

"It's a locked-room mystery," an observer says. Stabbing one's self in the chest seems like a curious way to commit suicide. But if not by his own hand, how had the room been locked? Many suspect a professional job. Or threats against Keeney's loved ones that forced him to do the job himself. Moosic, outside of Scranton, is near the home of one of the state's top dons, a junkyard operator with mysterious legal immunities, a successor to the Russell Bufalino crime family, which for years controlled the state's underworld.

So now the main supplier of girls to The Reciprocity Club was dead under mysterious circumstances. Leaving a wife, a silent partner high in York County law enforcement circles, and bank accounts filled with large, untraceable sums.

Dicky Parks, meanwhile, caused more alarm bells to ring in Stan Rebert's district attorney's office. Parks not only was involved in prostitution, but also the servicing of video poker machines, gambling, and money laundering. "Dick Parks was a collection guy for poker machines, and he used to take the money to Butler, Pennsylvania," one investigator told me. Butler has figured in recent mob escapades in Pennsylvania. A gambling center, its denizens had links to former Lackawanna County DA and state Attorney General Ernie Preate. Preate in the 1990s was prosecuted for links to underworld gambling. The mob likes vending businesses, as endless streams of coins are perfect for money laundering.

So with Dicky Parks, we had prostitution, gambling, money laundering. What organization sponsors such activities? The mafia.

Investigators began to suspect the mob had infiltrated the York County district attorney's office *and* courts.

"We started to see lots of flags," I was told. Flags involving not only the DA, but also York County judges.

Stories began circulating of cases with peculiar outcomes dating back to Stan Rebert's private practice. A jewelry appraiser was arrested in the 1980s as part of a crime ring. He'd appraise jewelry, then send thieves to steal the jewels at the homes of his customers. Hot jewelry was found in the safe of one of Rebert's closest friends, an attorney. Rebert unsuccessfully represented the jewelry appraiser before becoming DA. Later, after Rebert had become DA, the convicted jewel thief petitioned Orphan's Court and had the confiscated jewelry returned to him. In another case, a York County judge strangely ruled oral sex for money wasn't prostitution. "For a number of years you could get a blowjob in York County without fear of arrest," I'm told. This very accommodating court ruling immeasurably helped the sex trade, until a higher court overruled the county judge.

Stories abound of unusual drug arrests with no prosecutions. A man was arrested with a sack of marijuana in his car but was released, only to be arrested several more times, without prosecution.

A York bar openly known as a house of prostitution and gambling remains open and goes unprosecuted to this day, seemingly untouchable. One of the escort service providers told investigators the bar has links to the Baltimore mob.

"We started wondering which mob controlled York," I was told. Baltimore? Butler? Northeast Pennsylvania? It was starting to look like one big happy family, helped in no small part by corrupt York law enforcement and courts.

It's not only the mob that gets passes from Stan Rebert's DA's office, and county courts. Rebert's friends escape prosecution, and wag their tongues about it. One wealthy woman in the country club and fox hunting set tells me that's how York County operates. She explains she was arrested for driving under the influence one night on Route 74. The next day she telephoned Rebert. "We have a problem Stan," she says she told the DA. "Call Harry Ness, he'll take care of it," she says Rebert instructed her. She never had dealings with Ness before Rebert's referral, she tells me. Ness advertises himself in the phone book, in capital letters, as "former assistant district attorney."

"Ness and Stan took care of it," the woman tells me. She explained Ness had the charge reduced to public drunkenness, a charge not involving a motor vehicle and therefore not jeopardizing her driver's license. All she had to do was pay the lawyer's bill, she says. No ARD, no alcohol classes, like the rabble must endure. York leads the state in drunk driving incidents. One wonders about Rebert's political contributions, and similar contributions to county judges.

If you're part of the wealthy set in York County, you're protected, she goes on to explain to me. The country club-DA's office-court set considers itself above the law. By way of further describing the community, this woman adds that she was once sexually propositioned by a leading figure in the county Republican Party, a man *in his eighties.* "We were in Hershey, at a Republican Party function, and it was getting too late to drive home. He said he'd get me a room," the woman relates. "On the way to the room he said there was only one room left, and we'd have to share it. He opened the door and I saw it was only a single. He says to me, 'We'll just have to share this bed, won't we?'" The party official, who walks with a shuffle, shuffled off to the bathroom. The woman picked up her bag, turned and hurried from the room and drove home.

Such strange bedfellows in York County. Sex, alcohol consumption, and legal protection, are socially acceptable and an important part of life here.

The well-heeled country club set wants to keep the party rolling and keep the cash registers ringing. Dicky Parks, in 1997, threatened the party.

"I always got the feeling that Stan Rebert wasn't so much afraid of Senator Delp as much as he was afraid of Dicky Parks, and what Parks could say about Graff and others in the district attorney's office," one investigator told me. People began moving away from Stan Rebert; the rats began jumping ship.

"Political leaders from both major parties have scrambled to secure safe positions outside the center of the storm," the Daily Record reported at the height of Delp frenzy in 1997.

The most prominent ship-jumping rat was city councilman Tom Kelley. Somewhere in this time period Kelley began making arrangements to leave Rebert's office. Kelley arranged a job in private law practice with Hanover attorney John Mooney, to run Mooney's York office.

"The public story was that Kelley's wife was upset that Rebert wasn't cracking down on the prostitution," an observer tells me. Behind the cover story, Kelley, the newcomer to York, was beginning to see that the community, and Rebert's office, had a dark side. Kelley's own precious bullshit career and reputation were threatened.

Lucky for Tom Kelley, another dead body turned up. On June 16, 1997, at the height of the unfolding sex, money laundering, and political scandal, Dicky Parks, now forty-five, shot himself in the head with a 9mm. He died the next day.

"Dick just wanted this thing to end," his partner in Platinum Escorts, David Ness, says.

Others aren't sure it's so simple. State prosecutors and others wondered whether Parks had been pushed.

"In the back of my mind I can't stop thinking that Dicky was threatened," the observer says. "Some very big people were about to get drawn in. I can't help thinking someone came to Dick and said this better stop now, or one of his family members would die. So he killed himself to stop it."

Parks shot himself at home, in a scenic, fourteen-acre, country club setting. He and his wife for the past several years rented a nine-room section of a house owned by attorney Dale Anstine's in-laws. The week before Parks died, Anstine told the Daily Record that Parks "doesn't want to talk to anyone. The whole damn thing's a tragedy."

Anstine added he hadn't seen Parks in six months, since before the sex scandal. He'd last seen Dicky Parks on the golf course, he said.

I picture Dicky Parks at the course, smiling, holding a driver, the clubhouse behind him, the hills of York County rolling away. Something's wrong at the club.

Dead bodies were mysteriously turning up all around prosecutor Tom Kelley's place of employment, a predicament he shares with Charlie Robertson. All this was enough to make Tom Kelley exit stage any direction to get away from Rebert's office. Two weeks after Parks shot himself, Kelley announced he was leaving the DA's office for private practice with Jim Moody. Heavens to Murgatroid!

So a politician who'd been too cheap to pay a hooker more than fifty dollars led to Tom Kelley leaving the DA's office. If Kelley had stayed out, Lillie's case probably would never have been reopened.

Though he got away from Rebert's office, law enforcement officials chide that he didn't get far enough away from his duties as child-abuse prosecutor. They remember Kelley in private practice handling child abuse cases. Having renounced his public trust to protect children, he sees child abuse can be quite profitable.

That's how it is in York County. It's not about the kids, it's about making money from kids, exploiting them, or otherwise profiting from their disadvantage. I encountered a long-time associate of a particular York County judge who decides child custody cases. The associate openly peddles his influence with the judge. The judge, I was told, normally gets at least more than ten thousand dollars to fix a case when he works on his associate's behalf. Rumors circulate that these moneymaking relationships between York County judges, lawyers and associates are attracting investigation by our sharp-eyed friends in the FBI. But that's another story for another day.

James and Beatrice Mosley found out all those years ago. York County is not a safe place for children, or other decent people.

Councilman Tom Kelley remained in private law practice for just four months. He'd stay in private practice until the firestorm involving Senator Delp and Dicky Parks died down. Now that Dicky Parks was dead, the heat lifted from the DA's office. Meanwhile, at the York Dispatch, a top editor was fired, people say for his insistence on pursuing corruption in Rebert's office. Rebert's friends — among them some of the paper's top advertisers and sex club members — are said to have pressured the Dispatch to stop its probe of organized crime infiltration into the county DA's office and courts.

Once the dust had settled and the heat had blown over, a city council member tells me that DA Rebert came into a city council meeting to woo Tom Kelley to rejoin his staff. "Rebert came to the council meeting and afterwards they were talking together in the hall," an associate of Kelley remembers. "The next day Kelley said he was going back to work for Rebert."

Kelley, then 33 years old, announced in November 1997 he was leaving private practice to rejoin Rebert as the county's first deputy prosecutor, in charge of the trial units.

Back in the DA's office, the path would now be clear for Tom Kelley to attend to his favorite pet project: abusing his public trust and using the powers of his office to indict his political opponent, the mayor of York, for the murder of Lillie Belle Allen.

While discussing Stan Rebert and various other county elite, one of my sources suddenly grew quiet when talk turned to Russell Schaad, founder of the detective agency, father of the slain policeman.

"I was talking one day to Tom Chatman," he tells me, suddenly lowering his voice. "Chatman told me he and Schaad once investigated a Christmas Eve murder of an old woman. The old woman had this coin collection. Schaad told Chatman he could go home, and Schaad would finish up. The coin collection ended up missing."

My conversant went on, "Tom Chatman told me he suspected Schaad stole that poor old lady's coins. He said he always suspected Schaad had used the coins to start the detective agency."

# 4

## "Turn your backs and everything will be okay"

In July 1999, Stan Hough's Dispatch published several articles commemorating the 30th anniversary of the York riots. The articles concerning Lillie Belle had factual errors due, no doubt, to the suppression of the police records. The Dispatch, for example, had Lillie sitting between her parents in the back seat of Bubba's Cadillac, and not on the left hand side: "Lillie Belle, sitting between her parents in the back seat, had already scooted across her mother's lap...." reads a Dispatch article, incorrectly. The Dispatch also incorrectly reported that more than one tire was shot out, that the car drove off "on metal rims," and so on. But these are small mistakes, and honest errors, I think.

Overall, the reporting on Lillie Belle's life was excellent, even haunting. Particularly outstanding was one article penned by Lauri Lebo. Lillie Belle liked making a dish called Hoppin' John, with black-eyed peas, rice and peppers, Lebo discovered. Lillie would sit up nights talking with her girlfriend in Aiken about her hopes and dreams. Her daughter Debra has no photos of Lillie, and only a few knick-knacks by which to remember her mother. A wedding ring. Some costume jewelry. A blown-glass ashtray. Outstanding writing. If only the rest of the Dispatch's coverage rose to this level.

The people of York began to feel bad. Something about it didn't sit right. Lillie Belle Allen, it turned out, has a restless, powerful spirit. Was she an animal to be left on the street, or a human being, with rights to full justice?

As Shakespeare and Socrates knew, justice is divine, not merely human. It's something wrapped up in God. Our institutions our temples we have built to honor the ideal. When justice is not provided by our institutions, our spirits, our fragile bond to God, cries out for it, and seeks it. It is that divine spark that lifts us above animals. Not to seek vengeance, but to see right and dignity prevail over wrong.

Some in York, to their discredit, confuse vengeance with justice. Shortly after these articles began to appear, city councilman Tom Kelley approached his boss in the DA's office. Tom Kelley asked to reopen the Lillie Belle Allen case, Rebert says.

Rebert says Kelley asked for permission to "shake out" the case for new leads. From his seat on city council, Kelley began to ask people to come forward. People understood Kelley to mean here was an opportunity to stick it to the "buffoon," Mayor Robertson.

Kelley knew he could manipulate the case to make trouble for Robertson, while at the same time protecting the other policemen with much more direct involvement. As far back as 1970, a federal judge had criticized young Patrolman Robertson (and other cops) for attending white power rallies in Farquhar Park during the riots, and making white power salutes. Robertson, of all these characters, at least acknowledged he behaved wrongly and seems genuinely repentant.

Back in the DA's office, city councilman Tom Kelley wanted his foe's head, and set out to get it. It is to Stan Rebert's discredit that he allowed Kelley anywhere near this case. Putting a man's political opponent in charge of his prosecution is inexcusable. An honest district attorney with integrity would never have allowed this to happen. It gives the appearance a family's tragedy is being used to settle political scores. Which, of course, is exactly what Tom Kelley had in mind.

Sometime late in 1999 and into 2000, Kelley and his investigators requested the old state police and FBI reports, bureaucratically buried thirty-some years earlier. They began to read. It was easy to pick up where Creavey, Cronin and company left off in 1969. If nothing else, their latter-day work showed that prosecutions could have easily been brought all along.

Reading from the reports, Tom Kelley, county detective Rodney George and York city detective Dennis Williams, began making a list of likely witnesses and suspects, always mindful that their real prey was Charlie Robertson. Like their predecessors, they set out to protect other police officers.

In early April 2000, the detectives contacted Donnie Altland, now fifty-one, and asked him to come in for an interview. Altland showed up on April 10, without a lawyer. That interview of course didn't go so well.

"They overplayed their hand with Altland, and led him to believe they had more on him than they did," an observer close to the investigation tells me.

That night Donnie Altland went home and discussed the situation with his wife. A short while later he made two tape recordings, one for his wife, the other for police. The next day, Altland drove his pickup truck down to the Susquehanna River. On a napkin he wrote the words "Forgive Me God," underlining the word God twice. Then he walked down to the river and shot himself to death with a .22.

Much was made in the newspapers about the recordings left by Altland. The recording to his wife asked for her forgiveness. The Dispatch trumpeted the second tape contained new evidence, but that's not the case, as investigators know. The tape provided nothing police didn't already know, that they hadn't known for thirty years.

In their ruthless stretch to destroy Charlie Robertson, Tom Kelley and company had already underhandedly and needlessly driven one man to suicide. Altland felt compelled to kill himself, leaving behind a wife and two children who knew nothing about his dark night on Newberry Street. Another wrongful death.

On April 18, 2000, detectives George and Williams interviewed Gary King, who'd been sitting on the Slick family porch when he witnessed Lillie's murder.

On the same day, Williams and policeman Scott Nadzom interviewed William "Sam" Ritter, who Creavey and company had interviewed in '69. Ritter in 1969 had said he had been sitting on the Slick's porch and hadn't participated in the shooting. This time, he started out by saying he didn't remember a lot, and again said he'd been at the Slick's. But then, from the blue, came a confession. They mentioned the 1969 statement to Ritter. "After reading his statement I asked him if he saw who was shooting and he said, 'We were shooting down and they were shooting up,'" Detective Williams reports.

"When you say you were shooting down, what were you shooting?" Williams asked.

"A .22 rifle. I still have it," Ritter responded.

"How many times did you shoot?"

"About five or six."

"Were the other people with you shooting?"

"Yes, everybody was shooting."

"Why?"

"Because they were shooting."

This discussion suggests that Ritter could have been arrested at any time.

The detectives were concerned about Beatrice Mosley's sighting of cops mixed in with the shooters, even though she was dead, and couldn't testify. "I asked (Ritter) if he owned a motorcycle around July 1969 and he said he did, a 125cc Harley Davidson," William writes. "I asked him if he wore a white helmet and he said his helmet was blue. I asked him if he was on his motorcycle (just) before the shooting riding up Newberry Street and he said no, he was with friends in front of Billy Slick's house." Much to their displeasure, Sam Ritter, then eighteen, obviously wasn't the cop pushing the bike seen by Mrs. Mosley near the tracks. Later, they would find Randall Schouck, who'd say he'd come to the area on a motorcycle, but Schouck and his bike were at the corner of Newberry and Philadelphia when the shooting started. He wasn't the cop seen by the reverend's wife either.

About two weeks later, on May 9, 2000, detective George and state Trooper Keith Stone were dispatched to visit the object of Tom Kelley's desire, York Mayor Charlie Robertson. Trooper Stone had been assigned to the inquiry by his superiors at the Pennsylvania State Police. Once again, the city and state police, with the county DA's office, are back in the saddle for one more round-up. Bing, bang, boom! And they're shocked, shocked! to learn that policemen were anywhere near Newberry Street that night!

Robertson, to his credit, acted like the old policeman that he was. Robertson recounted responding to the radio call in the armored car. If Detective George and Trooper Stone were truly interested in solving the crime they should examine the police at the barricade, the mayor told them. Robertson pointed up to the intersection of Newberry and Philadelphia streets. With this interview, to my knowledge, Charlie Robertson turns out to be the only law enforcement officer, past or present, who actually sought a full accounting of the incident. Charlie Robertson acted like a cop. Now that Kelley had reopened this can of worms, Robertson pointed the way to a real investigation, one that could end up busting lots of cops. Does he hope that by pointing to other cops, his own culpability will be diminished?

Detective George's crime report of this interview with Robertson reads, in part, "Robertson stated that before Allen was shot, the police put up barricades and were not to let any black people up N. Newberry Street. Robertson mentioned Ronald Zeager who was Sergeant with the York City PD at the time of this shooting. He stated that Zeager was at the intersection of Philadelphia and Newberry when this incident occurred. He and Zeager have spoken periodically about this incident. This was an all white area and the Newberry Street boys were a gang in that area. Robertson stated while sitting in the armored car he heard one of the police come on the radio and say that a car, he believed it was a Cadillac, drove through the barricades and was coming up Newberry Street at a high rate of speed."

Detectives George and Williams, and Trooper Keith Stone, start out, like the others, apparently intent on a fair and even-handed investigation. Like the state and city cops before them, they quickly fall into the abyss. That corner of Newberry and Philadelphia streets remains, to this day, a cop trap. Detectives George and Williams, Trooper Stone and the others, like the cops before them, stepped right into the trap.

While they pulled out all stops to destroy Charlie Robertson, they'd turn a blind eye to the goings-on at the barricade, and down by the tracks. They would not interview retired York officer Ron Zeager for another *nine months,* until February 21, 2001. Zeager then would tell them he noticed, as the Mosley's Cadillac passed the barricade, everyone inside was black. As the massacre began, Zeager and the other cops, "took cover behind their cruiser," George's report states.

They never bother to ask Zeager why he and the other officers at the corner didn't come to the aid of the family. Zeager insisted the barricade was "not up yet," though he mentions standing on the corner with several state policemen, among them Trooper William Linker and, he thought, Corporal Rick Dressler.

As for the mysterious radio broadcast, George's report reads that Zeager stated, "no one called over the radio and stated that a car crashed through the barricades. (That was asserted by Charles Robertson in his interview of 05-09-00). He said that he was not sure if they had portable radios in 1969." This disagreement about the radio is at the heart of the case. Gabriel Mark Barr, in 1969, recalled he and Jim Messersmith, "walked across the street to see the guy with the two-way radio to see if anything happened to the lady who was shot." The police also had radios in their cars. More evidence about the radio was to come, but Kelley and his men would suppress it.

Zeager and Robertson over the years regularly took meals together. As the new investigation proceeded, Zeager would stop hanging around Charlie Robertson. Instead, Zeager hired a lawyer.

As I say, Tom Kelley's men wouldn't get around to talking with Ron Zeager for nine months. Instead, the officers under Kelley's direction concentrated on indicting Mayor Charlie Robertson. They would quickly begin to suppress evidence of wider police involvement. Unless it had something to do with Robertson, they weren't interested. Unless it could be used against Robertson, they didn't want to hear it. They would continually steer witnesses away from talking about policemen, unless that cop was Charles Robertson.

They began to interview the cops who worked that night with Robertson in the armored car: Jim Vangreen, Ray Markle and Dennis McMaster. Jim Vangreen, interviewed in May 2000, professed not remembering much, except that Robertson identified himself to the shooters when he got out of the armored car, and that the Cadillac subsequently drove away "on flat tires."

On June 1, 2000, Ray Markle was interviewed. Not surprisingly, he also says he remembers little.

A few days later, Detective Williams interviewed Dennis McMaster. By now McMaster was chief of police of East Pennsboro

Township, a suburb of Harrisburg. McMaster also had interesting things to say about the radio. McMaster recalled that after the ambulance carrying Lillie left he instructed the family to drive toward the barricade at Philadelphia Street, so he could follow and talk to them. "He then radioed the Police Station at Newberry Street and told them to stop the Cadillac when it reached their location. This failed to happen and the car continued on and left the area," Williams report reads. That car just couldn't be stopped. That car, that barricade, just didn't work together.

In late 2001, Chief McMaster would say he heard only static on the radio. While in Farquhar Park he heard a transmission about shots being fired, he'd say. The radio is at the heart of the case.

Curiously, in his first interview on June 4, 2000, Chief McMaster didn't say anything about witnessing Charlie Robertson handing out ammunition to the Newberry Street Boys. He never mentions it.

It's clear where this so-called "investigation" is going two days later, on June 6, 2000, when detectives George and Williams interview Rick Knouse. Knouse tells George that the Messersmiths had been listening to a police scanner to receive a warning that the Cadillac was coming. It wasn't information the detectives wanted to hear. When Knouse's taped interview begins, he makes passing reference to the police scanner.

Knouse explains that John Messersmith was barking orders. "It was like an order," Knouse says. "You go here. You, you, you, and you go down here and look for, wait for this Cadillac cause it's on the way. And I think that happened something to do with the police scanner that you known—." Here Knouse is discussing a police scanner and Detective George interrupts him and steers him away from the subject. "And a—," Knouse starts to elaborate.

"You guys went down to Cottage Hill Road?" George stops him, changing the subject.

Tom Kelley and Rodney George have knowledge of the scanner and they're suppressing it. Detective George doesn't want anything on the record about the Messersmiths listening to the police radio. No use getting more cops in trouble. No use solving the crime. Let's fry the mayor's ass, and move on.

The Rick Knouse interview is very damaging to Kelley, George and company. Knouse explains he and the other boys were taking hallucinogenic drugs, and drinking heavily that day. "There was a lot of idol time you know sitting on the porch drinking, smoking cigarettes this and that I mean getting tired there were drugs. There was speed there was crank there was acid," Knouse tells George. A burned-out acid head becomes star witness to indict a sitting mayor. Any cub reporter's dream come true.

It gets worse. Knouse's mind by 2000 is long fried. He says he remembers clearly John Messersmith telling him to "kill as many niggers as you can. And you know that would ring and ring in a person's head." In another minute, with the prodding of detectives, he would attribute this same statement to Charlie Robertson.

Knouse knows Charlie Robertson is mayor, and wants to drop some dimes on the town authority figure. But Robertson is only one of many cops Knouse wants to talk about. They ask Knouse whether he had a gun the day Lillie was shot.

Knouse responds, "Somebody gave me a gun, now that you're talking I remember somebody giving me a old like bolt action 30-06. I remember somebody giving me that. And a—."

"Where did that take place?" George asks.

"Right down in here."

"At Newberry and Cottage?" George asks, leading Knouse.

"Whatever day that I'd seen the police and— and Robinson," Knouse says. Knouse keeps calling Robertson "Robinson."

"It was not just Robinson. It was a crew of police down there, hollering what kind of gun do you got and this and that. He said, 'What are you shooting, Knouse?' I don't know much about it and I don't know who it was said he's got a 30-06 and he had shells for it. He threw a box of them down."

"What did he, back up a little bit. Who was that?" George asks. Rather than changing the subject, George encourages this line of rambling.

"Robinson."

"Who is…"

"Charlie Robinson," Knouse says.

"The mayor?" George asks, again leading.

"Who's the mayor right now," Knouse says. "He was a beat cop then."

"And he saw you at the intersection of Cottage Hill and Newberry Street?"

"Right here at this intersection."

"With the gun. Yes?"

"Yes, yes. He'd seen me with the gun and asked me what it was and this kid says a 30-06 and Robinson threw a box of shells down and then—."

"What did he say to you?"

"He said, 'Kill as many as you can.'"

George asks, "Referring to?"

"Referring to he used the word niggers."

So now Knouse attributes the phrase, "Kill as many niggers as you can," to Robertson, when, earlier, he attributes this to John Messersmith. A little more acid and, no doubt, he would have heard a lot more people saying it.

George keeps steering Knouse to talk about Charlie Robertson. He asks if Knouse knows Robertson, and Knouse replies Officer Robertson used to chase the kids for curfew violations and the like. "I was never like at a breakfast with him or anything," Knouse explains. "It was just from being a kid you know."

"But this time," George asks, "did it seem like your relationship with the police this time and the people down on Newberry Street, the kids—. Was it different then?"

"Yeah it was different," Knouse replies. "It seemed like everybody wanted to kill blacks." Knouse goes on to try to explain how he had been given ammunition. "I'm talking about fifty people around around these cops and they and they were talking just a lot of shit you know like keep white power and keep it together and don't you know and protect yourselves and we're with you and we're behind you and—."

"Who said that?"

"Charlie and there was a couple other cops with him. They was kinda like you know pumped up like rally type of thing you know."

Detective George doesn't even bother asking Knouse to name the other policemen he says are with Robertson passing out the ammunition, the "crew of police down there," Knouse says he saw. Instead, he has Knouse name the *kids* present. For the rest of the investigation, this is how it'd be. Name the kids, but keep talk of the police limited to Charlie Robertson.

"Do you remember a guy who was referred to by some other people as Fireman Jim?" Detective Williams asks Knouse toward the end of the interview, while they're having Knouse name boys. "Fireman Jim" was mentioned in Creavey and Cronin's 1969 interview of Gabriel Mark Barr as being on the roof with Barr and Don Altland.

"I don't, I remember that name yeah I know who you are talking about. He was, he was around there," Knouse tells them.

It would take several months before they'd learn Fireman Jim was James Frey. Before the grand jury, Frey would have interesting things to say about Newberry Street neighbor, Officer Wayne Ruppert.

But Tom Kelley wouldn't be interested in Ruppert. Kelley and company have pre-selected Charlie Robertson for punishment, and they're protecting everyone else.

It gets so bad that detectives George and Williams seem to resort to tacking on gratuitous attacks against Charlie Robertson at the end of their reports. They interview former Girarder Gary Moffit on June 12, 2000. Moffit says he was down by the railroad tracks, looking at warehouses, when the shooting started. The last paragraph of Moffit's report reads, "Moffit added that a couple of days after Allen was killed he was talking to Rick Knouse about what had happened the night she was killed. He stated that Knouse told him that shortly before the car came up Newberry Street, Charlie Robertson, who was a police officer at the time, was on Newberry Street passing out 30-06 guns to the kids on the street. He stated that Knouse told him that Robertson gave one to him."

Here Knouse tells a boy that Robertson passed out guns, when Knouse later says it was ammunition. Robertson denies handing out ammunition. "It didn't happen," he says. He says he was working the night shift during these days of the riots, and was home sleeping in bed in the afternoons, when others say he was passing out bullets.

George is gratuitously tacking statements damaging to Charlie Robertson at the end of his reports. Rodney George, I'm told, sought a job on Mayor Robertson's police force.

It happens again on September 21, 2000, when detectives George and Williams interview Glen Monday, who in 1969 was an eleven-year-old Newberry Street Boy. Monday's interview for the most part backfires on prosecutors. Monday talks about various white gangs coming together for meetings at Farquar Park. "Monday stated that he remembered some police officers being at the meetings," George writes. Again, they never ask Monday to list the officers.

Monday knows where the blame rests. The report continues, "Monday stated that he thinks that the police were partially responsible for the woman being killed because they were at the intersection of Philadelphia and Newberry Street(s) and should have stopped her from going down Newberry Street. Monday remembers that he and his younger brother were stopped by police at that same intersection and were not allowed into that area only days before the woman was killed. He stated that they put him and his brother in a police car and took them home. Monday could not recall the names of any of the police there but he did remember Officer Charlie Robertson. Monday stated that everyone on Newberry Street knew Charlie and that he knew everyone in that area." This, again, is tacked to the report's end.

Mayor Robertson, prominent in the public eye, has been made the fall guy. A type of mass hysteria has taken over. If any of the other officers on the scene had the visibility of mayor, those officers would have taken the flak, not Robertson. Then again, had not Charlie Robertson been elected mayor and raised the wicked ire of Tom Kelley, the case would never have been reopened, however egregiously.

The sad irony is that police and prosecutorial corruption kept Lillie from getting justice in 1969; police and prosecutorial corruption brought the case back to life three decades later.

*Justice* continues to elude Lillie Belle Allen. This time we're all along for the ride.

The business about passing out ammunition or yelling white

power the day before Lillie's murder, while illustrative of the big picture, is diversionary. It's one of *many* sideshow events of the York riots, dressed up as the main event. There's no direct connection between these incidents and the ambush of Lillie Belle Allen. It takes our attention away from the barricade, where prosecutors know the cops received warning of the ambush, and where the kids were running around with guns in plain sight of the cops. It diverts us from considering those cops who did nothing to help the family, who witnessed the murder from behind their cruisers, and who did not apprehend the shooters. To believe that Robertson's yelling white power drove the kids to murder diminishes the culpability of the other officers at the barricade, in the street, and elsewhere. Conversely, a hard look at the actions and inactions of other officers places Robertson's actions in proper context and weakens a murder charge against him.

That said, Robertson no doubt played some part in something here. Yelling white power may be construed as inciting riot, but the statute of limitiations for that has long since been allowed to run. Certainly Robertson't role should be fully known, as should the actions of *all* the police officers.

If any one of these cops had been elected mayor, the case would just as easily have been reopened. That's not justice. That's politics.

At some point, even the officers working for Tom Kelley on this vicious farce realize it's another phony Lillie Belle Allen investigation, and they're beginning to worry. They know that if the suppressed facts of the case are discovered by the public there could be real trouble for Pennsylvania and York police, and trouble for them. Perhaps civil rights prosecution. Anyway, they knew, Tom Kelley didn't want to go there. So the cover-up must continue to this day. What else can they do? It began to dawn on them the problem any honest cop had investigating this case in 1969. One can imagine all the detectives in 2000 turning to each other and asking, What have we gotten ourselves into? If we just turn our backs, maybe everything will be okay....

Five days after Jim Monday pointed his finger to the cops at the barricade, four months after Charlie Robertson pointed his finger to the cops at the barricade, detectives Rodney George and Dennis Williams decided they better go see retired Pennsylvania State

Trooper Gerald Roberts.

Roberts told them he was stationed at the barricade with Trooper Steve Rendish. George writes in his report that, shortly before Allen was shot, "Roberts said that as he and Rendish were standing on the corner, a white male in his twenties came up to them and said that they could turn their backs and that everything would be okay. No one would shoot at them. Roberts said that he turned to Rendish and they both said to each other, 'What have we gotten ourselves into?'"

Detectives George and Williams must have turned to each other and swallowed hard.

What had *they* gotten themselves into? They had turned their backs, yet everything was not okay. The police at the barricade violated basic trusts we expect when we encounter policemen. Now Tom Kelley and his detectives violated a basic trust we expect in prosecutors. Telling the truth.

For the next year, Tom Kelley and his fellow prosecutors would say they had no proof a barricade even existed on Newberry and Philadelphia streets. Tom Kelley damn well knew he had proof.

Like the others with something to hide, Tom Kelley was lying.

The question of the "barricade" seems at times to be one of semantics. It's really one of self-preservation. The issue becomes outright preposterous. We know from witnesses like Glen Monday, and officers McMaster and Robertson, and others, that a barricade had been in place for days, and that cars were being stopped. Whether there were yellow saw horses with the officers, as Lillie's family remembers, seems beside the point. It's indisputable that police officers were standing there, watching the murder, and doing nothing to help the family or apprehend the shooters. Police officers, not saw horses, have a sworn duty to protect the public, and arrest murderers.

Retired state Trooper William Linker, who was stationed at the barricade for several nights during the riot, says he doesn't remember much about the night Lillie died. He says he remembers being at the intersection of Newberry and Philadelphia, but says he was there for more than one night. He says he remembers a shooting on Newberry Street, but does not remember who was shot. He remembers hearing, after the shooting, that the occupants of the car were from out of town.

"Linker did not remember having specific orders as to what they were to do at the intersection but he thinks they were there to keep the blacks out of the area (and) the whites in the area," Linker told detectives George and Williams. This validates the memories of witnesses like Monday.

Wentz's TV shop, across the street from where the cops were standing, had a tv set in the window, and Linker remembers watching the moon landing while standing on the corner. But the actual moon landing and walk on the moon happened the day before, on Sunday, July 20. NASA's chronology states the Eagle lifted off from the moon early Monday afternoon, and had rendezvoused with Columbia later that afternoon. At the hour Lillie was shot, the astronauts were orbiting the moon, preparing for their voyage home. Not much would have been televised after nine Monday night, and the tv shop might even have been closed.

Only when reminded of their duty to protect the public do the officers begin to question whether a "barricade" was in place. Their statements at this point seem self-serving, meant more to protect themselves, than the public. Linker says he doesn't remember the car going down Newberry Street or having any orders to stop cars from going down Newberry Street. He says there were no barricades until after the shooting, at which time people were prevented from passing.

In July 1969 state police Trooper Michael Marchowski was a recent graduate of the State Police Academy. He was stationed at the corner of Newberry and Philadelphia with senior Trooper Linker. "Linker was the man," Marchowski says. "I was told to do what Linker says." Marchowski says he remembers being in York city several nights during the riots, but says he can't remember whether he was stationed at the same corner every night, or was moved around.

Marchowski recalled some type of barricade or fence where they stood on the sidewalk. He says this "barrier" was more to afford the officers protection, "some cover more than anything else." He says he can't recall if there were any type of barricades or road blocks actually on the street to stop traffic, but he does recall "some type of structure on the sidewalk the officers stood behind."

Interviewed by Trooper Stone and Detective Williams in August 2000, Marchowski's statement reads, in part, "Marchowski states he was at the location for a short while when he heard firing and commotion further down the street (Newberry St.) and he remained at his location the entire time and did not see what was happening or what had happened. He remembers the armored car coming into the area after the shooting and maybe an ambulance but had no recollection of ever seeing the victim's vehicle. Marchowski had no recollection of the vehicle passing through the intersection on its way up N. Newberry St. or seeing it afterwards when it came back south on Newberry St. after the shooting. Marchowski stated he did not recall himself stopping vehicles as they travelled (sic) through the intersection (nor could he) provide information whether other officers at the intersection were actually stopping vehicles and speaking with the occupants.

"Marchowski could not recall anything about a TV shop at the intersection with a tv on in the window showing the lunar landing (as previously described by Tpr. Linker who was at this intersection also)," Trooper Stone writes. "Marchowski could not remember seeing other citizens, motorcycle rider or any other persons interacting with the police on the corner. Marchowski points out that he just doesn't remember much of anything about that evening other than hearing the commotion/shots."

City police officer Ron Zeager says he was not given "any particular instructions before being stationed (at Newberry and Philadelphia streets), only that it was a trouble spot and officers needed to be there in case any trouble occurred." Zeager says he doesn't remember much. He thought a black male drove the car. "He only got a look at them from behind," his statement curiously reads.

"At one point during the evening Zeager remembered vaguely some cars sitting at the traffic light heading west on Philadelphia at Newberry. One of those cars turned down Newberry Street and before he knew it the car was halfway down the block. A few minutes later, he heard shooting. They took cover behind their cruiser," Zeager says. Like the other cops, he did not help the family.

In early August 2002 I visited retired state police Trooper Gerald Roberts, who was stationed at the corner with his partner, the late Trooper Rendish. Roberts lives in Boiling Springs, outside Harrisburg. He lives in a neatly trimmed ranch house overlooking a cornfield. An American flag waves from a planter on the porch.

Roberts remains in good health. His memory was obviously sharp and vivid. He's slightly shorter than six feet tall, with a heavy-set, stocky build, and gray hair cut in a close, butch crew. He came to his door without a shirt, and wearing khaki shorts. I asked him about his recollections of the young man who walked up to him and who had advised the police to turn their backs when the shooting started. Roberts became angry and at first denied this had happened.

I held up the one-page statement he gave to detectives.

"Give it to me," he said. "Isn't that a subpoena?" he asked. He pronounced it "subpoenee." He seemed to be expecting a subpoena.

I told him it wasn't a subpoena, but his statement to investigators.

Suddenly Roberts walked away from his door and disappeared into his neat and orderly house, leaving the door open. He appeared to go into his kitchen. It was a hot day, and I watched his shadow and his darkened outline as he came out of the kitchen, carrying an object in his hands. He stepped outside on to his porch with a pair of eyeglasses, put on the glasses, and read the statement.

Roberts' statement, written by Detective George reads, "On 09-26-00 at 0915 hrs Det. Williams and I interviewed Gerald Roberts at his home ... in Boiling Springs. Roberts is a retired PA State Police Officer and was on duty at the intersection of Philadelphia and Newberry Street the night that Lillie Allen was killed.

"Roberts remembered that on the night that this occurred, he and Trooper Rendish were sent to the intersection of Newberry and Philadelphia Street by Sgt. Tappe of the PA State Police. They were sent there and told to stay there until they were relieved. They knew about the trouble that was going on in the city, however he does not remember getting any specific instructions, only to have their presence in the area. They were never told to keep the blacks out and the whites in the neighborhood.

"Roberts stated that when he and Rendish got to the intersection there were no barricades there. He remembers parking the marked police unit facing West on Philadelphia Street, west of Newberry Street. He and Rendish were at the Northwest corner of Philadelphia and Newberry Street. Another State Police trooper and a York City Police officer were also at the intersection from time to time, however Roberts remembered that they were on a roving patrol.

"Shortly after arriving there, Roberts recalled that some one had shot up at them from the railroad tracks at Newberry and Gay. Roberts stated that it was a black male who ran down the right side of the railroad tracks. The two troopers took cover. Roberts stated that he could see the shooter was black. He does not recall if any other additional units came there to check for the shooter.

"A short time before Allen was shot, Roberts said that as he and Rendish were standing on the corner, a white male in his twenties came up to them and said that they could turn their backs and that everything would be okay. No one would shoot at them. Roberts said that he turned to Rendish and they both said to each other, 'what have we gotten ourselves into.'

"Roberts recalled that at sometime after that conversation, Lillie's car went past them heading north on Newberry Street. Roberts stated that there were a couple cars sitting in front of it at the stop light at Newberry and Philadelphia. They went straight and Allen's car turned onto Newberry Street. He noticed the car going up Newberry Street. He saw it turn and stop on the tracks and then all he heard was gunfire. He and Rendish took cover behind their car. The shooting lasted only a brief time. He thought that he remembered an ambulance or armored car going in and getting the woman but he is not sure.

"Roberts said that after the shooting he remembered that Rendish was interviewed about stopping someone with a gun. When we asked him if this was the incident where they stopped the brother of a York City Police officer. He was in a car and coming out of the area of the shooting. He had a shotgun in his car. Roberts then recalled that incident and said that it was the one he remembered."

Reading his statement as he stood in front of me, Gerald Roberts became angered, upset and, I saw, frightened. The statement obviously was his. He seemed betrayed that the statement now had seen the light of day, on his own doorstep, no less. He gave me the impression that Kelley's investigators had promised him some sort protection, and now he felt betrayed. "That's it, I'm not saying anything to anyone now!" he blurted. He turned and angrily stalked inside.

I became righteously indignant. "Why didn't you help those people in the car?" I asked, now angry myself.

Through the screen door Roberts said, "We did!" He smiled, and continued, "There's a lot that happened. You don't know. You weren't there." He waved a hand to indicate a lot had happened in the background. Roberts made it plain to me that he knows quite a bit more than had been recorded by detectives George and Williams. What that, Roberts angrily ordered me from his property and closed his door. He wasn't asking members of the community into his home to discuss the incident over tea, though by his own admission there's plenty more to tell.

Retired Trooper Roberts tells me "we did" attempt to help the family. I wondered. Perhaps Roberts was the officer seen by Beatrice Mosley, the cop who had come up to the car and looked inside after the shooting, before the arrival of the armored car. If so, why hadn't Roberts done more? Why had he not stopped the shooting, which he says he was warned about? Why had he not apprehended the shooters, when he witnessed the killing from behind the safety of his car?

"There's a lot that happened. You don't know. You weren't there," Roberts tells me. Well do tell, Mr. Roberts.

Driving away from Roberts' house, I felt sure that he would talk if given the proper incentives, by real lawmen. Talking with Gerald Roberts, I became convinced that this case needs to be reactivated by the Civil Rights Division of the U.S. Justice Department. Legislative hearings are also in order, to ensure thoroughness. We need the truth, which Tom Kelley and his men have proven incapable of providing, and which they are attempting to conceal. To tell his full story, Gerald Roberts obviously requires the services of a real lawman, one who will not turn his back on public corruption.

Such a lawman is in short supply in Pennsylvania.

# 5

# Indicting a ham sandwich in time for election day

A few days after they'd interviewed Rick Knouse and Charlie Robertson, District Attorney Stan Rebert and his top assistant Tom Kelley petitioned a York County judge to impanel an investigative grand jury. They petitioned Judge John Uhler.

John Uhler was the county district attorney in the late 1970s and early 80s. Now he was a judge.

DA Uhler didn't care enough about Lillie Belle Allen to open a file or simply inquire about the status of the most infamous, unsolved murder case in his trust. Uhler was the DA when the bullets were lost. As chief law enforcement officer, the buck stops there. Although the canons of judicial conduct obligate Judge Uhler to recuse himself, he would come to refuse to get off the case, further damaging the credibility of this already horrendously flawed and unraveling travesty. The perception grew that Uhler was not an impartial, disinterested, nor fair judge, but a man with something to hide, out to protect himself, and others, and willing to misuse his office and trust to accomplish this. Where have we heard that before in this story?

The grand jury convened in September 2000. This would be the first investigative grand jury in York County in over thirty years. In the end two million dollars would be spent. At times it took on a farcical air. State police would search Newberry Street for bullets. Divers would bob the depths of murky Codorus Creek, looking for the rifle used to shoot Henry Schaad. These boys were hot on the trail, all right. After thirty years at the bottom of the Codorus, it would have been just as useful to look for Blue Beard's treasure, the remains of Judge Crater, or the entrance to the Lost Dutchman mine.

Still, whenever a box this fascinating is picked up and rattled, something interesting is bound to tumble out. Residents never interviewed before now told prosecutors and grand jurors stories of hiding behind curtains and watching Lillie's murder on the street. Robert Meyers volunteered he saw Bobby Messersmith walk into the street and shoot at the car. Sometime afterward, Bobby told him "they shot because Lillie leaned across the hood like she was going to shoot." He'd say he didn't originally tell police because he was afraid.

Some old witnesses suddenly felt free to talk. James Rummel, who police interviewed in 1969, now said he saw Bobby Messersmith "fire a shotgun at Lillie right before all the shooting started." Perhaps he would have told this to a grand jury in 1969, or 1979.

Some of the new accounts seem somewhat apocryphal. Robert Stoner, a former YMCA outreach worker who first surfaced in newspaper accounts in 1999, told prosecutors he ran down Newberry Street after the shooting yelling, "What's happening to this community!" This seems slightly tailor-made for a tv movie. None of the other witnesses recall Stoner's starring role. Stoner spoke of kids, wrapped in gunsmoke, giving each other high-fives and whooping while Lillie lay dying. His name really is Stoner. The boys he saw with guns out on the street included Bobby and Art Messersmith and, he says, Greg Neff. Trouble is, everyone else seems to remember Neff shooting from a second story window. Even detectives George and Williams wondered why, if Stoner was such a conscience of the community, he waited *three decades* to come forward. Stoner replied he called York Police Captain McCaffery soon afterwards and then again, three days later, but McCaffery never got back to him.

Years later, Stoner says he was playing golf with Greg Neff, who he says told him, "That gun will never be found that killed that woman. It was destroyed." It seems fitting that this was supposedly said on a York County golf course.

Other accounts dredged up by prosecutors seem even more fanciful. Art Geiselman, in 1969 a reporter for the Baltimore Sun, told prosecutors he and his photographer were driving around King Street on the night of the murder when he heard a car "driving on its rims coming up behind them." The tires (plural) and windows were shot out, he said. The car, he said, was driven by a black minister who told them they had been shot at and their daughter was shot. Geiselman says they followed the car a bit until police turned it into the station.

Geiselman's story contains several glaring falsehoods. Only one tire was shot out. After the ambush Hattie, not her father, drove the Cadillac directly back to her Pershing Avenue home. They then took James Mosley's car to the hospital. Bubba's shot-up Cadillac remained on the street for days, not at the police station, and so on.

Other accounts have a haunting, urban myth quality.

Amy Lau was one year old at the time of the shooting. She told prosecutors she met Bobby Messersmith's mother in the city in 1989. In a house in the city, sometime in the timeframe of 1989 to 1992, the young woman says, she was shown the gun used to kill Lillie Belle along with several KKK outfits. Mrs. Messersmith told her that Bobby had shot Lillie Belle Allen.

All this is great fodder for oral history, or a psychologist's paper on mass hysteria. It's like the rumor game, where you pass a whisper around a room, except it's done over a thirty year period, and it's even harder to figure out what to believe.

The fascinating, enduring constant in this story, as Sgt. Creavey and the original investigators discovered all those years ago, is that witnesses invariably point to the role of *a large number of* police in Lillie's murder. And so it remains to this day. Witnesses invariably direct the authorities where they don't want to go: to the corner barricade, to police mixed in with the shooters. At some point, lost in their own heart of darkness, even county Detective Rodney George and the other investigators began to realize the police had a much greater role in the murder than prosecutor Tom Kelley was willing to flesh out. Detective George and the others began to realize that they, like policemen before them, have gone into the tank and were working on a sham investigation. Their investigative notes and questions seem to almost sigh as one off-limits clue after another drips from the lips of witnesses.

Stephen Noonan tells them he saw a police cruiser at Bobby's house shortly before the shooting. Glen Monday tells them he attended meetings in Farquhar Park with "some police officers being at the meetings." Rick Knouse mentions the "crew of police" inciting the boys to riot. Roger Kinard tells them he "got the impression police wanted (the boys) to back them up." Retired Trooper Gerald Roberts tells them they were forewarned of the planned murder. It goes on and on. All these leads go unexplored by Tom Kelley. "Kelley's got Robertson single-handedly running the police force back in 1969," one dismayed observer tells me. Kelley wants to present the big lie to the public that Mayor Robertson of 1999 was Mayor Patrolman Robertson in 1969, calling all the shots. As George Orwell pointed out, before dishonest men can control the present, they must first control the past.

Perhaps the officers working for Tom Kelley in 2000 weren't all bad cops, and came to resent being forced into the hole where the other cops had fallen.

When they finally track down James Frey, their hearts seem to have gone out of Tom Kelley's bullshit, smear investigation. Almost as an afterthought, they take note of Frey's encounter, shortly after Lillie's murder, with Wayne Ruppert, the future chief of police. "Officer Ruppert, shortly after, told them they did the right thing," they note Frey telling them. They know it's a dead letter. They know this isn't about Ruppert, or the other cops, or uncovering the truth. It's about destroying Charlie Robertson.

After all, this isn't the true or thorough investigation Lillie Belle Allen's family, and the public, have waited so long to see. This is a sham political investigation designed for the sole purpose of humiliating Charlie Robertson before the next mayoral election in 2001.

It's been said that a dishonest prosecutor can manipulate a grand jury to indict a ham sandwich. Here we have proof.

The indictments came rattling down the chute just in time for the primary election of 2001. Tom Kelley's ally, Ray Crenshaw, opposed Robertson in the Democratic mayoral primary. Robertson was daily pummeled in both newspapers. Having received regular leaks from Kelley's prosecution team, the papers trumpeted an imminent indictment of the mayor. Several witnesses interviewed by Kelley's investigators called in to the DA's office to complain after reading in the paper about their supposedly confidential interviews. It didn't help that Robertson kept putting his foot in his mouth. This was quickly turning into a national story, and Robertson didn't know how to handle the national press. Robertson is a bone-headed beat cop. This in no small part is what got him into political trouble with DA Stan Rebert's country club set. He wasn't one of them. But people in the streets of York knew where he was coming from, and understood him. Newsweek Magazine didn't.

Despite the amazing drubbing given Robertson, Ray Crenshaw turned out not to be the most dynamic candidate for mayor. At a debate with Robertson, Crenshaw appeared to nod off while standing at the podium. In the end, Robertson would beat Crenshaw in the polls by 127 votes even though everyone in the city fully expected their mayor to be indicted any day for murder.

The timing of Robertson's arrest was curious, and raised suspicion near and far. The affidavit seeking his arrest was filed on May 17, 2001, two days after the May 15 primary. Court papers handed down before the primary mentioned a white police officer who allegedly provided ammunition to rioters. Robertson's attorney wrote the prosecutors the week before the primary asking them not to file for his arrest until after the vote. This caused even The New York Times to wonder what was going on. If this was a legitimate indictment, what did an election have to do with it? Was this about law enforcement, or politics?

Things were so bad that District Attorney Rebert felt obliged to issue a press release denying he'd ever indict a man for murder based on political motivations.

True to form, they planned to arrest Charlie Robertson for murder on a day when a judge wasn't available for a hearing, so the Democratic mayor would spend a few days in the county prison — the York Republican party's gulag. A favorite York County trick. Robertson instead went away to Virginia for a few days before turning himself in. He ended up spending only a few hours at the state police barracks, driven there by Rodney George. Still, Robertson's humiliation was staggering. The world press turned out to see Charlie Robertson handcuffed after his arraignment and driven away through the town where he once had walked as a beat cop and presided as mayor.

In an age where journalism has been reduced to writing a two- or three-word caption beneath a talking head, Charlie Robertson's traducement proved irresistible. He became the Mayor Murder Suspect. At hearings in the courthouse, prosecutors would stand, point to Robertson and intone, *"Murderer* Charles Robertson." One would think he'd put a gun to someone's head and pulled the trigger.

Charlie Robertson tried to hang tough. He said at first he wouldn't resign, that he'd stand for general election in the fall. But people began to move away from him. For a natural politician, an old neighborhood gumshoe cop, that's hard. Like Willie Loman says, you're out there riding on a smile and a shoeshine, one day they don't smile back, and that's murder.

Charlie Robertson one day invited reporters from the York Daily Record into the mayor's office for an interview. He broke down and began to cry. He remembered when he was a boy, sometime in the late 1940s, when his father had been beset by several blacks, beaten and robbed. This caused him, he confessed, for many years to resent blacks. Tearfully he said he had come to realize over the years this was wrong.

At last the day came when the pressure became so great that Charlie Robertson announced he would bow out of the general election in November 2001.

"I look around the city and I see a lot of good things that Charlie did," one York political watcher tells me. "I think a lot of us feel bad for him." Another tells me, "You know, when Charlie left office, no one had a party for him, or a thank-you."

In the end, Robertson was indicted on the strength of questionable testimony given by Rick Knouse and Chief Dennis McMaster. McMaster suddenly decided he'd been with Robertson one night when he says he saw Robertson tossing a box of ammunition to James Messersmith. Yet James Messersmith wasn't at the killing. Outside the courthouse one day, James Messersmith loudly called Denny McMaster a liar.

And just what was Dennis McMaster doing while Charlie Robertson supposedly passed out ammunition? Filing his nails? Did Patrolman Robertson tie up and gag Patrolman McMaster? Perhaps McMaster was on his way to the doughnut shop, with the cops at the barricade, while the lawyers and judges took repast at the clubhouse.

Why had Chief McMaster waited *thirty years* to come forward? Why wasn't McMaster indicted? What deals or threats had Tom Kelley made with Chief McMaster? McMaster, for his part, trips the light fantastic, saying he didn't realize passing out ammunition to a law-abiding citizen was a crime.

McMaster had resigned from the York police department after Mayor Robertson passed him by for promotion. I'm told McMaster sought appointment as Robertson's police commissioner. McMaster remains chief of police of East Pennsboro Township.

The fix was in. Denny McMaster, the cops at the barricade, Tom Chatman, all the other suspect cops would continue to find unholy protection in the York County DA's office and courts. To paraphrase Tolstoi, there is one way to properly prosecute a case, and a thousand ways to fix one.

To fix this case, Tom Kelley relied on the old standby of crooked prosecutors everywhere: selective prosecution; manipulation of evidence and the grand jury; incomplete investigation; leaking to the press; installing a house judge.

And what of Judge John Uhler, the disinterested and uninformed DA who lost the bullets? Robertson's attorneys asked that the murder charges be dismissed, as too much time, they said, had passed to provide a fair defense. Thirty-years had been deliberately allowed to pass to protect unnamed guilty parties, the lawyers argued. Scores of prime players were either dead, missing, or victims of Alzheimer's, and evidence over the years had either been destroyed, lost, suppressed or just plain not gathered. Uhler for once did the proper thing and recused himself, and all other York County judges, from deciding this issue, since he and other county judges perhaps, he said, could be called as witnesses. Perhaps Uhler realized the pile of shit he was standing in, and hoped an honest judge would make it all go away.

The state Supreme Court thereupon appointed senior Bucks County Judge Edward G. Biester to hear what was called the time-delay argument. By this time Robertson had already removed himself from re-election and had been totally humiliated in his hometown.

Observers of the Pennsylvania judiciary expected Biester to throw out the charges, as the prosecutor's true goal — Robertson's destruction — had already been attained. The uncharged guilty parties — i.e. policemen, prosecutors and judges — would then find protection from further embarrassing inquiry in open court, with the world press looking on. The case dismissed, Biester, the theory went, would then get in his car and drive home to Bucks County as fast as he could. This is a common maneuver with political cases in Pennsylvania courts.

At a hearing, Judge Uhler took the witness stand and passed the blame for not prosecuting Lillie's case to the police officers working under him when he was DA. "I can assure you, " witness Uhler said, "if any information was filed, it would have been pursued." This was the same buck passing invoked by every other district attorney. And the city police pass the buck to the state police, who pass the buck back to the city police, and so on. That's what this story's all about. No one's held accountable.

At the same hearing, hoping to make their case, the DA's office trotted out none other than Thomas Chatman to speak on behalf of police. Chatman took the stand and swore the oath. As he'd been doing for thirty years, Chatman falsely blamed the *witnesses* for the delay. Tom Chatman's so smoooth. He's a glib talker, as the Mosleys discovered so many years ago. He'd make you think the building ain't burning while the floor's smoking at your feet. Chatman told the court the city police had been "stonewalled" by witnesses. He said the state police had taken over the case, but the witnesses stonewalled them too.

Chatman knew this wasn't true. For months in 1969 it was the *police* who stonewalled the FBI and the Civil Rights Division and refused to turn over their reports. They even lied about writing the reports. The police lied about identifying suspects and reading them their Miranda rights.

Chatman could get away with lying in open court because the DA's office continued to suppress the police and FBI reports from 1969 and '70. They have never been released to the public. Indeed, they are published for the first time in this book. The DA's office knows that Chatman was lying. DA Rebert has already been taken to the woodshed for keeping the truth from the court on another case. Rebert got into this growing mess because Tom Kelley's case from the start was all about getting Charlie Robertson, and not about getting at the truth.

These untruths on the witness stand, prosecutorial misconducts and suppressions of evidence I suppose directly affected Judge Biester's ruling on the time-delay argument. Biester on December 18, 2001 ruled that the trial should proceed, saying he had seen no evidence that the delay was caused by anything other than lack of credible eyewitnesses in 1969. "I can make no finding that the investigation of the York City Police Department was negligent or a failure to follow due diligence," he ruled. He's wrong. Maybe he's just a crackpot who writes the orders, a collector of a long-overdue bill.

Judge Biester then went on to observe that many people "may prefer to see the issues raised in these prosecutions buried or put away. But only after they are resolved can this be put fully and permanently behind this city." On that point he's exactly right. That's why Lillie's march to justice isn't going to end any time soon.

"This case has been delayed long enough," Biester told the courtroom. With that, Biester got into his car and drove away from York County as fast as he could.

And with that, John Uhler reinstalled himself as the judge who presumes to preside impartially over the trial. Uhler has violated at least three counts of the judicial canon, which supposedly governs the conduct of Pennsylvania judges. A judge may not sit on a case where he has a personal interest, even a *perception* of an interest. A judge may not sit on a case where his friends, associates or family have an interest, or even the *perception* of an interest. And a judge may not bring shame and disrepute to the judiciary. Uhler violates all of these.

Unfortunately, Pennsylvania judges in recent years laugh at the unenforced canon of judicial conduct. It's a quaint little document, like our constitution, kept in some butterfly collector's cabinet. They might as well make paper airplanes with the pages of the canon, or wipe their asses with it. In the 1980s, state Supreme Court Justice Rolf Larsen accepted an envelope stuffed with cash while he was sitting on the bench of the Supreme Court in Philadelphia. Larsen then was permitted to vote on whether this was acceptable. Larsen voted to exonerate himself. The entire affair was made secret by the court, following standard court secrecy rules. Larsen then proceeded to use the courts to punish anyone who stood up to him. Is this what Pennsylvania judges want? Rolf Larsen was finally impeached, but only because he publicly complained about another supreme court justice sitting on cases involving his own brother. The judiciary has become the most corrupt, unaccountable and tyrannical branch of state government. It's out of the financial and comprehensible reach of average Americans, supported by hidden contributions from lawyers working for wealthy clients. And that's the way they like it. Many of our judges don't even seem to view themselves as part of government, but rather as some sort of irreproachable deities, unencumbered by the rules of mortal men. Judges profess everyone in society must obey rules and laws, but them. And in so doing they diminish the integrity and independence of our courts. And they diminish society.

And why not? We're living in a topsy-turvy age when writers don't write, poets don't rhyme, and singers don't sing. An age when some firefighters see nothing wrong with setting fires. When millionaire ball players won't play ball, and tell fans to buzz off. When CEOs outright lie about their companies. An age when some policemen don't protect the public, and find protection from compromised prosecutors and courts. It's a time when priests sexually abuse children, and find protection in the bosom of mother church. An age when beauty, truth and justice risk going out of the world because they can't be easily packaged by corporate donators. Why should judges be impartial or honest? No one else is. Shouldn't judges too be as nasty as they want to be, black-robed Darth Vaders, lawless and feared, lords of all the other gangstas? They are feared, but not respected.

Everyone involved in the Lillie Belle Allen's murder, and the public, has a simple right to walk into a courtroom and expect impartial justice. Not perfect justice, just impartial. Founding jurists like John Jay and John Marshall, and latter day great bench setters, like Learned Hand, understood that people would only accept our courts if they perceived impartial fairness. "Thou shalt not ration justice," Hand once told the Legal Aid Society.

In the end, the great jurists understood they are our judges only because we allow them to be our judges. As our courts continue to lose moral high ground, and widen their disconnection with average Americans, there will be hell to pay.

Our canon of judicial conduct not only protects the public against the outright chicanery we see here, it protects against the *perception* of partiality or injustice.

Justice, let alone the perception of it, isn't going to be served while John Uhler sits on this case. He doesn't care about the rules of his own judiciary. As DA he couldn't keep tracks of the bullets, it's no wonder he can't find the canon now.

The stakes obviously are very high in York County for Uhler to foist himself on this case. It's not about race, as they'd have us believe. They love to play that race card. It's about unchecked lawlessness and corruption in our police departments, our prosecutor's office, and our courts. Will witnesses in Uhler's courtroom be allowed to speak of the bullets? Will witnesses be allowed to talk about the endless buck-passing between the cops and the DA's office? No way. What about the cops at the barricade, and what their superiors knew? Shouldn't the civil rights division attorneys be allowed to testify? They should be ordered to explain why they accepted the crock of bull that there were no suspects or cooperating witnesses when the thirty-three pages of police reports show otherwise. It certainly looks like Uhler is there to protect the truth from coming out. And that perception alone is enough to persuade an honest judge to step aside from this case.

Should a child of John Uhler's or Stan Rebert's suffer some great misfortune, these men would never accept second-class treatment like this in a courthouse. They would rightly demand an impartial judge, even-handed prosecutors, and equal protections guaranteed by our constitution. They would rightly demand to know the full truth, without a whiff of cover-up. Uhler and Rebert do not think a fair and impartial trial is necessary for the child of Beatrice and James Mosley. They have contemptuously decided to give Lillie Belle Allen a second-class trial, like the second-class citizen she was in the good ol' days. To do otherwise threatens too many York policemen, district attorneys, and judges.

And what of Tom Chatman, who Jerris Leonard, the former head of the Civil Rights Division, fears committed obstruction of justice back in 1969?

The day in late 2001 when Chatman testified in court about the "stonewalling" of witnesses, he didn't have far to walk to take the witness stand.

After 1969, Tom Chatman went on to become chief of the York Police Department. After many years he retired from police work. Today he works, pinch yourself, as a *bailiff for Judge John Uhler*. At least these boys know where to find each other. Long ago, Tom Chatman was in a dilemma, and the decisions he made brought him here.

I can't help thinking it's just as well that James and Beatrice Mosley have died. To walk into that courtroom after all these years and see Tom Chatman, of all people, pouring water for Judge Uhler at Lillie's trial, would be too hard for them to take. Years ago, on the darkest day of their lives, the Mosleys came to Tom Chatman and asked for his help, to please solve the vicious murder of their daughter. And Tom Chatman looked into their faces and did nothing to help them.

Tom Chatman enjoys the employment of the judge on this case and the protection of the district attorney. It would be almost too much for Beatrice Mosley to bear, watching Chatman pouring the water, bringing papers for the judge, swearing them in, asking them to tell the truth, the whole truth, and nothing but the truth. Yada, yada, yada.

# 6

# An overdue bill

In my mind that car forever rolls down Newberry Street, passing the expectant, turned faces.

I keep going back to Newberry Street, getting out of my car and walking the street, trying to catch some hint of the meaning of the event from the gritty pavement, the silent houses lurching on either side of the street like mishappen teeth, the dust-blown tracks.

I must confess I have found myself quite vexed by the simple case of The Wrong Car. For a long while I couldn't understand how someone could be shot like that, and why no one to this day has properly brought the case to full justice.

Finally I confessed to a life-long resident of York County that I have been unable to wrap my mind around the people of York and their treatment of Lillie Belle Allen. This man explained it to me in simple terms that he said even I could understand.

"Don't you get it?" he ruefully looked at me. "She's a nigger. They didn't give a shit about Lillie Belle Allen. They still don't." He gave a dismissive wave.

That sobered me up. In my mind it finally explained the thing. The deliberate mistreatment of Lillie and her case makes a statement.

And what of the participants on Newberry Street? Of the ten men eventually arraigned for Lillie's murder, police identified seven back in 1969. Could have been picked up at any time. Others were lost to time, others died.

One day in April 2001, Detective Rodney George and Trooper Keith Stone drove out to suburban Philadelphia with an arrest warrant to pick up Bobby Messersmith. Messersmith now is infirm, having injured himself in an accident. He has a home and a wife in

Montgomery County.

Handcuffed, placed in a police car, Bobby Messersmith began a long ride back to York County to finally face trial for the murder of Lillie Belle Allen.

In the back of the car, Bobby began to be scared. He saw that fate at last was catching up with him. It was as if, on a night long ago, he had made a deal with the devil, and now the devil had come to collect his due.

Bobby suddenly braced himself. He was not so alone after all. Driving back to York, Bobby Messersmith said something that rattled Detective Rodney George and Trooper Keith Stone to their cores.

Bobby Messersmith saw that George and Stone had fallen into the very heart of darkness, where so many cops before them had fallen. He squinted in recognition. It was then that he welcomed Rodney George and Keith Stone to the dark side.

Bobby Messersmith cocked his head. To this day Bobby has an uncanny, 1960s boyish quality about his voice and speech, like Beaver Cleaver or Brian Wilson gone very, very wrong. An eternity seemed to pass. From the depths of his soul, Bobby Messersmith stabbed at them.

"You guys don't want to know the truth," Bobby said matter-of-factly. "If you want to know the truth, how many police officers did you arrest?"

Times are bad when Bobby Messersmith gets to righteously scold society.